Endorsements for *The Art of Bohart*

'Art Bohart is one of those original thinkers who synthesises and integrates core ideas of diverse therapeutic communities and finds the through line to a new understanding of them all. This volume offers an inside look at his thinking process over the years and his steadfast dedication to ensuring that we don't forget the deep, transformative core of Rogers' work: that persons know where they are going and will self-right if we provide them a safe space and an empathic ear. In these times of hi-tech manipulation, the deceptive simplicity of this idea, spoken in Art's gracious and humble way, shines through this collection. It's a gift of a book.'

Maureen O'Hara, Professor of Psychology, National University and Director of International Futures Forum-US

This book brings together a dozen of Art Bohart's amazing, legendary and inspiring conference presentations from the past 30 years. Art is one of a small number of writers who, over the past 30 years, have made a real, generative impact on how we think about person-centred therapy and indeed psychotherapy in general. In these essays, he spells out a range of implications that flow from his central vision of clients as actively engaging with psychotherapy in order to change themselves. Art represents contemporary person-centred therapy at its best: provocative and passionate yet also open-minded, down-to-earth and full of compassion and common sense. I'm delighted that I will now be able to point my students in the direction of this lovely edition of his previously unpublished papers. Read these Artful essays one at time and savour them. An Art a day keeps the CBT away!

Robert Elliott, Professor of Counselling, University of Strathclyde, UK

An international treasure of humanistic psychology and psychotherapy integration, Art Bohart offers his poignant insight and clinical wisdom in this new volume. He's one of a handful of psychotherapists I always read, and I enthusiastically encourage you to do likewise.
John C. Norcross, Distinguished Professor and Chair of Psychology, University of Scranton, USA

Such a joy to have these unpublished papers by Art all in one place. When I've been lucky enough to go to international conferences, his presentations are top of my list to attend for intellectual stimulation, challenging insights and profound thinking about what it means to be human, the power of empathic listening and encounter and the potential and wisdom of organisms in growth-promoting environments. Art's style reflects his content – accessible, dialogic, deeply respectful of difference, humble, playful, imaginative and creative. This book will be inspirational and invaluable for those working in healing human relationships and living in the world today. Art is passionate, principled and committed to a person-centred mindset while being understanding, respectful and learned about other models and approaches to counselling and psychotherapy.
Suzanne Keys, counsellor working in education, UK

Art Bohart is one of the most influential and progressive thinkers within the field of psychotherapy. This book is a reflection of his true creativeness. These talks, a number of which I was fortunate enough to hear first-hand, show how he sees person-centred psychotherapy as a radical, deeply empathic process, focused on the subjectivity of clients, and placing absolute trust in the organismic wisdom of the person. As is so typical of Bohart's approach, he has developed his propositions in such a way that they are inclusive and expansive, creative and future oriented, while grounded in his firm belief in the power of personhood. This book will give any reader a real insight to Art Bohart's person-centred approach. Simply, fantastic!
David Murphy, Associate Professor, University of Nottingham, UK

The Art *of* Bohart

Person-centred therapy and the
enhancement of human possibility

Arthur C. Bohart

Foreword by Pete Sanders

First published 2021

PCCS Books Ltd
Wyastone Business Park
Wyastone Leys
Monmouth
NP25 3SR
UK

Tel +44 (0)1600 891509
contact@pccs-books.co.uk
www.pccs-books.co.uk

© Arthur C. Bohart
Chapter 5 © Arthur C. Bohart and Makenna Berry Newton

All rights reserved.
No part of this publication may be reproduced, stored in a retrieval system, transmitted or utilised in any form by any means, electronic, mechanical, photocopying or recording or otherwise without permission in writing from the publishers.

The author has asserted their right to be identified as the author of this work in accordance with the Copyright, Designs and Patents Act 1988.

The Art of Bohart:
Person-centred therapy and the enhancement of human possibility

British Library Cataloguing in Publication Data.
A catalogue record for this book is available from the British Library

ISBN   paperback 978 1 910919 79 8
        epub 978 1 910919 81 1

Cover design by Hugh Cowling
Printed in the UK by CMP (UK) Ltd. Poole, Dorset.

Product code – 01202550
This product has been assessed as low risk and can be used safely without safety information.
The manufacturer's authorised representative in the EU for product safety is:
Easy Access System Europe – Mustamäe tee 50, 10621 Tallinn, Estonia
gpsr.requests@easproject.com

Dedication

To my partner and co-thinker, Karen Tallman.

And to the memory of Peter Schmid, who not only influenced my thinking but was always generous in his support.

And to a long list of people who have impacted on my professional development, including my students, my clients, Bob Rosenbaum, Jerry Shapiro, Dale Larson, Marge Witty, German Lietaer, John McLeod, Seymour Feshbach, Gertrude Baker, Tamara Klumpe, Coleen O'Toole, Fran Miller, Les Greenberg, Robert Elliott, Pete Sanders, Maureen O'Hara, Beverly Palmer, Barry Duncan, John Norcross, Bruce Wampold, Jeanne Watson, Judith Todd, Rhonda Goldman, Gene Gendlin (deceased), David Rennie (deceased), Barbara Brodley (deceased), Charlie O'Leary (deceased), Hal Arkowitz (deceased), Al Mahrer (deceased), Jerold Bozarth (deceased) and many others.

Contents

	Foreword – Pete Sanders	*vii*
	Introduction	*1*
1	Person-centred therapy: a radical vision	*3*
2	Enhancing personhood: working with the one who does not get ill	*20*
3	Further meditations on clients' wisdom	*43*
4	Empathy-based psychotherapy: developing a model of person-to-person psychotherapy	*60*
5	Self-organising wisdom in psychotherapy: theoretical conception and early empirical investigations (co-authored with Makenna Berry Newton)	*78*
6	Some neglected insights of Carl Rogers	*90*
7	Becoming the self that one is: an implicational view of personal change	*113*
8	Listening to subjectivity	*123*
9	Of mindsets and meta-perspectives: person-centered therapy and assimilative integration	*133*
10	Listening as being: an alternative to hope	*142*
11	The pernicious idea of avoidance	*159*
12	Working with the internal critic	*170*
	References	*192*
	Name index	*203*
	Subject index	*207*

Arthur C. Bohart is Professor Emeritus at both California State University Dominguez Hills and Saybrook University. He is the co-author or co-editor of several books, including *How Clients Make Therapy Work: The process of active self-healing*, *Empathy Reconsidered: Humanity's dark side*, and *Constructive and Destructive Behavior*. His work has focused on empathy, the client's role in psychotherapy, client-centred therapy, psychotherapy integration and evidence-based practice in psychotherapy. Currently, he is semi-retired and doing part-time teaching at Santa Clara University.

Foreword
Pete Sanders

I first 'met' Art Bohart in the early 1990s when he made occasional contributions to the new email discussion group founded by tech-savvy members of the US-based Association for the Development of the Person-Centered Approach. Straight away, I was attracted by Art's thoughtful questions and responses among the discussions, which could, on occasions, become intemperate. To be honest, I didn't know anything about him. British counselling and psychotherapy were still emerging from their parochial beginnings. Then, suddenly, we could correspond instantly with people on the other side of the world, and Art's carefully considered contributions, delivered with what I grew to understand as characteristic humility, were gems.

When I first saw him speak at an international conference, it was immediately apparent that he was held in the highest regard by academics and practitioners from all over the world. While most famous professors were rather stiffly hailed for their incisive contributions, the reception Art Bohart got was warm, almost affectionate – as though he was a much-loved brother or uncle. I noticed that he was, indeed, friends with classical client-centred therapists and experiential therapists of every hue – a quality notably lacking in some of the early person-centered and experiential (PCE) conferences.

Then in 1999 came his (with Karen Tallman) seminal contribution to psychotherapy literature, *How Clients Make Therapy Work: the process of active self-healing*. If anything could be said to be a timeless classic, this is one, and it's a must-read for any aspiring therapist. Art and Karen put clients first in a way that, even in person-centred psychology, was ground-breaking – a genuine 'Why hasn't anyone done that before?' moment – while therapists took the back seat.

Fast forward to 2008, when Art gave two presentations at that year's PCE conference in Norwich. The hall was packed to the gunnels. The second presentation, which attendees believed was going to be the last in his career, received a long standing ovation. I had never seen anything like it. And I would not have seen the like of it again were it not for his gracious acceptance of the invitation to be a keynote speaker at the British Association for the Person-Centred Approach annual conference in 2013.

Sadly, many UK counsellors and psychotherapists will not know Art's work because almost all of it is located behind paywalls or in expensive, difficult-to-obtain books published in the US. The unique collection published here brings Art Bohart's work within affordable reach of the average UK therapist. Whether you are person-centred, experiential or integrative, there is a wealth of thought-provoking and challenging ideas for you here. And in these pages you will meet a man who has continued to champion clients as persons, active agents in their own healing, when the fashion increasingly is to see them as faulty machines in need of correction.

Pete Sanders
Spring 2021

Introduction

In the autumn of 2019, I started looking through papers I had presented at conferences and conventions but that had never been published. I discovered that these papers had ideas that had never made their way into any of my articles and books in print. Or, if I had published something on an idea, I found that I had elaborated on it in a presentation in a way that carried it further. I decided to ask PCCS Books if they would be interested in publishing papers based on these presentations. I am grateful that they have taken me up on that. I am quite excited to see these papers in print.

The first 11 papers I have selected focus on things of relevance to the practice of psychotherapy, but particularly to person-centred therapy. I have tried to arrange the papers so there is some continuity. Various ideas appear in different papers, but they are considered from different angles. I believe that, when the reader has finished reading the whole package, they will have a comprehensive understanding of what I think about such things as the role of wisdom in psychotherapy, the role of empathic listening, the idea of therapy as a meeting of persons, the contrast between a person-centred way of looking at therapy and an interventionist way, how to practise integratively from a person-centered point of view, the role of mindsets in how therapists proceed, the place of subjectivity in both psychotherapy and psychology, client courage, hope, and the nature of the self and self-development. I hope that my thoughts will provide some insights into all of these topics.

The final paper is a combination tongue-in-cheek/serious paper on self-criticism. It represents my interest in psychotherapy integration. After a (hopefully) 'light' look at self-criticism in the theories of different approaches to psychotherapy, it takes a more serious look at the topic in terms of these same theories. This is the only chapter where I have left the references tied to the chapter instead of including them in the master reference list. This is because this chapter stands alone from the other ones and I wanted to make it easier for readers to find the references specific to it. I have collated all the references for Chapters 1–11 in one master list at the end of the book.

The title of the book was PCCS Books' idea! I have convinced them to let me sub-title it 'The enhancement of human possibility' because that is what I think therapy is all about. I wish to thank Pete Sanders, Catherine Jackson and all the PCCS Books team for bringing this to life. I also wish to thank my wife, Karen Tallman, for her help in thinking through some of these ideas, as well as for helping edit the manuscript.

1 | Person-centred therapy: a radical vision

This paper is based on my presentation at the Conference of the World Association of Person-Centered and Experiential Psychotherapy and Counseling, Vienna, Austria, 8–12 July, 2018. There are so many 'either/ors' in the world that I have long been wanting to extol the unique virtues of the person-centered approach while also preserving the valuable insights of other psychotherapy approaches. This presentation was my most recent attempt at that.

I have two purposes in this talk. The first is to spell out a significant conceptual difference between the way person-centred therapists see the process of therapy and the way just about everyone else does – the 'dominant' paradigm. I think a pure person-centred approach is often misunderstood. It operates from a different mindset than do most other therapies.

I am not going to say that the person-centred approach is superior to other approaches, and particularly not superior to those in the person-centred/experiential community who do not adopt the pure person-centred approach. It is 'both/and', not 'either/or'. Other approaches are valuable, but in different ways. I believe in the idea of the tribes of the person-centred approach, or the 'tent' of the person-centred approach, and include within it emotion-focused therapy, Gendlin's focusing-oriented therapy and approaches such as that recently advocated by Finke (2017), about blending it with the dominant paradigm in the mental health establishment.

A long time ago, I made a presentation at the American Psychological Association Convention. I argued that the category 'psychotherapy' is a 'granfalloon of practices' (Bohart, 2006). I adopted that term from Kurt Vonnegut's book *Cat's Cradle*. A granfalloon is a category whose members are in it on a superficial basis. An example given by Vonnegut is the category 'Hoosiers' for people who come from the state of Indiana in the USA. They may share nothing in common except that they come from Indiana. I believe the category 'psychotherapy' is similar. In some cases, the only thing that practice A and B have in common is that they both call themselves 'psychotherapy'.

The category 'psychotherapy' is, if not a granfalloon, such a broad category that it tells us very little about its members. It is like the category 'sports'. In the USA, fishing is considered a sport. Lawn bowling is also considered a sport. So is automobile racing. So is soccer. So is sailing. And so is badminton. So is rock climbing. So is ice dancing. So is curling. Many consider chess a sport. Yet these 'sports' have virtually nothing in common. Some involve competition; others do not. Some involve strenuous physical activity; others do not. Some are done in a team; others are not, and so on.

While some of us may prefer one sport over another, we typically do not seriously argue over whether one sport is better than another. Yet we do argue over whether one approach to psychotherapy is better than another. We do this even in the person-centred community, where we argue over how person-centred therapy should 'really' be and attack those who do not agree with our version.

If we realise that the category 'psychotherapy' is a granfalloon of practices, then we can realise that the class members are different practices, each of which has its own unique identity and own virtues, just like individual people have their own, unique identities and virtues, yet they may not share very much in common. We can then perhaps appreciate each practice for what it uniquely offers.

Classical person-centred therapy is one form of practice. By 'classical', I mean that the therapist proceeds largely through empathic understanding responses. They have no agenda to 'fix' or change the client, or even to facilitate a certain kind of process. This differs somewhat from other forms of practice found in the person-centred community, such as emotion-focused therapy, focusing-oriented therapy or Finke's approach. It differs from other forms of practices in the larger humanistic psychotherapy community, such as existential psychotherapy and Gestalt psychotherapy. It also differs from other brands of therapy, such as the psychodynamic therapies and the cognitive-behavioural therapies. Yet each form of practice has value in its own right.

Let me delineate the difference between virtually all other forms of practice in the granfalloon 'psychotherapy' and the classical person-centred approach. In doing this, I am not going to say anything new that has not been said before by Peter Schmid, Barbara Brodley, the late Jerold Bozarth, Kathy Moon, Marge Witty, Barry Grant and many others. In contrast to other approaches, person-centred therapy focuses on the dialogue between two whole persons. I emphasise the idea of two whole persons. I am not saying that practitioners of other persuasions do not relate to clients as whole persons. Good therapists of all persuasions relate to their clients as whole persons. However, that is not their primary agenda, and it is the primary agenda of person-centred therapy. The theories of other approaches focus their practitioners' attention elsewhere. Their theories focus attention on aspects of the client – that is, clients as collections of various structures, behaviours and processes. And those therapists do relate to clients in such terms, even if, at the same time, they also relate to them, at least in part, as whole persons. It is a question of what the primary agenda is, what the therapist is up to. For the person-centred therapist, the dialogue with the client as a whole person is the agenda. That is what is figural, commanding the therapist's whole frame of attention. This is not true for other approaches.

A cartoon entitled 'Brain on a stick' by Jorge Cham (2009) illustrates this point. In the first panel of the cartoon there is a drawing of a person as they understand themselves – in terms of their dreams, hopes and so on. In the second panel is a drawing of the person as a university professor sees them. The drawing is of a brain on a stick.

If it were my cartoon, I would add a third panel. It would say, 'How psychotherapists see you.' It would include:

- disorders and diagnoses
- defence mechanisms
- internalised objects
- transference
- dysfunctional self-structure
- compromise formations
- primitive drives
- fused self-other object representations
- weak ego
- dysfunctional internal working model
- insecure attachment
- dysfunctional cognitive schemas
- conditioned dysfunctional emotional responses and behaviours
- dysfunctional skills and habits or missing effective skills and habits
- resistances and avoidances
- inauthenticity
- bad faith
- responsibility avoidance
- collusion
- dysfunctional narratives
- experiential avoidance
- primary and secondary emotional responses
- dysfunctional emotion schemes
- over- or under-regulation of emotion
- low differentiation
- unfinished business
- self-critical split.

As an example, let us say that the client says, 'I hate myself. I am a miserable son of a bitch. I don't deserve your attention. I might as well kill myself.' The person-centred therapist is listening to understand the client – to get the client's message, or, in the words of Marge Witty (personal communication, undated), to get the point the client is trying to convey. It is a dialogue. By contrast, an emotion-focused therapist, while also trying to understand the person's pain, would have part of their attention focused on something else besides the dialogue: the idea that the client is exhibiting a self-critical split. This may mobilise the emotion-focused therapist to intervene with the two-chair technique, while the person-centred therapist is purely focused on understanding the client. Similarly, the psychodynamic therapist might 'hear' an internalised critical object, possibly serving a defensive function against some disowned feeling. The cognitive therapist may 'hear' a dysfunctional thought to be combatted. None of these therapists would be primarily engaging in dialogue, as in two persons talking to one another. That is not what they are up to. Dialogue may also happen, but it would, at least in part, be secondary to the primary agenda of identifying markers in emotion-focused therapy,[1] defences and transferences in psychodynamic therapy, and dysfunctional cognitions in cognitive-behavioural therapy.

This is not bad. It is not that focusing on these things may not be useful, it is that it is not the person-centred therapist's agenda. The person-centred 'practice' is to listen to, connect with and relate to the whole person as a creature of hopes and dreams; as an authentic agent trying to make their way in a difficult and sometimes incomprehensible world; trying to find a way to fit their way of being effectively into that world; trying to make sense of their problem, themselves, or their life situation, to get their 'take' on what is going on with them and their world. And to hear it and share it through dialogue as fully as possible. The person-centred therapist wants to hear the person. That's it.

In her recent book *The Gardener and the Carpenter*, Alison Gopnik (2016), a developmental psychologist at the University of California, Berkeley, discusses 'parenting'. She contrasts a

---

1. Robert Elliott, one of the co-founders of emotion-focused therapy, who heard this presentation, told me afterwards that, for him, dialogue is primary, intervention is secondary. I would still argue that this leads to a split in attention, while the classical person-centred therapist's attention is wholly focused on the dialogue.

'carpenter' approach to parenting with a 'gardener' approach. I believe that most approaches to therapy, at least in part, adopt more of a 'carpenter' mentality, while what she says about the gardener mentality fits perfectly with the person-centred point of view. We can call what I am going to quote an evidence-based approach, since Gopnik is a well-regarded developmental psychologist researcher. She says that 'to "parent" is a goal-directed verb'. She goes on to say:

> … it describes a job, a kind of work. The goal is somehow to turn your child into a better or happier or more successful adult… The right kind of parenting will produce the right kind of child. (2016, p.3)

This is what she calls this the 'carpenter' model of parenting.

By contrast, Gopnik argues for the metaphor of parent as gardener. She writes that parenting:

> … is not a form of work, and it isn't and shouldn't be directed toward the goal of sculpting a child into a particular kind of adult. Instead, to be a parent… is to be a part of a profound and unique human relationship, to engage in a particular kind of love… Love doesn't have goals or benchmarks or blueprints, but it does have a purpose. The purpose is not to change the people we love, but to give them what they need to thrive. (2016, pp.9–10)

She continues:

> So our job as parents is not to make a particular kind of child. Instead, our job is to provide a protected space of love, safety, and stability in which children of many unpredictable kinds can flourish. Our job is not to shape our children's minds; it's to let those minds explore all the possibilities that the world allows. Our job is not to tell children how to play; it's to give them the toys and pick the toys up again after the kids are done. We can't make children learn, but we can let them learn. (p.20)

I would say, no better description of person-centred therapy exists.

To carry this contrast further, I'm going to compare the person-centred paradigm to the paradigm that is dominant in the field today. In the dominant paradigm, the therapist observes, at least to some degree, the client from outside and looks for signs of dysfunction. The therapist's job is to find ways to 'correct' this dysfunction. There are two forms of this paradigm. The stronger form is the 'treatment' paradigm. The treatment metaphor is patterned after medical doctors, who 'treat' disorders. From the person-centred point of view, I don't 'treat' anyone for anything.

The 'interventionist' paradigm is the weaker version. The therapist 'intervenes' with 'interventions' to make changes in clients. This focuses the therapist's attention on what needs to be 'intervened on' in the client and on the use of interventions. So the therapist's attention, when they're listening to the client, is, at least in part, on how to intervene, while the person-centred therapist's attention is wholly on hearing and receiving the client's message and story. While therapists from the dominant paradigm may also be listening to the client as a whole person in part, their focus on intervention, at the least, is going to cause a split in attention. I can guarantee that, because I've tried functioning in terms of the interventionist paradigm. At various times in my life, I've tried looking for transference, markers of self-critical splits, dysfunctional cognitions, avoidances and so on.

This is different, for example, to when I'm sitting with my wife and listening to her talk about a problem at work. I'm not thinking about what she's avoiding. I'm not thinking about what emotions she's not in touch with; I'm not thinking about her dysfunctional cognitions; I'm not thinking about whether she's transferring. I'm trying to listen to her as a whole person expressing her concerns. We are engaged in a dialogue. It is not an intervention. This also happens when I have a good dialogue with someone at lunch, say, at a conference. I'm trying to understand what the other person is saying. Just as, I hope, you're doing with me right now. I want to respond in a responsive way to what the other person is saying, thinking and experiencing, and that is what the person-centred therapist is trying to do.

I don't see myself as intervening. I'm certain Carl Rogers, at least later in his life, didn't either. I can't speak for him in the 1940s and early 1950s. But by the late 1950s, as his writings demonstrate, he did not see therapy as intervention.

I want to reiterate that there is nothing wrong with thinking of therapy as intervention. It makes perfect sense. It is a legitimate, useful way to proceed. Many professions do not focus on their work with a client as a person-to-person dialogue either – not doctors, dentists, tennis coaches, guitar teachers and so on. They focus on your bodily symptoms, your teeth, your stroke, or your fingers. Appropriately so. They may also engage you as whole persons and you may have wonderful dialogues with them, but that is not the primary reason you are together.

The point is that it is perfectly reasonable for therapists from other points of view to function in a manner similar to good tennis coaches, guitar teachers, doctors, dentists and so on – to focus on aspects of the person in order to correct dysfunction, promote better performance and so on, while also treating them as persons and engaging in some dialogue with them. And, therefore, it is perfectly reasonable for them to think in terms of what interventions will be useful.

However, for the person-centred therapist, therapy is a meeting of persons. Carl Rogers (Cissna & Anderson, 1994) said that therapy is actually a by-product of a meeting of persons. In other words, focus on the meeting and not on interventions, dysfunctional client processes, what to change and correct and so on.

So what do pure person-centred therapists do? In one sense, they do not 'reflect feelings', 'establish a therapeutic relationship', and so on. They do not have a goal of helping the client actualise, get in touch with feelings, become more process-oriented or explore themselves. Those things are likely to happen, but they are by-products.

Person-centred therapists want to meet in dialogue with this other person in their otherness and understand them, and that is it. They want, in one sense, to hold a very deep conversation, really get to know the other person, and give them a chance to hold the stage and present themselves and their ideas, thoughts, reflections and experiences to another person. The ideal person-centred therapist is, first and foremost and most basically, a witness.

I have previously, in a joint paper with Maureen O'Hara and Larry Leitner (Bohart et al.,1998), contrasted the medical-like model of therapy with humanistic models in general (of which person-centred therapy is a part):

> First, psychotherapy is not disorder-driven. The goal is not to alleviate a disorder, nor cure a condition, nor even to solve a problem. The goal is to provide a relationship as an optimal context within which an active, agentic client can reflect upon the patterns of his or her life. The therapist interacts with the client and through that interaction provides the client with an opportunity to experientially explore, examine, reflect, have a creative, co-constructive interactive experience with the therapist, and through all this, re-evaluate whatever life choices the person has made/is making, and revise if necessary. This may be motivated by the client's experience of distress, and one goal of the therapy may ultimately be to help the client alleviate the distress. But the focus of the therapy is not the distress, as if the distress were a 'pathogen' to be removed, or a 'condition' to be diagnosed and 'treated'. Rather, distress is seen as secondary to the individual's pursuing a more satisfying, meaningful life, and that is the primary focus of the therapy.
>
> There is thus no a priori reason why anyone could not avail themselves of such a relationship, regardless of their diagnosis. All people experience, value, set goals, make choices, evaluate, reflect, and are therefore potentially capable of utilizing the kind of experience a humanistic therapist provides. (Bohart et al., 1998, pp.144–145)

And how and why does this help? As I have just said, I believe that the process of meeting provides a place where the client feels recognised as a person, as an authentic agent, and listened to. That provides a safe space where the client can relax their defences and operate in a more 'intelligent', wise and creative fashion. As Maureen O'Hara (2018) and Bernie Neville (2018) have discussed, person-centred therapy (as well as emotion-focused and focusing-oriented therapies) leads to a heightened state of consciousness. We have a small bit of evidence that person-centred therapy indeed leads to this. I and my colleague Makenna Berry Newton rated three transcripts of person-centred therapy sessions (two of them with Carl Rogers as therapist) on wisdom scales and found that the clients showed signs of engaging in a process designed to lead to a wiser, heightened stage-of-consciousness way of living. These results were presented at a Society for Psychotherapy Research conference (Bohart & Berry, 2011; see also Chapter 5 in this volume).

Person-centred therapy essentially works by fostering creativity. However, the paradox is that the person-centred therapist is not trying to do this. They are not trying to get clients to relax their defences, promote more intelligent and wise ways of functioning or promote creativity. Those are by-products of the fundamental intention, or practice, which is to meet, listen to and share with another person, just like creative playing with one's child is good for the child but the best play is when the parent genuinely is playing with the child, not when the parent is 'intervening' to 'programme' or shape the child.

So, as Gopnik says about parenting – you parent by not parenting – the person-centred therapist does therapy by not doing therapy. It is actually quite Zen-like. And, if you do this, paradoxically, clients find their own way. Clients change but the therapist isn't changing them.

Therefore, there is no reason to talk about intervention, even though, despite what I just said, we actually do respond in terms of empathic responses. But empathic responses are not interventions. They are not to do something to the client or for the client. They are for the therapist. They are to do something for me – to help me, the therapist, understand the client. Carl

Rogers said towards the end of his life that empathic responses were how he tested his understanding (Rogers, 1986). If I'm intervening with anyone, I'm intervening with myself. This is a non-instrumental paradigm. It is an attempt to engage in a whole two-person I-thou – or, as Peter Schmid says more accurately, thou-I – dialogue (see Chapter 2, this volume).

A few years ago I was talking to Bruce Wampold. Bruce is the researcher and statistician who has most convincingly demonstrated the existence of the 'dodo bird verdict' – that all *bona fide* psychotherapies work approximately equally well for almost all conditions. Bruce suggested that he and I write an article on therapy as just talking. He said, 'What is wrong with just talking to someone?' I think that is what many clients want. We vastly underestimate the importance of that. Just talking, sharing, having another person hear you. Especially in a world where the fact is that most people don't listen. So what is wrong with having a practice where someone just listens? And we can have all these other interventive practices as well. It is not either/or.

I'd like to move on and talk about other aspects of person-centred therapy that follow from this. First, one derivative from what I have said is that person-centred therapy is a phenomenological approach. By this I mean that its level of focus is at the level of people's phenomenological experience of the world. It is interested in how people experience themselves and their world, as creatures of hopes, dreams, disappointments, frustrations and so on. This is true even at the philosophical and theoretical level. Rogers was always talking about what the whole person did: hold constructs tentatively, be open to internal experience and so on. Many other approaches describe the person in terms of underlying mechanisms. There is nothing wrong with this. It is perfectly valid and useful to try to understand persons at these other levels, but I would call these what the philosopher David Livingstone Smith (2013) has described as the 'sub-person' level – the level of underlying mechanisms.

I was struck by this when I was part of a symposium at a conference of the Society for the Exploration of Psychotherapy

Integration in 2018 (Holland et al., 2018). The cognitive-behavioural presenter, Steve Holland, presented a case of a man with 'social anxiety disorder.' He talked about how the man's dysfunctional schemas would get activated. This is a perfectly fine, useful way of conceptualising what was going on with the person, but it is in terms of a 'sub-person' mechanism. It is not how the person experiences themselves. I was socially anxious as a young man. I didn't experience my schemas getting activated. I experienced myself as a person who would become anxious when I faced certain social situations, and I wanted to understand that at the person level – in terms of my hopes and dreams and fears – not at the level of underlying schemas.

The person-centred therapist relates to the client at this level. In other words, the person-centred therapist works with the client at the level of the client as agent, in the terms that people use to describe themselves and their own experience. In so doing, one of the advantages of the person-centred approach is that it relates to the client as a whole person, which means that it also relates to the client in terms of the person's capacity for agency, and it is through mobilising client agency that I believe therapy works.

One more point about person-centred therapy. Person-centred therapy is a liberation philosophy. Its focus is on the uniqueness of the person. It does not compare one person with another, nor by some standard of behaviour. The goal is to understand the person in terms of their phenomenal world.

Most other approaches rely on normative judgements in one form or the other. The person and their problems are compared with some normative standard and judged to be inappropriate or dysfunctional in some way or the other. The goal is then to bring the person within the normative standard. The normative standard can be what society thinks about what a person should do or be, or what some professional diagnostic system says, or what some theory says.

I was struck by this too in the same symposium at the conference of the Society for the Exploration of Psychotherapy Integration. The case presented by Stephen Holland was of Sam. Sam was diagnosed with social anxiety disorder. He feared being judged as inadequate and undesirable. He showed avoidance. He had limited social interactions. He tended to avoid parties and other social situations, and did so when he could. He had dated women but no relationship had lasted longer than six months. He was not currently dating. He expressed anxiety about doing so. Sam had reported being introverted as a child.

It appeared to me that all these things were automatically taken as dysfunctional: fears of being judged as inadequate, showing avoidance of social situations, not having had a dating relationship longer than six months, and so on. I didn't get the sense that anyone questioned that assumption. The goal of the therapy then became to get him over these fears. There was no question raised as to whether or not there actually was something wrong or inappropriate about the way Sam was. That was taken as a given. The therapy then became the process of making him not doubt himself, have confidence, and learn to be a good conversationalist and outgoing and unafraid in social situations. In other words, to become a confident extrovert.

The point I want to make is, what is wrong with Sam being the way he is? What is wrong with him having fears about being judged as inadequate and undesirable? What is wrong with him avoiding social interactions, parties and the like, other than that he doesn't like it? What is wrong with him having anxiety about dating situations? Who says Sam should be confident, outgoing and the like? It is a social standard that says one ought to be confident and outgoing in social situations, particularly in the USA, where being an extrovert is valued.

My view of Sam is that there is nothing wrong with him. My view of working with him would not be to try to re-arrange him to fit some cultural norm. Rather, I would want to listen to him and hear him as the unique person he is. Through that, he might come to decide that he doesn't want to become more outgoing. Perhaps he might even decide he is comfortable being more shy and quieter, or perhaps having one or two friends but not a lot of friends. Perhaps he might find out he is not that interested in dating. Perhaps he then takes the pressure off himself to date, to have friends and so, and begins to feel fine. His anxiety goes away. Perhaps it is a 'should' that he is putting on himself, based on what others tell him he should be, implicitly or explicitly. What we person-centred therapists believe is that, by prizing and accepting the person just as they are, they will come to change, if they choose to. Of course, Sam may decide he still wants to change these things, in which case using some of the cognitive-behavioural stuff might be a great thing for a therapist to do.

We believe there is an intrinsic growth tendency, and when the organism is not turned against itself, it will spontaneously move to a better personal organisation and better-organised interface with the world to meet the needs of the person better. In order to do that, the person will take account of the world more, perceive it more accurately, and weigh and balance more wisely how they want to be with the world. They take care of themselves better vis-à-vis the world, because, after all, we are embedded in the world, as Martin Heidegger (1927/2008) said. Our being is 'being there'.

This is in contrast to other approaches that have an 'engineering' component, where the person is being engineered to respond in one way or the other. Again, I do not denigrate such approaches. Not only are they useful but many clients want and like them. In this particular case, Sam did want that. What I am saying, is that person-centred therapists have something unique to offer – an experience of being listened to and prized and accepted unconditionally as we are. This allows us to bring ourselves into a better balance with ourselves and our environments in a way that is more intrinsically wise for us – in ways that fundamentally respect who we are.

I would like to give a terrifying example of the engineering idea carried to an extreme. It's said that China is developing the technology to be able to implement a system using artificial intelligence and facial recognition to monitor, reward and punish its citizens' activities according to how they conform to the ideology of the state (Goldberg, 2018). It would not be too far afield to suggest that I could see therapies doing the same thing, shaping us into 'socially appropriate behaviour'. It already happens in mental hospitals, where withdrawn patients earn rewards when they come out of their rooms and socially interact because someone else thinks they should. Contrast this with Gendlin's (1967) report of the Wisconsin Project, in which he collaborated with Carl Rogers, where he worked with very withdrawn and uncommunicative people diagnosed with schizophrenia. He describes how he respectfully met them where they were, respected their space, respected their experience, and did not try to coax or force them to behave otherwise.

The core idea of person-centred therapy is a) a respect for persons, and b) the idea that people need to have the freedom to create their own paths, in dialogue with the world. In contrast, most points of view put an outside perspective on the client. We work from within their perspective, their world view, with how they understand themselves and their world. It is a matter of working organismically with them to assimilate a dialogue with us not only as an empathic other but as a representative of the world. Some interventionist approaches decide in advance a way of being and then try to shape you in that direction. Person-centred therapists are really trying to respect the person's path.

This becomes important now, in the era of neurodiversity. People are asserting their rights to be as they are: people called autistic, people who hear voices, deaf people and so on. Person-centred therapy is right in there. The core idea of person-centred therapy, as I see it, is valuing diversity and different voices and different paths. That is the core insight, even before the relationship idea.

Some of you might bring up problems like, what if your client is a child molester, or anorexic, starving themselves to death? In one sense, this changes nothing. Even a child molester or someone with an eating disorder should have the chance to have the experience of engaging in a meeting of persons, a dialogue, with an empathic witness. So should a person labelled schizophrenic. There are those who claim that such meeting can only reinforce dysfunctional behaviour. However, the Wisconsin Project, as well as other studies, have put the lie to this. Rogerian empathic responding does not reinforce dysfunctional behaviour. On the contrary, treating another person as a person mobilises that spark within them to move towards more effective personal organisation, which includes becoming more socially responsive. Research by those who do motivational interviewing (Miller & Rollnick, 2012) has demonstrated that empathic listening mobilises growth more than does confrontation, and does not 'reinforce' denial, avoidance behaviours and the like.

At the same time, we may have to step out of our role of purely trying to meet the person as they are in order to protect others in the social environment, or to keep them from hurting themselves. I will not dwell on the problems that causes for us here. I just note that it is a separate issue from whether they too deserve to have a meeting of persons.

In this regard, person-centred therapy is a liberation philosophy. It is an approach that helps people develop and explore their personal freedom and its boundaries. One of its goals, such as it has a goal – or perhaps it is better to say one of its outcomes – is to liberate people from restrictive shoulds and models of how one should be, as well as restrictive and oppressive social judgements.

Conclusion

I would like to conclude by briefly commenting on how what I have said fits with other approaches that I see as person-centred at base – not pure dialogical approaches, but where the therapist uses techniques to facilitate various kinds of self-exploration processes. I am most familiar with emotion-focused therapy and Gendlin's focusing-oriented approach. I value both approaches. Gene Gendlin and his ideas were the single most important influence on me as a would-be psychologist, even more than Rogers. And I strongly advocate emotion-focused therapy to my students. I see both approaches as important and necessary variants of the person-centred approach, along with many of the other variations, including Finke's approach of integrating person-centred values and ideas into practice in the mental health establishment, as well as motivational interviewing.

Going back to my starting point, I see them as different forms of practice that actualise person-centred values in different ways. I think this is necessary. I applaud efforts to bring person-centred values into the mental health system. I do believe that person-centred therapists and emotion-focused therapists can use diagnosis to help work with and understand their clients. However, they are no longer doing classical, pure person-centred therapy, and that is okay. They are doing a somewhat different form of person-centred-based practice, and that is also okay. All I am trying to do here is preserve the vision of a kind of 'pure' person-centred approach as offering something unique in its own right.

At the same time, I am glad variants like emotion-focused therapy and focusing-oriented therapy are around. We should be proud to have them as members of our community. I feel the same about motivational interviewing, which is increasingly coming to be called a directive form of client-centred therapy. I believe that to be an accurate description. We need all these forms of practice, which all basically honour the importance of empathic listening, acceptance and the idea that the client is the author of his or her own life. They are different ways forward, but all are valuable.

2 | Enhancing personhood: working with the one who does not get ill

This is a slightly modified and updated version of a talk given at an event to honour Peter Schmid's being awarded the Carl Rogers Award from the Society for Humanistic Psychology, Division 32 of the American Psychological Association. The event took place in Vienna, Austria, 7–9 May, 2009. I was honoured to have been invited to participate. It was a lovely 'meeting of persons' over dinners and through having many good talks, in a lovely city. I have changed the original title, which was 'Person-making: working with the one who does not get ill'.

> When Dongshan was unwell, a monk asked, 'You are ill, teacher, but is there anyone who does not get ill?'
> Dongshan said, 'There is.'
> The monk said, 'Does the one who is not ill look after you?'
> Dongshan said, 'I have the opportunity to look after him.'
> The monk said, 'How is it when you look after him?'
> Dongshan said, 'Then I don't see that he has any illness.'
>
> (Cleary, 1990, case 94, p.402)

This Zen story is sometimes interpreted as meaning that, when the monk is sick, he takes care of the part of himself 'that does not get ill'. In other words, he supports the strong or healthy part of himself. This is who the person-centred therapist might be said to take care of: the one who does not get ill. The person-centred therapist responds to the person inside. That includes that part of the client who is wise and intelligent – the part that can 'look out for the rest of the person' if given half a chance. The therapist does this by responding in an unconditionally positive regarding way. To respond in an unconditionally positive regarding way to another person is to treat them as a person; it is to treat them as an authentic source of their own experience (Bohart & Greenberg, 1997). It is also to respond to them with fundamental trust in them. The therapist also responds by prizing and understanding where the other person is coming from. This is to treat them as an implicitly sensible, fundamentally intelligent other, again – as an authentic source of experience. Finally, the therapist is congruent and genuine, which is yet another way of treating another as a person, worthy of being responded to as a person.

The person-centred therapist can do this, no matter what the person's 'problem' is. They listen and work with the one who does not get ill, no matter what that person is struggling with: anxiety, depression, borderline personality disorder, schizophrenia, anorexia, or terminal cancer. For instance, I talk to that sensible person inside the person labelled as schizophrenic, inside the person with Alzheimer's (Sabat, 2001), or inside the person labelled borderline.

Therapy, then, works by supporting the client's intrinsic capacity for self-righting and meaning-making. This does not mean that the therapist does not also listen to the 'hurt' parts, or the so-called irrational parts. The therapist tries to listen to and understand *all* of the person, but in so doing is supporting the intrinsic wisdom-making part of the person. And it is that intelligent person inside who ultimately knows what to do to best cope with whatever adversity the person is facing.

And is there such a wise person inside? Carl Rogers believed so. To quote him:

> I had been working with a highly intelligent mother whose boy was something of a hellion. The problem was clearly her early rejection of the boy, but over many interviews I could not help her to this insight. I drew her out, I gently pulled together the

evidence she had given, trying to help her see the pattern. But we got nowhere. Finally, I gave up. I told her that it seemed we had both tried, but we had failed, and that we might as well give up our contacts. She agreed. So we concluded the interview, shook hands, and she walked to the door of the office. Then she turned and asked, 'Do you ever take adults for counseling here?' When I replied in the affirmative, she said, 'Well then, I would like some help.' She came to the chair she had left, and began to pour out her despair about her marriage, her troubled relationship with her husband, her sense of failure and confusion, all very different from the sterile 'case history' she had given before. Real therapy began then, and ultimately it was very successful.

This incident was one of a number which helped me to experience the fact... that it is the client who knows what hurts, what directions to go, what problems are crucial, what experiences have been deeply buried. It began to occur to me that, unless I had a need to demonstrate my own cleverness and learning, I would do better to rely upon the client for the direction of movement in the process. (Rogers, 1961a, pp.11–12)

This quote expresses the crux of the person-centred point of view. Key to this point of view on psychotherapy is the idea that the therapist is not the one who solves the client's problems. Rather, the therapist is someone who, through their rapt attention, presence, empathic listening and positive appreciation of the client, provides the kind of relationship within which the person's own capacity for self-healing and self-righting can take over.

Put another way, the therapist relies on the person's own potential for making wise decisions for themselves. In essence, the therapist relies on the 'wisdom of the organism'. The individual is seen as having vast resources 'inside' them for productive, constructive and creative action, albeit they may not be apparent in the moment.

Such wisdom is not only the property of individuals. It can also be found in groups. To quote O'Hara (2008) with reference to some of the large-group work that she and Carl Rogers and others engaged in:

> ... there had emerged a shared intuition that if faith in the basic relational principles central to the person-centered approach... could be sustained long enough... somewhere along the way, a shift in our consciousness took place and we began to understand what we were doing less in the terms of an instrumental and causal phenomenon and more as an emergent process by which a vast, implicate wisdom might be apprehended and brought to the service of a suffering world, and ultimately to the evolution of consciousness. (p.vii)

It is not only Rogerian theory that holds that there is a kind of wisdom, or potential for wisdom, 'inside' the organism. A common exercise used in hypnotic and guided imagery approaches to therapy is to have a person learn how to relax, and then to imagine that they are visited by a figure who will turn out to be their 'inner guide'. The inner guide is often able to give the person wise advice and/or insight into what their problem is. It is not unheard of for a client to say something like, 'I just met the wisest person I've ever known' after doing the inner guide exercise (e.g. Zilbergeld & Lazarus, 1987).

Two other demonstrations of the existence of this potential for inner wisdom can be found in Gendlin's (1996) focusing exercise, and in approximately 50% of the clients who make progress in eye movement desensitization and reprocessing therapy (EMDR) (Shapiro, 1995). Gendlin's focusing exercise has been empirically demonstrated to be useful. Yet, although in therapy it is accompanied by a therapist who sits nearby, the process is entirely inner. The therapist may suggest the steps, but what emerges comes from the client. Similarly, in EMDR, the client is asked to keep a problem situation in mind, along with the feelings, while they then follow the therapist's moving fingers. All the therapist does is then say, 'What comes up for you now? Stay with that,' and institutes another round of eye movements. An unfolding process takes place where the person spontaneously goes through a series of healing steps that make sense in retrospect, but that cannot be predicted in advance (Bohart, 2001). Again, since all the therapist is doing is saying 'focus on that' and 'follow my fingers', this too is an inner and self-generated healing process. Approximately 50% of clients are able to resolve their problems with no other assistance. According to EMDR therapists (Shapiro, personal communication), the other 50% need additional assistance from the therapist in the form of the 'cognitive interweave'.

Others also work with clients from the assumption of a potentially wise, generative, client self-healing process. The co-founders of motivational interviewing, for instance, say:

> We believe that each person possesses a powerful potential for change. Your task as a therapist is to release that potential, to facilitate the natural change processes already inherent in the individual... (Miller & Rollnick, 1991, p.62)

And Orlinsky, Grawe and Parks (1994), in their review of the literature on how psychotherapy process relates to outcome, quote Arthur Kleinman (Kleinman, 1988a, p.112) when they say:

> We view psychotherapy as 'the activation through the process of interpersonal communication of a powerful endogenous therapeutic system that is part of the psychophysiology of all individuals and the sociophysiology of relationships'. (p.278)

This meaning of organismic or implicit wisdom refers to the person's potential for mobilising a forward-moving, generative, wisdom-developing process by engaging in an unfolding process of discovery, creativity and new meaning-making. It is this meaning and process that I wish to focus my attention on.

There is, however, a companion meaning that I wish to note. That is that there is already organismic wisdom in the person's present behaviour, no matter how dysfunctional, unwise or destructive and cruel its manifestation is. What 'organismic wisdom' refers to here is that a person's present behaviour, feelings or thoughts are based on some implicit effort on the part of the person, or organism, to take care of itself, based on how it sees, perceives and experiences the world in the moment, in the context of its own values, beliefs, history and goals.

On this meaning, several authors have held that there is always a bit of wisdom in even the most dysfunctional or destructive behaviour. Marsha Linehan (1997), from a radical behavioural perspective, holds that there is 'wisdom' in the moment in dysfunctional behaviour. She notes that many have held the idea that dysfunctional behaviour was once wise in the past, but is no longer wise. To the contrary, she holds that there is wisdom in it even in the present moment. She talks about the need of the therapist to dig for the 'nugget of gold in the bucket of sand' in order to help clients. Gendlin (1968) has talked about a 'positive thrust' underlying dysfunctional behaviour. Duncan, Solovey and Rusk (1992), from a strategic/solution-focused perspective, also hold that we need to respect and seek out the wisdom in the client's dysfunctional behaviour in order to help them change. As Bohart and Tallman (1999) have said:

> A core principle is that the client is *intelligible*. There is some reasonable component to their behavior patterns from within the clients' understanding of the world. There is some coherence and purpose to their dysfunctional behavior. (p. 239)

In this presentation, I will primarily focus on organismic wisdom as part of the growth process, in terms of the human's intrinsic capacity for proactively and creatively dealing with problems, creating new meaning and moving forward in an 'ecologically wise' fashion. However, this second meaning of organismic wisdom also will play a role.

Unpacking 'organismic' wisdom

What is this 'internal wisdom', or 'organismic wisdom' (as person-centred therapists are wont to call it)?

Note that Rogers says that 'it is the client who knows what hurts… what problems are crucial'. This implies that it is the client, at some level, who has a 'map' of the problem, has some kind of implicit understanding of what it consists of, what 'makes it up'.

This knowing is not necessarily conscious, left-brained, spelled-out knowing. For Rogerians, as well as for others, such as Milton Erickson and Carl Jung, what is 'in the unconscious' is not necessarily only repressed, avoided or primitive stuff. To the contrary, it is often the wisdom or the capacity for wisdom. Rogers says that the client 'knows what experiences have been deeply buried', but this knowing is not necessarily explicit. The person may vaguely sense the problem but not yet be able to identify it or articulate it in words. They may also vaguely sense the direction that healing or resolution will take, but not know yet how to put that into words or symbols, let alone how to enact it. In this sense, the wisdom that the person has is similar to the kind of wisdom Einstein had when he was working towards his theory of relativity by 'following a feeling' (Holton, 1971).

This is a crucial assumption: that such knowing or wisdom is, to use Maureen O'Hara's term (2008, p.vii), implicate. For Rogers (and Gendlin), this wisdom is also referred to as 'organismic', meaning that we can often feel or experience what we need to know to resolve our problems 'there' – where we experience things. Gendlin's (1970) theory of experiencing helps, in that it provides one explanation of what this 'organismic wisdom' is – the fact that we know more than we can say at a felt, bodily level, and that this knowing always has the potential to be explicated in words and symbols that carry forward the body's (and the organism's) capacity to understand, cope with and experience in a fuller, 'ecologically wise' fashion. This also relates to John Wood's (2008) contention that therapy consists of helping restore the dialogue between two modes of consciousness: the analytic and the holistic.

Rogers not only emphasises that clients know what hurts; they know what will help. He says that clients know 'what directions to go in'. Again, this does not mean that they know this explicitly. This breaks down into two components. First, they can sense or feel what will help. If a therapist suggests something that does not fit, the client may well have an organismic sense that it does not fit. I will call this more of a 'fitting' function: clients can know implicitly what is wise for them, what will nurture them, what will carry forward their experiencing. The second component of knowing what will help is what I will call the 'creative' function.

As I have already mentioned, clients, like Einstein, can feel or sense the directions they need to go in. That means they are capable of creating the steps needed to be taken to move forward, if given the proper room, space or supportive interactions. Where they go, where they may end up, is not necessarily predictable in advance (Bohart, 2001). As Gendlin has said:

> ... Roger's method brought it home that the decisions a person must make are inherently that person's own. No book knowledge enables another person to decide for anyone. That goes for life decisions and life-style as well as, moment by moment, what to talk about, feel into, struggle with. Another person might make a guess, but ultimately personal growth is from the inside outward. A process of change begins and moves in ways even the person's own mind cannot direct, let alone another person's mind.
> (Gendlin, 1984, p. 297)

The process, however, is not one of simply tuning in and finding that the steps are all there, already formed, ready to appear (Gendlin, 1990). Rather, it is an organismically wise, intelligent *process* of 'feeling one's way', by taking one step, learning from that step, taking the next step, and so on (Bohart, 2007). It is not like Einstein knew all the steps already towards his theory and he just had to recover them. Rather, he was guided by a feeling of where he was going, but he had to create the steps by taking a step, investigating what he had learned from that step, make mistakes, take the next step and so on. But he was able to check each step against that implicit felt sense, to know if it was a step in the right direction.

The final component of Rogers' view of organismic or implicit wisdom is that it is intrinsically pro-social – that is, that the actualising tendency has a tendency to produce movement in a pro-social direction. Although people often do not act in kind, prizing and pro-social ways towards others, Rogers asserted that, as individuals grow in therapy, they invariably move towards being more pro-social in their behaviour. This implies that a part of their potential for organismically or implicitly wise movement is the potential for becoming more kind, caring and prizing towards others.

So what is organismic wisdom? Karen Tallman and I (Bohart & Tallman, 1999) have preferred to call it 'ecological wisdom', to get at the fact that the person's behaviour is always directed toward and arises from that person's ecology (see also Zimring, 1995). We understand a personal ecology to be what is present and available in a person's current life world (in terms of people and physical world), as well as the ecology of their values, beliefs, goals and previous experiences. In terms of the 'wisdom' in a person's dysfunctional behaviour, we have said that:

> A client's behavior is ecologically wise within the constraints of his or her subjective world as he or she perceives it. We need to understand the ecology of the problem. Plus [as therapists] we need to take the time to let clients explore the contextual factors that keep them stuck. (Bohart & Tallman, 1999, p.240).

Furthermore, therapy is the process of helping the person to unfold that implicit ecological wisdom. As we have said:

> Often clients themselves are not aware of or do not take seriously the ecological wisdom of their own behaviors. It is often implicit and tacit. They have been too busy defending themselves or criticizing themselves to access it. When individuals are being self-critical, they do not pause to reflect in a way that leads to accessing the behavior's implicit logic. (Bohart & Tallman, 1999, pp. 241–242)

One example is of a woman living with a physically abusive husband. Friends tell her to leave him, but she finds herself unable to do it. She is highly self-critical for this, saying, 'I know I should.' As the therapist helps her unfold the implicit 'wisdom' of staying, she gets more fully aware of how constraining are the forces in her ecology keeping her in the relationship: the presence of children, lack of money and job skills, and pressures from friends and family. She is so busy self-criticising that she does not fully take these seriously. As she is able to unfold her implicit wisdom and take these factors seriously, she is able to evaluate them and begin to generate creative solutions to deal with them.

To unfold the idea of implicit, ecological or organismic wisdom further, I am going to rely on Robert Sternberg's ideas on wisdom. For Sternberg, wisdom is most fundamentally the capacity to *balance* various factors. He has emphasised, for instance, balancing the three components of intelligence (Sternberg, 2007): analytic intelligence (rational, left-brain, logical reasoning), practical intelligence (the ability to think practically about issues in one's life), and creativity (holistic, right-brain functioning). Elsewhere, he, like Rogers, has defined wisdom as including a pro-social element:

> ... people are wise to the extent [that] they apply their intelligence, creativity, and wisdom toward a common good by balancing their own interests, the interests of others, and the interests of organizations or other supra-individual entities; over the long and short terms; through the infusion of values; to adapt to, shape, and select environments. (Sternberg, 2004, p145)

It is important to note that wisdom is not *just* personal creativity. A person can be highly creative without being organismically wise, as they can also be highly intelligent in an analytic, intellectual sense, or high in practical wisdom, without being wise about taking care of either themselves or others.

As I have considered it here, organismic wisdom, or ecological wisdom, using the idea of balance, is a process that involves the person's unfolding and articulating what they know implicitly so that they can more proactively examine, sense, evaluate and balance all the factors in their life. This is done in order to come up with balances that optimise moving forward in terms of goals, values and past experiences in their experiential worlds with all of its constraints, while also 'taking care' of self, others and things that exist in their world. What happens in therapy is that the person is able to 'bring forth' that which is implicit, and that allows a kind of 'opening up' so that the whole 'space' of things can be considered, its contents evaluated against one another and balanced. Such balancing is enhanced by bringing things forth into conscious awareness, but the balancing itself is an organismic, experiential process that includes dialogue between both rational, left-brain elements and practical and creative right-brain elements (Wood, 2008), as well as with the world and with the therapist. And from this process often emerges, in the literal sense of new emergents, new creative insights and solutions that have existed as implicit potentials in the person's sense of the world before, but that have not previously had the space, the attention and the care to come forth and form.

If therapy at heart works through the process of relating to the one who does not get ill, to the implicitly intelligent, wise person inside, then we might expect that the therapy process will serve to enhance intelligent functioning, at least in the moment. There is some evidence that this is so (Zimring, 1990). In a series of studies using Gendlin's (1996) focusing technique, Zimring found that focusing led to improved use of attentional resources, improved complex problem-solving (doing maths problems), and improvements in memory. Given that the therapy process includes focusing on felt meanings (Gendlin, 1996) as a part of it, we might expect therapy also to enhance these functions.

Acting unwisely

However, a problem with the idea that we have this capacity for implicit wisdom has probably occurred to some of you already. If we do have this capacity, why is it that we act unwisely so often? It is not hard to demonstrate this. I suspect that if any of us reflect over the last few days we will find at least a few incidents where we did not act wisely, even if it was eating that fattening and unhealthy food that we know we should avoid (parenthetically, I keep being troubled by the thought that it would be boring to act wisely all the time, but that is another story).

I do not know the exact proportion of the time we act wisely to the time we act unwisely, but I suspect that unwise behaviour is quite frequent. People act impulsively. They act against their better self-interests. They are cruel to themselves and others. They make short-sighted decisions. People with anorexia sometimes starve themselves to death. People drink themselves to death and in the process ruin their relationships and their children's lives. Although they have the capacity for empathy, people frequently do not reach out to others; indeed, throughout history, they have treated 'the other' in dehumanising, violent and vicious ways, whether 'the other' be women, members of another tribe or ethnicity, people with disabilities, people who do not fit a given society's view of how one is supposed to look, or those of an alternative sexual orientation or lifestyle. Given that nearly 100 million people were killed in wars in the 20th century alone, and 10 million in the last decade of it (Hedges, 2003), it is not hard to argue that people frequently do not act in a wise way.

So how is it that we, who have this capacity for self-organising wisdom, so often act unwisely? And how does that fit with the idea that there is a bit of 'wisdom' in even the most unwise behaviour? How is it that people's inner guide gets so easily blocked? First, I suspect that, when we say there is some wisdom even in the most dysfunctional behaviour, we mean to say that the person, from within their subjective world view, is making decisions based on their felt understandings of their place in the world and on what will help them make their way better. This knowledge may be felt, implicit or impulsive. But it is 'wise' to the extent that it is based on some quick, organismic, implicit way of balancing what the organism thinks it needs in that moment. That it can be selfish, cruel, against one's own better interests, and even, from the outside, stupid does not obviate the fact that, from the Rogerian perspective, it is coming from the actualising tendency – the tendency of the organism to try to forward itself, to try to decide what is best for itself, given its immediate understanding of its self and its ecology.

In that case, why is it so often unwise? I think there are at least two reasons for this. First, Rogerian theory has focused on rigidity and lack of openness. Rogers' answer to why people are unable to act in an ecologically wise fashion was simple. He believed that, because people were treated with conditions of worth as children (and as adults), they have lost touch with their organismic valuing process. They get lost in rigid 'shoulds', and so are unable to act wisely. All that is needed to restore this capacity, according to Rogers' earlier theorising, is to treat them with unconditional positive regard so they can get over their conditions of worth and learn to trust themselves. In other words, it seems as if Rogers believed that children would have the capacity to act in an organismically wise fashion – i.e. score highly on the process scale (Rogers, 1961a) – right from the start if they weren't 'interfered with' by parents who imposed conditions of worth on them.

Perhaps I am caricaturing Rogers' view a little. But this view seems to imply that the process of therapy is simply one of the therapist, through providing the conditions of unconditional positive regard and empathic understanding, releasing the client from conditions of worth so that this organismically wise process can naturally operate. From then on, the client can move to solve their personal problems. Rogers' portrayal of psychotherapy, in essence, was that the goal of the therapist was to *get out of the client's way*. This implies that this self-healing process, this organismic wisdom, lies *within* the person and just needs a kind of space within which it can operate. Once freed up, it operates independently of the other person in the room – the therapist.

Now, I note before I continue that this is not entirely fair, because Rogers changed his views later in his life to emphasise more the idea that therapy is a 'meeting of persons' (Anderson & Cissna, 1997). Although I do not believe Rogers ever fully explored the implications of this, it would seem to me to suggest that more is going on than merely that the therapist is a 'releaser' who provides a space for clients to actualise.

However, Rogers' earlier view that organismic wisdom is somehow just 'within' the person creates the conundrum that I am left with: if so, why do people not act wisely more often? Is it such a special 'seed' that it can only grow in the rarified soil of psychotherapy? Or is it that we are all so screwed up from our childhoods that *without* therapy we will not act wisely? But that does not work either, because most of us act wisely at least some of the time, and some individuals become paragons of wisdom.

Nonetheless, there can be little doubt that one reason people do not act in an ecologically wise fashion is that they may have internalised rigid constructs that get in the way of this process operating in an optimal fashion. We (Bohart & Tallman, 1999) have emphasised a second reason for why people may not act in an ecologically wise fashion. That has more to do with situational reasons. That is that, when people feel threatened, defensive, under high stress or have little safe time and space in their lives to think and reflect, they are more likely to act rigidly, impulsively, cruelly and in an ecologically unwise fashion. However, it should be noted that some people under stress are still able to act in an ecologically wise fashion (Leicester & O'Hara, 2009).

Both of these reasons emphasise that something gets in the way of an inwardly open process. Rogers stressed the need for inner openness. Indeed, Rogers' process scale is a measure of inner openness and receptive listening. I have emphasised over and over the importance of a receptive listening process to productive change in therapy (Bohart, 2007, 2008), as have others (Wood, 2008). In order for a person to move forward in a creative, constructive process, they must hold their constructs tentatively and *listen* receptively to themselves and to others. This condition can be found in Rogerian therapy, the focusing exercise, EMDR and the inner guide exercise.

This inwardly open, receptive listening process allows things to 'bubble up' and for creativity to emerge. What is needed to facilitate it is a safe space and empathic listening. I particularly emphasise the need for some space. I believe it is quite literally having some space within which to reflect, feel and think that allows one to move from implicit, encapsulated, reactive functioning into a fuller openness that allows dimensions of problems and experience to be felt, explored, sensed, travelled, integrated and balanced.

Enhancing personhood

However, even though I believe that a safe space and empathic listening (self-listening, often) is a necessary pre-requisite for promoting the unfolding of self-organising wisdom, I do not believe that, by itself, it is necessarily sufficient. I believe that these conditions foster the emergence of creative functioning, but not necessarily of what I would call a wisdom-facilitating process. By a wisdom-facilitating process, I mean more than just a process that helps a person move beyond old forms and find new and emergent solutions to problems. I mean a process that helps the person more productively locate themselves as persons in relationship both to themselves and to others. And to locate oneself as a *person* in relationship to others is to recognise the 'person-ness' of others, and to come more and more to prize them as persons.

It would seem that therefore the process is more than fostering conditions for creativity. It involves conditions that foster what I would call, after being influenced by Peter Schmid, 'enhancing personhood'. Peter has been the foremost theorist of 'the person' in person-centred thinking (Schmid, 2002, 2003, 2006, 2007; Schmid & Mearns, 2006). Specifically focusing on psychotherapy, I believe that we must see therapy not merely as the process of releasing the organismic wisdom-facilitating process from its shackles, but more as a sophisticated process of 'enhancing personhood'. Now I realise that the 'enhancing personhood' metaphor has problems. Probably it is more accurate to say that therapy is the process of providing a relational space, or dialogue, within which a process of the person emerging, or developing, can take place. The person in therapy is already a person. The process is that of being recognised as a person, which allows the self as a person to emerge and develop more fully.

Peter Schmid has fleshed out the notion of 'person' and, in so doing, has provided a new lens through which to see the nature and practice of person-centred psychotherapy. His notions help us understand the issue of organismic, intrinsic or ecological wisdom and how it unfolds in therapy, as well as to begin to understand how and when it might be more likely to happen outside of therapy.

Here, I will only briefly outline the key points. First, Schmid points out that the notion of the person includes both the notion of the substantial or individual aspects of a person and the relational or dialogic aspects. The substantial or individual aspect has to do with autonomy and independence. This includes ideas like uniqueness, freedom and dignity, 'unity, sovereignty, and self-determination…' (Schmid, 2007, p.35). As Schmid notes, this was a particularly influential conception in Rogers' early period: '[Rogers] consequently sees therapy as a process of the… development of personality…' (Schmid, 2007, p.35). It includes ideas like the person being self-determined, the actualising tendency, trust in the organism and experience, authenticity, and incongruence between various aspects of the self as psychological dysfunction. From this point of view, therapy works by strengthening the individual aspects of the person – helping them become congruent, more autonomous, self-determined, able to trust their organism and experience, and so on.

However, Schmid points out that the relational notion of the person is equally important, and is as much a part of the notion of person as is the individual or substantial part. As he (Schmid, 2006) has noted, persons *are* dialogue. Being a person means being from and being in relationships. It is through relationships and towards relationships with others that we become persons. 'We are not only *in* relationships; as persons we *are* relationships' (Schmid, 2007, p.36). This is characteristic of Rogers' later phase, as he emphasised groups and 'person to person'. This includes the emphasis on person as process, presence as openness to others, authenticity as congruence between experience and communication, and immediacy. 'Consequently, mutual encounter is a decisive element in therapy and personal development, and Rogers now considers genuineness as a pre-eminent facilitative condition' (Schmid, 2007, p.36).

Schmid goes on to emphasise that it is the tension between self-reliance and commitment that characterises the human being. What it means to be a person is characterised by the actualising tendency and the fully functioning person on the one hand and encounter and presence on the other.

For Schmid, psychotherapy is encounter. Encounter is acknowledging the otherness of the other. It is not merely 'being alongside' (i.e. the supportive function I have discussed above that

Rogers discussed), but also 'being counter to', which means being face-to-face with (Schmid & Mearns, 2006). Being with another person means to acknowledge them as an 'other', to acknowledge their fundamental difference from you, to *recognise* that fundamental difference. As such, the movement of psychotherapy is from the other to the self. It is an opening to the client and to whatever the client presents. This is the process that could be described as helping the person become a person, and that is the goal and process of psychotherapy. Parenthetically, I note that, for Schmid (and for me and most person-centred therapists), acknowledging the other and encountering the other is an enriching experience – unlike for Sartre, for whom it created nausea.

Schmid says that it is this face-to-face encounter, in dialogue, that creates the condition for self-consciousness, or reflection. Creating the condition for self-consciousness and reflection is creating the condition for a good 'workspace' (Bohart & Tallman, 1999), within which the person can come forth. Schmid also says that 'encounter is the core of an *intersubjective, co-creative process of personalization* (i.e. becoming a person) through meeting at relational depth or encounter' (Schmid, 2007, p.41). Therapy thus becomes a fostering of the process of 'becoming a person' (Rogers, 1961a), because 'being a person means: to disclose, to reveal oneself to oneself and to the Other, thus enabling "co-experiencing"' (Schmid, 2003, p.113, italics removed).

> Standing face to face avoids both identification and objectification. It enables encounter… The awakening from the totality of the being-caught-in-oneself does not happen through 'being independent'. Rather, the Other is the power which liberates the I from oneself… Thus, encounter in dialogue turns out to be a condition for self-consciousness. (Schmid, 2002, p.63)

And further:

> Being able to be touched, impressed, surprised, changed, altered, growing and also being able to stick to one's own experiences and symbolization… to value from within (without judging the

person of the Other), to have one's point of view. This is what being present means and what being a person means. (Schmid, 2002, p.63)

In sum, psychotherapy can be called, in one sense, the process of 'enhancing personhood'. Becoming a person happens through the process of encounter. We have to remember that people are dialogue, so this process of encounter is dialogue. As Peter Schmid points out, it is not that the therapist 'creates a dialogue', or that they 'bring the client into dialogue', but rather that the encounter between therapist and client already is dialogue because persons are dialogue, and as long as there is encounter, there is dialogue. Finally, I want to note that Schmid observes that this is not a process of the therapist projecting their own self into the client to understand the client, but rather a process of opening up to the client.

In other words, as I interpret Schmid, becoming a person happens by being related to as a person, which means face-to-face, in dialogue. This means recognising and opening up to the uniqueness of the other and the otherness of the other. It also means letting them recognise you as an other to them. I think of Martin Heidegger's well-known metaphor of the clearing (for example, Heidegger, 1971/2001). It is as if, in this kind of relationship, the other person's 'person-ness' is able to emerge out of the shadows into the clearing, or the space between the two of you. As I carry my imagination further on this, I imagine, as Schmid says, that this is an optimal condition for self-consciousness or reflectivity – not just reflectivity in terms of themselves, but reflectivity in the context of an other. In other words, the reflectivity is shared in the space that the two people occupy together. One is not just reflecting upon oneself alone, but in the context of the other. It is shared. It is 'co-reflecting', or reflecting together. And this is the process within which the deepest sense of accessing and recognising oneself as a person occurs, in the context of an other. In so doing, as we access our inner wisdom, we do so in the context of enhancing personhood, in the context of me becoming a person in the sharing and relationship with an other.

The person becomes more self-aware as they also become more other-aware (of you, the therapist, as a person). As this happens, they are able, in relationship, to get out of themselves, but also to gain a clearer sense of their own uniqueness, their own distinctiveness, their own values, their own life space, their own 'there-ness', so to speak, in relation to the other, the therapist, because to really know oneself as a person is to know oneself in relation to other persons. As this happens, as the whole Gestalt of *the person* emerges into the clearing, the whole Gestalt forms. The person becomes more organised, more coherent. They become more aware of their own experiencing; they become more aware of the ecological context of their lives. In my imagination, they come more into focus, both to themselves and to others. As they become more aware of you the other person, their awareness stretches outside of themselves. As Peter Schmid says, they are able to escape from being-caught-in-oneself, and the 'I' gets liberated from oneself. 'I' becomes more the reflexive awareness of the whole field of relationships, which is self, past experience, current values and goals and myself-in-relationship, not only to you the therapist but, by extension, to others in my life and to my care for the world.

It is then the process of developing the personhood of the person, which also is the self-organising wisdom process. It is the process of creativity emerging as part of the 'dance' of discovering/actualising oneself in the context of and presence of other persons. Thus, actualisation, or the 'activation' of organismic wisdom, is *a part* of becoming a person, and happens in relation, in dialogue. This is why it can also happen in groups (O'Hara, 1997; Wood, 2008). It is the sharing of experience that seems to most deeply facilitate the developing of organismic wisdom in the context of person-making.

This does not mean that people can only access their potential for ecological wisdom in the 'enhancing personhood' context of therapeutic relationships. Clearly people do act ecologically wisely outside of such relationships (Leicester & O'Hara, 2009). I will not examine this issue in detail here. It would be interesting to examine the contexts in which people do act ecologically wisely outside of therapy. I suspect that at least some of them are contexts that support people's 'personhood'. Some self-help procedures, such as Gendlin's focusing technique, the inner guide exercise or journaling seem to have an implicit person-enhancing component. These activities do confront the self with the self in an empathic context. These may foster the self taking care of and listening to the self. The process may not be as powerful as it is in the context of another person. Gendlin has often noted that focusing seems to work better when another person is sitting next to you, even if that other person is saying nothing but just keeping you company (e.g. Gendlin, 1990). Similarly, EMDR appears to work better when it is another person guiding your moving eyes with their fingers than if you are using a machine to do it.

Finally, there is some research supporting the idea that, when people are made aware of their 'personhood', they are more likely to act in a pro-social, moral fashion. A number of studies on 'de-individuation' found that, when people were unaware of themselves and their identities, they were less likely to act in a pro-social fashion, although the results depended on other factors as well (e.g. Diener, 1979). The most cited example of this has been the Stanford Prison Experiment (Haney et al., 1973), which purported to show that the depersonalisation of both guards and prisoners in a simulated prison setting led to brutal behaviour on the part of guards and psychological breakdowns on the part of prisoners. However, recent archival research has revealed that these results may have been due more to demand characteristics and compliance with authority than de-individuation (Le Texier, 2019).

Person-centred psychotherapy

Organismic wisdom, or 'self-organizing wisdom' (Wood, 2008), then, can be said to be a product of dialogue, of encounter, and of the process of enhancing personhood or becoming a person. In this sense, person-centred therapy works by speaking with the wise person 'inside' or, perhaps more accurately, by being open and receptive to the person as they come forth, and that *is* speaking to the wise person inside. The therapist receives the other as a sensible, sense-making person.

Therefore, the process of enhancing personhood in therapy is not simply a process of *releasing* the organismic wisdom that presumably exists in a blocked form in the client. Rather, it is a whole-person process of two people engaging with one another and it is that engaging, in the right kind of relationship, that facilitates and mobilises the organismic wisdom of the client. There is research to support this. Staudinger and Baltes (1996) found that people made wiser decisions when they *imagined* talking to a wise friend about a dilemma than when they merely thought about it without imagining such a dialogue. Bavelas and colleagues (2000) found that people's conversations were richer and fuller if someone was listening to them, as evidenced by simple responses that showed they were listening, than if the other person appeared distracted. I have already mentioned Eugene Gendlin's oft-made observation that, when people focus, which is an entirely internally directed process, it works better if someone is sitting with them, even if that other person doesn't say anything.

In this regard, we need to rethink the roles of unconditional positive regard, empathic understanding and congruence. Unconditional positive regard must be seen as a matter of two persons relating to one another. It is not merely a process of one person 'providing' a non-judgemental atmosphere for another. Rather, it is a *meeting* of two people in which one person relates to the other with unconditional respect, *as if the other person is a person worthy of being respected, of being listened to and of being able to make responsible and logical decisions for him or herself.* In other words, unconditional positive regard does not merely remove conditions of worth; it is an active process of appreciating the other as a person. Similarly, empathic understanding is not merely a process of one person helping the other explore themselves; it too is an active engaging process of encountering the other person in order to understand them. To be understood by an other, or to have an other try to understand oneself, is a process of being responded to as if one is a person – a person who has their own ideas, own thoughts and own experiences that are worthy of being understood by an other. In that context, the active enhancing personhood part of the self comes to the fore and operates in the context of sharing one's personhood with another, through the sharing of experiences. The person 'rises to' the other, and moves towards them in an active form of self-creation and self-carrying-forward. Finally, congruence is the core act of *being* a person with the other.

We also need to rethink what the client is doing in therapy. A typical view is that the client is engaging in a self-exploration process and is accompanied by the therapist, who is basically just sitting there and being a companion while the client introspects. While there can be some truth in this description, it misses another component: that even when the therapist is responding with empathic understanding responses, they are still interacting *as a person* with the other, and what is healing is in part the fact that the client is being received *by another person*, not just being an 'empathy machine' that is helping them self-explore. Even while the client is self-exploring, they are also *speaking to* a person. In one research study that I conducted with Gayle Byock (Bohart & Byock, 2005), we came to believe that 'Gloria', in the famous film with Carl Rogers (Shostrom, 1965), was not primarily introspecting while being accompanied by Rogers. Rather, what she was primarily doing was trying to *explain herself* to Rogers, to *get herself across* to Rogers, and, in order to do that, she was introspecting. The process was highly interactive and, in that context, 'Gloria' did experience the kind of process movement that characterises the organismic wisdom-facilitating process, resulting both in her eventually making a decision as to what to do about her daughter and in her accessing and evaluating her feelings towards her father, and making a decision to do something that would help her cope in the future. In doing all of this, she was also 'enhancing personhood', revealing herself to an other and, at the same time, developing and discovering her personhood in the context of an other.

To bring us full circle to working with the one who does not get ill, the process of therapy is that of listening to the potentially wise person inside. Therefore, when I talk to the *person,* I am talking to that sensible person inside the individual who has been diagnosed as schizophrenic, as borderline or as having Alzheimer's (Sabat, 2001). The whole idea is that, no matter how 'broken' they are, you give them a chance to stand up, show themselves, explain themselves and make sense to you and to themselves, and you open up to them and the two of you come to make sense together.

Conclusion

Although humans have the capacity for organismic, or ecological, wisdom, they do not always act in accordance with it. We have seen that, in psychotherapy, it is through the process of being related to as a person, as the 'one who does not get ill', that the person is able to emerge, and that this emergence is the process of the individual coming to act and decide in a wise fashion. It is through dialogue that this process happens. It is through dialogue that implicit wisdom is able to unfold into explicit wisdom.

It follows that, when people do not act wisely, it is in part because they are not being treated as a person, or are not treating themselves as a person. This can happen for many reasons. Among them may be that they are in relationships where people do not relate to one another in a 'thou-I' fashion, where they do not open themselves up to the other, or where they do not treat the other as a person. Or where they relate to themselves in this same manner, perhaps as an object to be manipulated or to be acted upon. Or where stress and circumstances interfere with the person's ability to create that clearing, that space, where they can hear themselves and be in touch with themselves as a person. Or where, because of the way they have been treated in the past, they relate to themselves (and maybe to others) in critical, dehumanising ways. Or where, because of earlier experiences, they are shut off to their own capacity for empathic listening, for listening to others as persons, because they have not had that experience themselves. In conclusion, the wisdom-enhancing process is part and parcel of the enhancing personhood process.

3 Further meditations on clients' wisdom

Much of this paper was going to be presented at a meeting of the Society for the Exploration of Psychotherapy Integration in Vancouver, Canada, 28–30 May, 2020, under the title 'Psychotherapy Integration and the Facilitation of Clients' Creativity and Self-Organizing Wisdom'. However, the conference was cancelled due to the coronavirus pandemic. I have modified it to both be a follow-up on the 'Enhancing Personhood' paper that I presented in Vienna in 2009 (see Chapter 2) and to focus on person-centred therapy.

As stated in Chapter 2, person-centred theory emphasises people's capacities for self-organising wisdom (Wood, 2008), alternatively sometimes termed 'organismic wisdom', or the actualising tendency (although I see self-organising wisdom as a component of the actualising tendency). In this paper, I reflect further on the issue of why people act unwisely. I also consider the idea that, even if they are behaving unwisely, there may be some 'wisdom' in what they are doing, from their point of view. Finally, I go on to further consider how therapy facilitates growth in wisdom.

One problem that arises for person-centred therapists is, if people have an intrinsic capacity for thinking and behaving in 'wise' ways, why do they so often behave unwisely?

There are different forms of unwise behaviour. Examples include doing the same thing over and over when it is not working, not paying attention to reliable information (such as on global warming), making unwise relationship choices, being insensitive and intolerant, and engaging in cruel or abusive behaviour. Unwise behaviour can manifest in addictive and other self-harming behaviours, such as eating disorders and destructive self-criticism. Suicide may, under some circumstances, be an unwise choice. Acting unwisely can also include acting in ways that disrupt and tear down the humane fabric of society: war, murder, robbery, environmental destruction, lack of charity towards others, totalitarianism, inquisition, torture, violation of civil rights, racism, sexism, and oppression of gays, lesbians and transsexuals. Figures such as Pol Pot, Stalin, Hitler and Donald Trump come to mind, as well as some of those who have supported them.

There is a possibility that there is some 'wisdom' in even the most dysfunctional or immoral behaviour. What this means is that, in many cases, persons could be said to be acting 'wisely' from their point of view, even if they are acting in a narrow, short-sighted way in terms of the world. Even with self-destructive behaviour, we can assume that, in the moment, the person implicitly believes they are acting wisely in terms of their place in the world – in terms of the pressures on them, the opportunities and limits available to them, their values, aims and goals and their perceived deprivations. They choose the behaviour that their organism decides best meets its needs in terms of maintaining a balance between themselves and the stresses and strains of their world. We can call it impulsive, unwise or cruel from the outside, but in that moment, it is an emergent from the whole person's experience of self and world in their context.

Consider an example. A client – let's call her Maria – continually beats herself up emotionally, even though, objectively, she is doing well in life. It seems irrational from outside. If you try to convince her she is doing fine, she resists and argues back.

A cognitive-behaviourist would see the client as engaging in 'dysfunctional thinking'. I would suggest that there is some sense, or even functionality, in the client's behaviour from within her point of view. Her 'radar' is particularly attuned to danger. Maybe this came from having been abused as a child. Wherever it came from, the client sets her perceptual detection devices high to make a priority of picking up danger. She particularly notices when she makes a mistake. Then she berates herself for that. Why? First, she is highly attuned to personal failings because she feels unsafe. Her way to keep herself safe is to make sure she does everything properly. Second, feeling unsafe, she then picks on herself to try to whip herself into shape. She does not know how to do it any better than to severely castigate herself for screwing up. After all, it is a matter of life and death to her. If you try to reassure her or talk her out of this, it does not work. Why? Because you are threatening her life support. She does not want to give up her vigilance. She is afraid you are mollifying her, or sugarcoating things. She wants to be a tough realist with herself and not make excuses for herself.

You might accuse her of being a perfectionist. Yet why is she so obsessed with perfection? Because she is afraid of the consequences of not doing something right. From her point of view, her 'dysfunctional' self-criticism is an attempt to 'right' her ship and to keep her safe and on the planet. That it may have harmful side effects – making her feel bad and worthless, perhaps causing depression and anxiety or even, in the extreme, making her feel suicidal – is an unfortunate side consequence. But it would be worse, from her implicit point of view, not to be honest with herself.

Underlying all this is most likely a belief that she is basically bad or incompetent (again, possibly learned in childhood). At an implicit level, she probably believes that, because she is bad and incompetent, she has to struggle hard even to succeed at all. She needs to keep up her vigilance constantly just to stay afloat. Imagine yourself on a make-shift raft in the middle of the ocean, constantly having to check for every little leak. That is how she experiences the world. And if she misses a leak, she berates herself, because it is so important to stay vigilant to any water coming in.

From within her world view, her destructive self-criticism makes perfect sense; it is 'wise'. Or at least it is functional, even if only in part. It is helping her deal with her perceived sense of threat, no matter how inefficiently. Yet at the same time, from outside, her self-criticism is 'unwise', 'irrational', and perhaps even self-destructive.

How does this view of client 'wisdom' fit with the idea that clients have an actualising tendency that manifests itself in their capacity for self-organising wisdom? It is a part of it. From Carl Rogers' point of view, even destructive or self-destructive behaviour comes out of the organism's attempts to actualise itself. A tree may have to grow in distorted or twisted ways to get enough sunlight. The organism is doing the best it can to actualise and preserve itself, given its prior experiences, its 'view' of the world and its current circumstances. That its behaviour may be twisted, harmful, or awful, is another story. But it is this capacity for trying to act wisely as best it can that allows the organism, under proper supportive circumstances, to grow towards more truly wise behaviour. So how does psychotherapy help with this? I shall discuss that later.

I will now turn to the question of why, if we have this capacity for acting wisely, we so often act unwisely. In order to do this, I must consider the concept of wisdom itself.

Wisdom

What is wisdom? There are a number of different conceptualisations. I will base my discussion on the ideas of Baltes & Staudinger (2000) and their Berlin Wisdom Paradigm, and the work of Robert Sternberg (1998). From the perspective of the Berlin Wisdom Paradigm, wisdom is defined as 'expertise in the fundamental pragmatics of life'. This refers to the person's ability to show good judgement, make good decisions and give good advice with regard to important areas of life, particularly those in which there is uncertainty.

There are five dimensions to wisdom (Staudinger et al., 1994). The first is rich, factual knowledge about life. This includes knowledge about 'human nature and the life course' (Anonymous, 2016). The second is rich procedural knowledge, which has to do with knowledge about effective strategies and behaviours for making decisions and dealing with life's problems.

The third is life-span contextualism. This includes 'having an awareness and understanding of the many contexts of life; how they relate to each other and change over the lifespan' (Anonymous, 2016). The fourth is relativism, which includes 'an acknowledgment of individual, social and cultural differences in values and life priorities' (Anonymous, 2016). Finally, the fifth component is uncertainty: 'knowing the limits of one's own knowledge' (Anonymous, 2016).

The other concept of wisdom I use is that of Sternberg (1998). For Sternberg, wisdom is basically balancing the factors involved in making a decision. It is balancing one's self-interest with the interests of others; balancing the use of different types of intelligence in making a decision – analytic intelligence, practical intelligence and creativity – and balancing thought and emotion. By extension, one can imagine that it would also include trying to find the best balance between different principles of morality when they conflict, different goals in one's life when they conflict, different values, different legal principles, different wishes and aims, long-term aims and short-term aims, and so on.

Implicit in Sternberg's model, and explicit in the Berlin Wisdom Paradigm, is the idea of 'heightened consciousness'. Sternberg's model implies the ability of the person to take a broader perspective: to get 'above' the various components of an issue and to see them in context, and then try to find the best way of balancing, coordinating or choosing among them. The Berlin Wisdom Paradigm emphasises contextualism, relativism and uncertainty, all of which imply the need to 'get above' and adopt a meta-perspective from which one can take multiple issues into account. This includes the ability to reflect, integrate different ideas and bits of information together, and rise above splitting and compartmentalisation.

These wisdom models have much in common with other conceptualisations of cognitive development. These include Lawrence Kohlberg's model of the development of moral thinking (Kohlberg & Hersh, 1997), Jean Piaget's model of cognitive development (Cowan, 1978), William Perry's (1970) model of the development of thinking during the college years, and Belenky and colleagues' (1986) model of development of women's ways of knowing. In all these models, higher-order thinking involves the ability to think multidimensionally – to 'stand above', to take multiple dimensions on a situation into account, and to integrate them (i.e. 'balance' different factors). These models are similar to Carl Rogers' (1959) process scale, which is, in my view, a developmental scale of more effective information processing as well as of ways of relating to one's self and experience. For instance, on the process scale, one moves from holding constructs rigidly through to the higher end, which emphasises holding constructs tentatively. All these models hold that higher-level functioning includes moving out of rigid either/or ways of thinking and of experiencing the world – getting out of rigidly held rules and beliefs or a belief in the absolute truth of one's convictions – and becoming able to see multiple perspectives and try to take them into account, realising that, in some sense, all knowledge is ultimately tentative and uncertain. In fact, those working in the Berlin Wisdom Paradigm have acknowledged that their ideas were influenced by Carl Rogers.

Turning to psychotherapy, Sprenkle, Davis and Lebow (2009) have stressed the importance of helping couples in therapy achieve a meta-perspective on their problems. Wile (1993) uses a colourful metaphor for the same idea: helping couples to 'get up on a platform'. Somewhat related is the idea of helping clients develop their capacity for reflective functioning and mentalizing (the ability to perceive that other people have different 'minds' and perspectives than one's own (Luyten et al., 2020)). There is evidence that facilitating mentalizing improves therapy outcome.

I distinguish wisdom from everyday effective functioning. It is possible that one is able to function effectively without being 'wise' in the sense that I have considered it here. One might be able to get along without rich factual and procedural knowledge of the pragmatics of everyday life and without the capacity to take a perspective. One might be able to function effectively with rigid either/or rules if one's life situation fits them and nothing too untoward happens. Wisdom particularly shows up when one is confronted with a dilemma, particularly a dilemma that does not have an obvious or easy solution, where one's normal operating rules don't work. The 'Judgement of Solomon' is a good example.

Unwise behaviour and decisions

I return to the question of, if people have a capacity for self-organising wisdom, why do they often act unwisely? I suggest that unwise behaviour occurs in part because of shrunken or narrowed consciousness. All forms of unwise behaviour have one thing in common – an inability to take the larger context or picture into account, and try to contextualise, balance and integrate different perspectives.

Using ideas from the Berlin Wisdom Paradigm, let me consider why this may happen. First, there is learning. The individual may not have acquired rich factual or procedural knowledge in the fundamental pragmatics of living. Consider my client, Maria. Perhaps she grew up in an abusive household where she was under constant threat. She learned to view the world as dangerous. She never learned to think in terms of possibility. Her knowledge of the pragmatics of life will be limited to those things that help her protect herself. Furthermore, she has learned rigid either/or thinking: either you are 'good' or you are 'bad'. She has not learned the 'richer', more differentiated knowledge that there are gradations and nuances in life and in self. She has not learned there are multiple perspectives on things, or that there is an inherent uncertainty in life. Both her self-knowledge and her knowledge of the world are probably limited. She may not even know how to take a perspective, even if she values it. She may not have learned how to stand above her experience, open up to it, listen to it and then reflect and dialogue with it. Similarly, she may not have learned to take a perspective with others either ('mentalize'). For instance, she may not know how to get up on a platform and consider both her emotions in a situation and her thoughts.

The life rules, schemas and values that we learn, our 'life-operating principles', may thus blind us to learnings that would lead to a more richly differentiated view of self and world. They can become self-fulfilling prophecies. If we see the world in terms of 'eat or be eaten', we will see other people as either loyal allies or enemies. But this undifferentiated view will, in turn, influence how we treat others, thereby creating a dangerous world in which we turn others into enemies.

The second reason we may act unwisely is because of threat. When we perceive ourselves to be threatened, we act to protect ourselves. Our attention focuses on danger. We miss the opportunity to see positive opportunity. Our consciousness shrinks down. We do not have the luxury of getting up on the platform and thinking multidimensionally. It is too dangerous. We become defensive. Under enough threat, any one of us may become defence-oriented and act unwisely.

Defensiveness can manifest itself in many ways. One is to attack. Another is to constantly look for danger. Another is to pick on oneself. Picking on oneself is a form of defensiveness because you are trying to protect yourself against threat. I believe that many things we consider 'psychopathological' are forms of defensiveness, arising out of the organism's natural desire to protect itself, coupled with a knowledge base of ideas and schemas that limit its ability to think multidimensionally.

Threat not only narrows our attention, it also narrows our sense of time and space. We do not feel we have the time or the space to get up on the platform and think multidimensionally. In some real-life circumstances, this is literally true. We need to act quickly. In such situations, we need to act on stored knowledge and hope for the best. We may end up acting unwisely, but that is because we did not have the luxury of engaging in multidimensional thinking.

This can happen when immediate needs in the moment are overwhelming, or we perceive them as overwhelming. If we feel desperate to eat, to feel loved, to get water, to get help, to protect ourselves or whatever, we will act on 'impulse', or on stored knowledge, and not take time to think multidimensionally. Overwhelming emotion can affect us this way as well, although I do not believe it is the emotion *per se*. Rather, I believe it is an implicit accompanying belief that the emotion means something important, or an implicit accompanying belief that we are unable to control the emotion, that leads us to act on it rather than reflect.

Ultimately, then, I believe that the inability to act wisely arises whenever we unable to take a higher-order perspective. We are not able to 'decentre', to see things in context, to see things from different points of view, and then to work to integrate and balance different perspectives. This implies that one key component of wisdom is empathy – the ability to 'reach out' and take into account the impact of one's decisions on others, their needs and so on. This would include empathy for the planet, not just empathy for the individual.

Therefore, unwise behaviour is more likely to happen when people are mired in their perspectives. This is likely to happen when a) they see no way out from their perspectives, b) they believe they are doing the right and proper thing from their perspective, c) their attention is narrowed due to threat or overwhelming feelings of need or emotion, d) they do not know how to reflect on their experience in a functional way, or e) for any other reason, they are unable to get up on the 'platform' and see things in terms of a meta-perspective. Pressures towards uniformity can play a role. It is not only individuals who act unwisely. Larger groups and nations act unwisely as well. Pressures towards uniformity and conformity also serve to narrow attention and interfere with multidimensional thinking.

I have framed this in terms of thinking. But what about emotion? Here is where the idea of 'organismic wisdom' comes in. The kind of thinking I am talking about is not merely logical left-brain calculating. It is more like a kind of 'allowing' of things to enter into awareness, a kind of open awareness. 'Thinking' in this regard sometimes includes things spontaneously 'bubbling up', as Carl Rogers was fond of saying. This includes the openness that allows the creative emergence of new ideas and perspectives. The kind of thinking I am talking about is holistic. We 'think' with more than our intellectual, analytic calculators. We also 'think' with our organisms. For Rogerians, feelings include more than emotions. Following

Gendlin (1970), feelings are 'felt senses' – that is, they are ways of knowing the world (for example, we talk about 'feeling your way'). Thinking is both right-brain and left-brain (Wood, 2008). It consists of a dialogue between analytic, bodily and holistic ways of knowing. When one is 'thinking' multidimensionally, what one is doing is both thinking in an analytic left-brain way and 'feeling' in an organismic holistic way. It is the productive, integrative dialogue between those different modes of knowing that leads to 'wiser' behaviour and decisions.

The value therapists place on getting in touch with emotions is because it is important to be able to feel emotions – that is, to have one's emotions. Emotions are an important source of bodily felt knowledge. They often tell us about where we are in life, or where we are in the moment, even if they are not always accurate in that regard. It is important to allow them to have a voice, to be one of the things that the whole organism considers in its multidimensional 'thinking', or blending of different ways of knowing, although it can be unwise to blindly follow emotions.

With this in mind I turn to how psychotherapy facilitates wisdom.

Psychotherapy as facilitating self-organising wisdom

I believe psychotherapy works in part by enhancing people's capacity for wisdom. In an earlier version of this idea, Diane Henschel and I proposed years ago that many psychological problems involved ways of thinking and experiencing that represented pre-operational or concrete-operational levels of thinking in Piaget's model of cognitive development, or pre-conventional and conventional thinking on Kohlberg's moral development scale (Bohart & Henschel, 1984). These ways of thinking created problems when they did not match the challenges of a person's life. We then argued that psychotherapy worked in part by promoting and providing opportunities to develop thinking and experiencing in higher-order, more formal operational ways.

I now suggest that we think of psychotherapy in terms of promoting wise ways of thinking, feeling and behaving. Two ways are through a) providing a place where clients can enhance the richness of their factual and procedural knowledge in the pragmatics of life, and b) through stimulating, facilitating, enhancing or supporting their capacities for multidimensional thinking. These two are intertwined. As we promote clients getting up on a platform and reflecting on their lives, we simultaneously promote the kind of exploring that leads them to develop more richly differentiated knowledge about themselves, others and the world. They not only develop their capacity for multidimensional thinking (Rogers would say they move higher up on the process scale) and their ability to see multiple sides of issues, to see things in context, to recognise the relativism of knowledge, and to recognise the uncertainty of knowledge; they also develop a bodily felt, or organismic, understanding of the importance of 'open' multidimensional thinking and experiencing.

From a Rogerian perspective, although therapists may promote or support clients expanding their knowledge base and their capacity for higher-order thinking and experiencing, it is still clients who ultimately solve their problems. It is only they who have the rich knowledge of their lives (often implicit at the start of therapy) and of themselves and can integrate the disparate aspects of their experience when they are up on the platform in order to develop new life solutions. It is only they who, through being open to think multidimensionally, may find new, creative solutions and bodily felt life changes emerging as they reflectively think about and experience themselves, the therapist and their lives. Even though the therapist's interactive presence (in person-centred therapy) and interventions (in other forms of therapy) may support and promote wisdom-making activities, it is still the organism and its capacity for self-organising wisdom that moves forward to create more differentiated, integrated, fulfilling and effective ways of living life.

More concretely, what do therapists do to support or promote clients' capacity for self-organising wisdom? I will consider person-centred therapy first and then briefly comment on other approaches.

What does the person-centred therapist do?

The person-centred therapist relates to the person with unconditional positive regard. That means that they actively prize the person they are working with, no matter what that person has done (this does not mean they approve of what the person has done). They treat them with respect, as an 'authentic source of their own experience' (Bohart & Greenberg, 1997).

Second, they actively strive to 'hear' where the person is coming from and to get the person's view of things and how the person feels about things and bring them into dialogue. They try to empathically understand where the client is coming from. This is not 'empathising with' the client in the sense of 'feeling their pain', or feeling compassion for their plight, although the person-centred therapist may do this also. Rather, empathic understanding is primarily a receptive kind of listening, dialoguing and understanding on the part of therapist. It is 'opening up' to hear the client in the client's own words in terms of how they are experiencing themselves and the world, and responding in a reaching out, sharing and co-constructing way to the other.

Finally, the person-centred therapist is congruent. This does not necessarily mean they self-disclose, but it does mean they are not playing a professional role. It means that they themselves are there as a person. They are a person listening to a person. Even when Carl Rogers was primarily in an empathic listening stance, it always struck me that he was there as a person. He seemed genuinely interested in what the client had to say. It was not an act, not something he was trying to do to 'be therapeutic'. It is this kind of genuineness that clients sense, even if the therapist is not sharing aspects of their personal experience or personal history. Congruence means the therapist sends clear signals so that clients can trust that what they are saying is what they really believe and feel.

What is helpful is that the therapist's interest in the client is genuine, and that their attempt to understand is because they are really interested in the client as a person. How does this help? It creates a 'safe space'. To the degree that clients are feeling under stress, threatened or defensive, this safe space allows them to relax and drop their defences. Over time, their vigilance levels will drop too. This should allow them to turn their attention inward and to reflect on themselves and their experience and to introspect. They do not need to look outward for danger. This should allow them to 'get up on the platform' and broaden their perspective. They are able to turn from a narrow, threat-oriented, defensive perspective to a broader, more open one.

This relates to Rogers' contention that therapy helps people move up on the process scale and become more open to their experience. They should also be able to become more curious about their experience rather than be threatened by it.

It may take a distrustful client a while to believe this, but over time even the most vigilant of clients will 'test the waters' and begin to feel they can trust this safe space. Feeling safe, they can take the chance of holding constructs tentatively. They will not feel they have to rigidly hold onto beliefs, perceptions, points of view and ideas in order to protect themselves or hang onto themselves. They will be able to 'turn them over', so to speak, and look at them. They will feel safe to explore painful experiences that they have not previously felt safe enough to look at before, not because they were 'afraid of the pain', as so many other theories hold, but because a person needs to feel enough ground under their feet to be able to hold pain and explore it. Exploring painful experience when one already feels under threat is to invite getting overwhelmed. It helps to have another person there to help bear the pain while you deal with it, whether it be physical or psychological pain.

As clients tell their story, they are able to reflect on it and turn their attention inward. Through exploring their experience in the context of sharing it with the therapist, they are able to develop a richer understanding of themselves, the people in their world, the events they have experienced and so on.

Furthermore, the therapist's empathic responses help the client develop rich knowledge. By bouncing ideas off the therapist, then hearing what the therapist says back, typically 'in other words', clients are able to see nuances in what they were saying. Clients are better able to get in touch with implications in their experiences and in what they say. They are able to think, 'Maybe I don't mean it quite that way,' and thereby expand their understanding. They are thus able to develop a more richly differentiated understanding of their 'story' and to see it in new ways.

So the therapist will be fostering intelligent processing. All this also feeds into their ability to begin to look at their lives in a more contextual, multidimensional sense. By turning ideas and perceptions over, by seeing them through the eyes of the therapist, they begin to broaden their perspective – to see things from different sides. They learn that there is usually more to the story than they thought. This will lead them to realise that ideas and perceptions are not fixed in concrete; they are perceptions, and they can be wrong or, when seen from a slightly different angle, they can look a little different. This helps them realise that there are multiple ways to look at things. This will be facilitated by their unearthing bits and pieces of memory of experiences and incidents that they had forgotten about, or neglected. It will also be facilitated by their getting in touch with feelings and emotions, even intuitions, that they had neglected or overlooked. All these things will broaden their perspective.

Ultimately, it is the open atmosphere that is most therapeutic. As they open up, they begin to notice possibilities neglected before. New perspectives emerge. This should all work to help them spontaneously and naturally begin to hold more tentatively their rigid, simplistic notions about themselves and life. They should be able to expand their 'schemas'.

The empathic listening component of the therapeutic relationship also contributes to clients being able to take a wider perspective and think contextually and multidimensionally. First, the sheer presence of an empathic witness does this. Just the presence of an empathic listening other, even if they say very little, helps expand consciousness. Just the act of my sharing with you my story, knowing that I am sharing it with you, and you are not judging but listening, helps me 'hear' it in a different way. In effect, I hear it through you, even if you don't say a word. I therefore get out of my skin and see it as someone else might.

This happens more and more the less defensive and threatened I get and the more I share. It is like me coming out into a clearing from being hidden in the bushes, through being seen by you. Through my hearing, you share my experience – we co-share it. We experience it together. Again, this facilitates perspective-taking. Through your accurately hearing what I am trying to convey, I get to sharpen my experience of what I am saying. It becomes more differentiated. If you make a mistake and don't get me, but you continue trying until you do, that helps me 'get above' my experience, look at it and find new words to say it. And that helps me take perspective.

Finally, there is simply a relief in sharing one's story with an empathic listening other. There is a genuine sense of unburdening. In 'letting go' of our story, we are able to rise above it and see it in perspective. 'Getting it out on the table', getting above the shame and pain in telling it, allows one to bring it forth more. Not only does it come out clearer as a result, but we are better able to take a perspective as well. Contextualising it helps 'contain' it.

The last part of the process I wish to mention is the creative part. As we are able to explore all aspects of our experience, as we are able to get it all out on the table, as we are able to turn things over and look at them, we are then able to begin to balance things, to compare and contrast things, and begin to find 'ands' where there were previously either/ors. Or, in a dialectical fashion, we are able to integrate things to create new syntheses, new ideas, new ways of being and paradigm shifts that bring new perspectives.

I wish to stress again that this process is not as 'intellectual' as I have made it sound. It is the organism that does the balancing. I do not know how we do this. I do know that it is our whole organism that ends up balancing all the factors and creating shifts in experiencing, thinking and behaving that lead us to new and more effective ways of being. We do the thinking, reflecting, looking, becoming aware of emotions and experiencing, turning things over and so on, and it is ultimately the organism that takes all that and does the integrating and balancing. Thus, creative ideas are usually experienced as just 'bubbling up' (Loesch et al., 1996), as are insights. Or we may just find ourselves being different in a positive way, and not know how it happened. In other words, wisdom is an organismic process.

What do therapists using other approaches do?

I would like to conclude by briefly considering how other approaches to psychotherapy might facilitate clients' self-organising wisdom. Behavioural exercises typically allow clients to develop more richly differentiated knowledge. Practising assertiveness allows clients to develop more richly differentiated knowledge about the pragmatics of social interaction. Additionally, because it allows clients to practise alternative ways of being, it opens up possibilities for the client, implicitly teaching them that it is better to think multidimensionally, not to believe too much in their previous ideas but to see things more contextually. Exposure techniques, where clients are exposed to their fears in order to overcome them, are done in bits and pieces. Again, clients learn there are shades in their experience; it is not either/or. And they develop more differentiated knowledge about their fears as well as about their strengths in confronting them. Finally, Socratic questioning used by cognitive therapists invites clients to get up on the platform and think contextually about their beliefs and experiences.

Emotion-focused therapy uses chair work to help people resolve conflict issues. 'Two-chair' work is used to help clients deal with internal splits. A person who is self-critical might be asked to role-play a dialogue between the critical side of themselves and the other side, which might be the defensive side, the excuse-making side or the beaten-down, apologetic side. 'Empty-chair' work is used to help a person deal with 'unfinished business' with another person. The client is asked to role-play a dialogue between themselves and the other person, in which they play both parts. Emotion-focused therapists (e.g. Elliott et al., 2004) have their own theories about how these exercises help.

From the point of view of this paper, I suggest that these exercises help by promoting clients' self-organising wisdom. I have always thought that the chair exercises are exercises in perspective-taking and creativity. It is true that they may help clients access and process emotions, as the emotion-focused therapists assert, but they also encourage clients to practise taking multiple perspectives on their problems and to explore and 'play with' their thoughts and feelings. It is not surprising that creative insights and ideas 'bubble up', as I have seen happen in videos of emotion-focused therapy. Nor is it surprising that clients leave with more richly differentiated knowledge about how they, other people and relationships operate.

I close by mentioning a study I conducted with two graduate students (Bohart et al., 2010) that supports what I am saying. Using the scales for rating wisdom from the Berlin Wisdom Project, we rated a case study of the client Jane (Mackrill, 2011), seen by an existential-psychodynamic therapist, and discovered that Jane moved upward on the scale over the course of therapy. In sum, whatever other benefits psychotherapy provides, it has the capacity or potential to facilitate clients' wisdom.

4 Empathy-based psychotherapy: developing a model of person-to-person psychotherapy

This paper is based on a presentation at the World Association of Person-Centered and Experiential Psychotherapy and Counseling, New York, July 2016. I was trying to build a bridge between my cherished person-centered point of view and other points of view. It represents my view of how to practise integratively from a person-centred base. In the audience for the presentation were Robert Elliott, co-founder of emotion-focused therapy, and William Miller, co-creator of motivational interviewing. I was pleased that they both responded supportively to the presentation.

Three weeks ago I was in Dublin, Ireland for the conference of the Society for the Exploration of Psychotherapy Integration. Now I am in New York for this conference of the World Association for Person-Centered and Experiential Psychotherapy and Counseling. Presenting at these two conferences illustrates the wave-particle nature of my identity for most of my professional career. Although I've considered myself fundamentally person-centred in my attitudes, I've also had an integrative bent. By 'person-centred', I mean that I see the relationship between myself and my client as the primary thing that contributes to the client's self-healing. It is not my techniques or my interventions. It is most fundamentally our meeting as persons.

In this regard, I do not see myself as the expert on my client. I believe that the client has an implicit potential for creative wise behaviour and I see myself as being a catalyst for that potential to come out. However, I catalyse it not by being an expert interventionist but through my being there in a certain kind of life-promoting way.

At the same time, I exist in a world where therapists are supposed to be expert interventionists. Furthermore, I know that therapists from other persuasions have developed ideas and procedures that clients can use to help themselves grow. I know that many clients actively want these things. I have had such clients. Furthermore, I know that when clients use them, they can find them useful.

So this has posed a dilemma for me. How can I best be there for my client? In order to answer this, I want to suggest a different mindset from which to do therapy than the dominant mindset in the field – the model that views the therapist as the expert who intervenes to creates changes in the client. The mindset I want to propose is based on my interpretation of Carl Rogers' views. I have no illusions that this mindset is going to replace the interventionist one. Still, I believe it is important to say this, and I believe it is how most good therapists actually practise.

I have previously argued that it was compatible with person-centred therapy principles to be integrative (Bohart, 2012). What I mean by integrative is that I, as the therapist, am willing to share the knowledge I have of other approaches with my client. In my 2012 article, I provided several quotations from Carl Rogers that supported my view.

However, there has been a debate over this for probably 40 years, with some arguing that person-centred therapists should stick to non-directive therapy and empathic reflections and not offer any responses from their own frame of reference. The debate will probably never end. My purpose here is not to try to convince those who are strong believers in the classical non-directive point of view, but to elaborate on what I think person-centred therapy is and how I believe we can operate in an integrative fashion and still be true to its principles. Furthermore I want to argue that I think it is important that we are able to do so.

In that regard, in 2012 I said:

> I wish to close by making a pitch for providing integrative forms of person-centered therapy to the world. If we refuse to allow there to be integrative person-centered practice, restricting person-centered practice to classical non-directive therapy, we deny clients and the world something very valuable. We leave it to others to provide the value of deep empathic listening, truly prizing people as people, and trusting people's self-organising wisdom by happenstance, when they provide their techniques and procedures. We are not going to change all the world into non-directive person-centered therapists. That means many clients will not get the experience of being prized and related to in the way we prize and relate to persons. We must find a way to integrate the use of techniques together with our belief in these fundamental attitudes so that clients have the right to get everything they want and need from therapists. This will provide an expansive, inclusive frame, which in my opinion is representative of the underlying thrust of person-centered thinking, which has always been towards openness and inclusivity. (Bohart, 2012, p.12)

This does not mean I want every person-centred therapist to do what I do. I prize classical non-directive therapy. If I were able to practise exclusively that way with my clients, I probably would. However, I have wanted to be responsive to my clients, and my clients have often wanted other things besides empathic witnessing. I do not know if that is because perhaps I am not as good at staying with my clients in a purely empathic, following way, like Barbara Brodley or Carl Rogers. However, I have come to be comfortable with viewing therapy as an ongoing dialogue where I can offer my ideas and knowledge in an empathically responsive way, while respecting the client's self-propelled growing edge. I want to point out that I *really* trust my clients to decide what is best for them regarding what we are doing in therapy.

I have argued elsewhere (Bohart, 2018; see also Chapter 1) that it is not either/or. Other approaches are valuable. It is simply that they do not offer the unique thing that classical non-directive person-centred therapy offers. I would like to see a world where there are diverse ways of being and practice. That is the best kind of world. However, in this presentation, I want to 'get under' all approaches and present what I call 'empathy-based psychotherapy', an integrative approach that is based in person-centred principles. This is compatible with what some major psychotherapy integrationists also think, who say that psychotherapy integration is based in the person-centred relationship (Gold & Stricker, 2020).

What I'm arguing for is a kind of 'meta-model' of therapy that could accommodate practice from a variety of points of view, although it is more of an underlying structural model. This has to do with the *kind* of relationship the therapist and client have, theoretically. I say 'theoretically' because I believe that, in practice, good therapists actually function in terms of the model I am going to propose, although they often talk in terms of the other model. The model I am going to propose is that of therapist and client as co-creators of therapy in the truest sense – that of two genuinely co-equal collaborators working together to create a process and climate of change. In order to do this, I'd like to contrast the core values of person-centred therapy with the dominant, interventionist model. In the interventionist model, the therapist is the expert on what the client needs to do. The therapist looks at the client and assesses what is wrong with them and what they need. This is the mindset that leads to diagnosis and identification of client dysfunctions, such as personality disorders, attachment disorders and so on. Based on what the therapist decides that the client is missing or what they deduce is wrong with the client, the therapist decides how to intervene. This may include empathic responses designed to help clients feel safe and validated, help them become more securely attached and so on.

By contrast, the person-centred model relies on the belief that the client is the ultimate expert on their own lives, not merely because they know more about their lives than the therapist but also in the sense that they are the co-creators of their lives. They, as Carl Rogers said, have intuitive, implicit knowledge of what is best to help them grow and what directions to go in. Therapists need, at least in part, to co-ordinate with this in order to make therapy work.

Many interventionistic therapists will agree, superficially, with the client-centred position that the client is ultimately the expert on themselves. They may even claim they are 'person-centred'. However, what they mean by this is that clients are experts on their life experience. Clients are not experts on what they need to do in order to change. The therapist is the expert, although the therapist may need to coordinate with the client in order to facilitate change. However, this is a different philosophical position from the one I am advocating.

I do not want to say that there is something wrong with the interventionist mindset. That mindset has made many positive contributions to therapy. However, I believe that person-centred therapy comes from a fundamentally different mindset and the one it comes from is important. What I believe happens in person-centred therapy is that it, most clearly of all therapies, prizes and allows the client to have and to hear their own voice. The client is able to sort out the 'me' or the 'I' from competing voices and 'shoulds'. I can hear my own voice. In fact, I may discover that I *have* a voice. I become more person-centred myself. And when that happens, I become able to think and perceive more wisely. New ideas surface. New perspectives emerge. I am able to move on from old constructs and forge new ways of being. I believe that all the techniques of other approaches ultimately contribute to this also, but primarily in the context of an empathic listening relationship.

The concept of 'hearing one's own voice' may be troubling for some, but phenomenologically, from both my own experience and working with clients, I know that it is real. This is not to deny that there are other 'voices' inside (e.g. voices of parents, bosses, partners, one's culture and so on (Stiles & Glick, 2000)). It is to assert that there is an experience, which I and many others have had, including my clients, of 'coming home to myself', of knowing when I am 'hearing my own voice'. It is unmistakable.

In the person-centred model, the client is expert on themselves. That does not merely mean they are expert in terms of what they know *about* themselves. They are the process experts as well. Only they know ultimately what is wrong for them, what needs to change, and how it needs to change. This does not mean they consciously know it. In a sense, it is misleading to say that they 'know' it. For instance, when the client comes into the counselling room, it is often not the case that they know what is wrong and what needs to change. What they know maybe is where they need to start. They have some intuitive sense of the direction they need to go. But it is still a journey of discovery.

It is in this sense that the client is the expert. Only they can take the steps. Only they ultimately know what the shape of the emerging outcome is going to look like, and only they know what steps along the road are useful. And, if they are not distracted by the 'expert' opinion of someone else, and if they are given the space to listen to themselves, they have the capacity to recognise when a step is in the wrong direction, or whether they are on track or not, or whether an idea fits with them or not. The client takes one step after another; some go in the wrong direction, but there is this intuitive self-correcting capacity that shows up in therapy, in the presence of an active, engaged, non-judgemental listener. From the outside it may look like the client is meandering off in the wrong direction; the client may not see what seems obvious to the therapist, but in the long run there is an intuitive logic to how personal truth unfolds. This has been most eloquently articulated by Gendlin (1990).

My work since 1996 has largely centred around documenting the evidence that supports this view of the client: that it is clients who make therapy work. They are in some sense, the therapists (Bohart & Tallman, 1999, 2010).

The job of classical person-centred therapist is primarily to be an engaged, empathic witness – to carefully listen to the client in a non-judgemental way. This is not a matter of 'being supportive'. Yes, be supportive, but it is more, and it is the more that is most important. It is the act of being empathically engaged with what that other person is struggling with that is the real core of change. It is active, engaged listening. It is not mechanistic, passive reflecting. If you watch Carl Rogers in that well-known film with 'Gloria' (Shostrom, 1965), you will note how actively engaged he is, and how his empathic responses are attempts to reach out and actively connect with her. It is not a technique. In that kind of interaction, the client comes to hear their own voice, and through that change occurs.

The person-centred approach is a *whole-person* approach. I contrast that with models that focus on the therapist's fixing, working through or enhancing parts of the client's functioning. It contrasts with the idea of intervening to change structures in the client, or to enhance process. In the interventionist model, the therapist may be trying to modify dysfunctional cognitions or ego structures or defences. The therapist may decide the client needs to take responsibility or to access feelings and sets out to help them do that. In that sense, the therapist is not relating to the person as a whole person who is trying to make their way in the world and trying to hear the person in that struggle; rather, they are focusing their attention on aspects of the person that need to be changed. This does not preclude listening to the person as a whole person, but that is not the primary focus of their attention.

By a whole-person approach, what I mean is you are in dialogue with a person who is trying to sort out their life. Then it is you listening and them talking, and you talking and them listening – i.e. it is the dialogue that is therapeutic. This is different from focusing on changing ego structures, strengthening self-structure, changing attachment patterns or challenging dysfunctional cognitions. In the whole-person model, it is two people talking over one person's problems in order that one of them can find a more satisfactory accommodation with themselves and life. The focus is on two *people* talking. In this context, it is the client who evaluates and decides: Am I out of touch with a certain feeling? Are there internal voices I want to change? Am I thinking *dysfunctionally*? Am I resisting? And so on. It is not the therapist taking away the client's power to be in charge.

That implies that therapy is a meeting of two persons. If we go back to the Carl Rogers-Martin Buber debate (Cissna & Anderson, 1994), which took place in 1957, the same year that Rogers published his article on the necessary and sufficient conditions for personality change (Rogers, 1957), that is what Rogers said. Therapy is a by-product of a meeting of persons. Put another way, therapy *is* a meeting of persons. It is not a technological enterprise.

How does this operate? There has been a recognition for a long time from many theoretical points of view that you can think of the person at two levels. At one level are the person's typical programmatic ways of relating to people. These can include the defence-driven stances the person takes, their routine schemas for operating and, in some theories, their 'false-self' patterns of relating to people. Underneath that is the deeper, personal level, which consists of what deeply means the most to the person. Different points of view formulate this level differently, but it is at this level where the deepest needs, hurts, wishes and dreams live.

Typically, in most encounters, we relate in terms of the superficial forms and not at that deeply personal level. It was Rogers' insight, as well as Eugene Gendlin's, that it is when we are able to get below the superficial forms to where people have room for the deeply personal to emerge and be shared in a person-to-person encounter that people meet and change takes place – both change within persons and change between persons. This was Rogers' insight, not only from his work in individual therapy but also from what he was trying to achieve in the encounter groups he did across the world. He was trying to set up conditions where people of different backgrounds and fashions could express themselves from their deeply personal levels; to get beyond their group identifications or political identifications and say what most personally mattered to them: 'what I want', 'what most matters to me – or to us', what was most deeply relevant. When that happens, people change, both within themselves and between themselves and others. In that regard, accessing emotion isn't so important in terms of emotion *per se*. Rather, accessing emotion has to do with accessing what is deeply personal to us – what means the most to us. Accessing emotion, therefore, is accessing the deeply personal.

Therefore, it follows that what is most therapeutic is to be deeply known in the context of a relationship with another person. It says a lot about our society and world that we have to have a special profession in order for this to happen.

As I said, in 1957, Rogers also published his necessary and sufficient conditions article. There he argued that what made therapy work, from the therapist's side of the coin, were three basic therapist attitudes: experiencing unconditional positive regard, or respect and acceptance, towards the client; empathic understanding of their experience, and being personally congruent in the relationship. If you think of those in the context of a meeting of persons, it is clear that they are attitudes, not behaviours, not strategies, and not techniques. They are what *constitutes* effectively meeting with and engaging with another human being and knowing them.

Many person-centred therapists took Rogers' necessary and sufficient conditions statement as a warrant for integrative practice. If you 'provide' the attitudes, then you can also use techniques. The book *New Directions in Client-Centered Therapy* (Hart & Tomlinson, 1970) was based on that idea. Rogers himself, in several writings, agreed that person-centred therapists could offer clients techniques.

However, I believe that some interpretations of the necessary and sufficient conditions article have been in part mistaken. From a person-centred point of view, you don't experience unconditional positive regard towards your client because it is a strategy or because it is 'effective'. Although it has the effect of validating the person, making them feel safe and secure, providing a corrective experience and so on, that is not the point. The point is that you hold unconditional positive regard because you are interested in them as persons. It is *because* of that, because you are genuinely interested in them as a person, that unconditional positive regard makes a client feel safe, provides a corrective experience and so forth. It is similar with empathy, which I will come to in a minute. As far as congruence goes, congruence matters because a deeply engaged meeting of persons means that the two persons must be honestly there with one another, not engaged in playing roles.

We listen empathically because we really want to hear the client's point of view, not because we are trying to do something to make the meeting go better. Congruence may not necessarily mean the therapist has to self-disclose; I agree with those who have argued that Rogers was being congruent even when he was not self-disclosing. However, it does imply that, in a meeting of persons, being transparent yourself, responding to the call of the other *as a person yourself*, is what it is all about. It is *human* helping that matters. It is human caring. I'm sure many therapists have had the experience of clients wondering if the therapist cares because they genuinely care or because it is their job. Guess which one clients find therapeutic?

So, as I am trying to meet the person, what if what comes up in me is something I know could be valuable to them? Should I not consider sharing it? Is that not responding to them? And what may come up in me is the fact that I know some stuff. I have, for instance, theoretical knowledge that might be of assistance. I also have some research knowledge about techniques that can be useful to a person struggling with a given problem.

So how do I do this? It is here that empathy becomes most important. It is my ability to be empathically in touch with the other, to really hear them *in this moment*, that matters most. If I am empathically in touch with them, then I can respond in terms of what they need. By empathic listening and responding, I do two things. First, I am engaging with the person: I am meeting them and listening to them. Second, I am responding to their call – I am, hopefully, sensitively offering something that they may need or find useful, even if it is primarily just being with them.

In that context, I offer my knowledge, including techniques or 'tools' I know of that might be of help. However, I am not playing the role of the expert interventionist. They are the deciders; they are the ones who will take the tool and use it, not infrequently in ways that I didn't intend – creative ways I haven't even thought of. Perhaps I offer the use of the two-chair technique when I see them struggling with their critical self. It is up to them to decide to use it. And if they do use it, it will be they who mine it for what it can offer them and creatively produce the outcome, no matter what our theories say, or research says, is useful for the average client.

This supersedes expert knowledge. I may 'know' from research that the process is supposed to go this way or that. I may 'know' that the two-chair technique is what to do to heal a split. If you are coming from an expert interventionist stance, you may even 'use' empathy to implement the procedure. You use empathy to time the intervention so the client will accept it. You use empathy to tailor it to them. But you are still the expert and your theoretical knowledge is superseding theirs.

By contrast, in empathy-based psychotherapy, my empathic listening to them comes first. *They* come first. Expert knowledge is never expert knowledge until they operate on it, until it's true for them. That is because the meeting of persons comes first.

I call this talk 'empathy-based psychotherapy'. What I mean by that is an alternative to the way we typically think of how to proceed in therapy. In the typical interventionist model, the expert therapist may listen empathically to the client, but he or she will also have a theoretical schema in mind for what needs to be done to get the client to change. This schema supersedes the client's ongoing expert knowledge. Empathy is used to tailor or adjust the intervention to the client. That puts the meeting of persons second to the therapist's machinations.

By contrast, I flip that around. It is empathy that is the primary determinant for what I do. Offering a technique becomes a way of meeting, of being-in-relationship, just like helping your friend or child or sitting with your dying parent is. Empathy becomes the touchstone for whatever I do. Anything I offer becomes a way of responding to the *person*. This means I am staying in touch with the client moment to moment as an active, intelligent struggling being, and what leads me to suggest something is my real, moment-to-moment interaction with them.

The common definition of empathy has to do with trying to step into someone else's shoes, to get what they're feeling from their point of view. But there are different ways you can step inside another person's shoes (by the way, for some clients it feels too crowded to have another person in their shoes with them). Not all ways are person-centred. You can use empathy strategically. Most therapists talk about it that way. You use it as an intervention. For instance, physicians are often trained in using empathic reflections to make the relationship better with their patients. The focus is on improving the relationship so that the physician can achieve their aims. The focus is not on person-to-person meeting. (Parenthetically, nor should it be. That is not the primary purpose of why physician and patient are together.)

There is a distinction between 'empathising with' and 'empathically listening to'. You can use 'empathising *with*' as a strategy. This is not what Rogers had in mind. He was not trying to empathise *with* people. There is nothing wrong with that, but I think Rogers was trying to empathically listen *to* people. To get to know them. To empathically understand them. The direction is from the person to therapist, not from the therapist to the person. Empathising *with* someone is from therapist to the person. You can empathise with someone while believing that you know better than them. Empathically listening *to* someone in order to really get them, to receive them, is from them to the therapist.

In this regard I have come to believe that Rogerian empathy is better construed as what Belenky and colleagues (1986) call '*connected knowing*'. They make a distinction between that and '*separate knowing*', which is looking at someone and analysing their behaviour from an external perspective. This is the kind of thinking stressed in school – analytic knowing. The kind of knowing therapists are taught includes looking at the client in terms of diagnosis, transference, resistance, being out of touch with feelings, thinking dysfunctionally, having poor social skills, being enmeshed and so on. All include looking at the client from outside and analysing what the client needs. By contrast, connected knowing involves trying to hear the person from within their frame of reference. This involves really being interested in hearing from the person in their own terms, and getting a felt sense of how they experience themselves in the world. It includes being connected with them in a mutual way. It includes suspending one's external point of view and trying to understand the other, no matter who they are or what their diagnosis is – to get *inside* the frame of external points of view, to get *them*. It includes believing at some level that there is some intrinsic sense in the other person's point of view, no matter how 'crazy' their behaviour may seem from outside, or at least granting them the courtesy of trying to hear the personalised sense in it.

Empathy is therefore a two-person enterprise. To be trying to *connect* in this sense means that it is mutual (see Cornelius-White et al., 2018). Connection involves two points meeting. It means to be willing to be 'penetrated' by the other. To hear them means allowing them to hear *you*. It means to take them seriously and then, in that sense, to communicate back to them in a way that 'meets' them on their terms. We are there holistically together. We are picking up information from one another non-verbally as well as verbally as we interact. As I am getting to know my client, my client is getting to know me, through the 'music and dance' of how we are non-verbally together. As Maureen O'Hara (1984) has said, we are trying to get inside the skin of the relationship, not just inside the skin of the other. But through this being together, each getting to know the other, *through how we interact together,* getting to know one another not only through my listening to my client but through my hearing and seeing how my client is reacting to me, anything I say or do is a sharing, in resonance or dialogue with the client. We get to know each other through our 'dancing' together – I know you through your knowing me through my knowing you and so on. We are co-constructing a shared ground of understanding (Clark & Brennen, 1991).

So, if I offer a technique, I am not intervening; I am offering something that emerges from our being together. It emerges from the 'experiential commons' that we keep co-creating as we go along. And if the client uses it, they are the 'interventionist', not me. They are the ones who can activate it and use it. It is inert until I hand it to them. It is a tool that is useless unless they use it. And they often use it in their own creative ways. I honour them as persons by honouring this.

This means the therapist is themselves always a learner – learning the terrain, so to speak; learning about the client; learning from the client as they move forward, and using their expertise *in response* to the terrain the two of them are treading. The terrain is the unfolding path that emerges from their joint dialogue. And it is through gathering that richening knowledge of one another that solutions emerge. As Weitzman (2016) has said, '… the terrain is teaching me how to walk on it if I pay attention' (p.136).

Does this mean the therapist cannot use separate knowing – i.e. diagnosis, analysis in terms of theoretical constructs and such like? If we think in terms of the primacy of connected knowing, the issue of being integrative becomes not whether the therapist engages in separate knowing but how they incorporate separate knowing into therapy. Do they co-ordinate separate knowing with connected knowing, respecting the client first and using separate knowing notions second? Do they, perhaps, use separate knowing as a general guide to what they do, but always coordinate it with, and even privilege, connected knowing when dialoguing with the person that is their client? In this regard, are they operating like Schön's (1983) reflective practitioner? He gives the example of an architect who has to build a building on a slippery slope. The architect may have a general schema in mind but they must responsively 'listen to' the slope itself and tailor what they do to that slope. In one sense, it is the slope that dictates what the architect does. Or, put another way, what emerges is a joint product of the slope and the architect.

I would like to briefly mention here a little research study that I and my students did on connected and separate knowing in therapy (Bohart et al., 2016). We watched videos and read transcripts of emotion-focused therapists – an existential therapist, a psychodynamic therapist, Carl Rogers and Fritz Perls. Carl Rogers was seen as primarily coming from a connected knowing mindset, but he did step out of that frame once or twice to offer a separate knowing comment. However, it was always subordinated to connected knowing. For the most part (but not as much as Carl Rogers), the emotion-focused therapists and the existential therapist subordinated separate knowing to connected knowing with their clients. By contrast, Paul Wachtel, a psychodynamic therapist, was empathic and exhibited connected knowing, but seemed to subordinate it to separate knowing. Fritz Perls, in his session in the 'Gloria' films (Shostrom, 1965), was rated as engaging in almost purely separate knowing. There was more to the findings and there was more complexity, but what they do show is that it is possible to combine separate and connected knowing in ways that honour the primacy of connected, empathic ways of relating to the other person.

So this is how I believe a person-centred therapist can stay person-centred and offer ideas and techniques from other points of view. It is how I have practised over the years 1990 to 2004 (when I retired from private practice). I call this empathy-based therapy. Is it client-centred therapy, classical person-centred, non-directive therapy? No. It is person-to-person therapy, person-centred based, but it is not classical person-centred therapy. And this is the message I would like to give to therapists: to move out of the expert-on-the-client stance, to see the client as the expert and to see themselves as a colleague, with some expertise of their own, including their own experience, to share with the client in a collaborative dialogue where, ultimately, the underlying healing element is the person-to-person relationship itself. What I am getting at is that, over and above anything else we do, treating others as authentic centres of their own experience (to paraphrase Bohart & Greenberg, 1997) is the most primary healing thing we do. We do not want to take away their power. But if we do this in the context of a person-to-person relationship, I believe we can expand what we do in therapy and still be true to person-centred principles, provided we are empathically listening.

However, there is a complication. Therapy does not exist in a vacuum. It is a professional activity whose purpose is to help one of the two people involved. In Western society, people see therapists as experts. So, if I suggest a technique, will clients not possibly buy into it because they see me as the expert rather than because they are authentically interested? That is a possibility, especially early in therapy. However, if we as therapists genuinely respect their decision-making, genuinely listen to them and genuinely treat them as authentic centres of their own experience, in my experience they come to experience themselves as co-equal partners in the encounter and then act that way. Imagine the therapist being interested in what the client as a whole person means when they say X, rather than on whether X represents a dysfunctional cognition, an avoidance, an out-of-touch with feelings and so on. Imagine that I am trying to grasp them in their authenticity. Imagine that I make it clear by my actions, over time, that we are equals in power-sharing and decision-making. They pick this up and respond accordingly.

I suggest that therapists who use techniques routinely can also function in an empathy-based fashion. You can respond either to the person or mechanistically. I can imagine a therapist doing motivational interviewing (Miller & Rollnick, 2012), or emotion-focused therapy (Greenberg et al., 1993), or Gendlin's (1996) focusing-oriented therapy from either a professionally oriented expert stance or from a meeting-of-persons stance. From a meeting-of-persons stance, you would not mechanistically offer the two-chair dialogue technique, even at a therapeutic marker of where it might be appropriate (Greenberg et al., 1993). Instead, it would be used responsively, in response to the call of the person. Marker information might help you hear the call of the person, but the marker information would be secondary to hearing that intrinsically unique call of the person, no matter what the superficial schema of the presence of the marker implied.

By responding in dialogue with the other from our empathic connection between us, person to person, I am not taking away the client's power. I particularly like what Jerold Bozarth often said about person-centred therapy: it is not what the therapist gives to the client, it is what they don't take away. Power issues are impossible to avoid. The client may see the therapist as the expert, no matter what we do. So all we can do is respond as best we can in a personalising thou-I/I-thou way, in such a way as to help create a level playing field. What we have to do is act in ways that don't take away their power. But this doesn't mean we can't share our knowledge base in a given moment.

Let me give you an example. I had a client who initially came to me wanting emotion-focused therapy. He was a young college professor and was worried about getting tenure. I am not a specialist in emotion-focused therapy, but I did not know of an emotion-focused therapist in the area. I informed him of this. I then described my point of view. I told him I have a 'general practitioner's' level of knowledge of emotion-focused therapy. I told him that I worked primarily from an integrative person-centred point of view. We dialogued a little about how I worked and how emotion-focused therapy fits with person-centred therapy. I pointed out that emotion-focused therapy is based on person-centred therapy but adds on some useful techniques. I told him that I had experience with many of the techniques (e.g. chair work and focusing), even though I had not had formal training in just how emotion-focused therapy sequences their use. I told him that, if he worked with me, it would be a blend of person-centred therapy and emotion-focused techniques. I would use my knowledge to bring up techniques at particular points that he might want to use, but it was up to him to say yes or no, or to try them out and find out if they worked for him. It would be collaborative work together to find out what worked best for him. He decided he wanted to work with me.

I started out doing my traditional person-centred listening approach. Eventually, when particular therapeutic markers appeared, I suggested various emotion-focused techniques. A few sessions in, the client talked about having problems managing his anxiety when he made presentations at a conference, and he was going to have to do that in a few weeks. At this point, I brought up the possibility of using some cognitive-behavioural techniques to help him manage the anxiety. I described them to him, and asked if they interested him. He answered that he wanted to try them.

The techniques helped him manage his anxiety for the presentation and he decided he would use them in the future. However, he didn't want to switch to cognitive-behavioural therapy. He knew what was best for him and he returned to the personal exploration path after that. However, our sharing the cognitive-behavioural experience did not just help him with the presentation issue; he discovered that using the techniques not only helped to engineer the anxiety away, it helped him understand at a deeper level that there were deeper issues involved. The experience of using the cognitive-behavioural techniques helped him sharpen what he wanted. He got a clearer sense that the anxiety was connected to issues of whether he was being true to himself or not in the career path he was pursuing. That is what came up for him after his cognitive-behavioural experience. It wasn't me who brought it up. We thus reverted to more deep, self-exploration work.

So, how did I decide to offer the cognitive-behavioural stuff? I listened to him and took him seriously as an authentic source of his own experience. It was the 'call of the person' to me for help that I listened to. Then, as we worked with the cognitive-behavioural stuff, it was my empathically hearing him in the moment that helped us adjust the techniques and fine-tune them so he found them useful. Then, I heard that he didn't want to continue with the cognitive-behavioural track after it had helped him through the tough spot at work. So it was through my empathic connection with him that we further adjusted what we did.

I want to stress that my empathic listening is not magic and nor do I have this great capacity to tune into what is true for my clients. To do that would be to fall back into the expert therapist trap. Rather, empathic listening is an ongoing, self-and-other, mutual correction process of tacking this way and that, continually testing out our understanding of each other's communications and where each other 'is at'. It is a mutual process (see Cornelius-White et al., 2018 on mutuality in psychotherapy).

I suspect that good therapists of all persuasions do at least some adjusting like this, although they may not venture outside the confines of their point of view like I did. This is how I have seen Leslie Greenberg operate in videos of emotion-focused therapy in practice, and it is how Robert Elliott, co-founder of emotion-focused therapy, has told me he operates also. They carefully and sensitively modify what they do to fit the unique 'terrain' of the client they are working with. The terrain teaches them how to walk. Although my point of view emerges from the person-centred point of view, I believe that what I have said in this paper could be used as a basis for practice from many different points of view.

5 | Self-organising wisdom in psychotherapy: theoretical conception and early empirical investigations

This paper recounts a little research process I and some graduate students did to begin to develop a scale to measure self-organising wisdom. Due to circumstances in my life, I never pursued this further. Still, I think it is interesting and am glad to see the ideas in it get into print. The paper is based on a presentation at the International Society for Psychotherapy Research Conference in Bern, Switzerland, 29 June–2 July, 2011. I co-authored the presentation with Makenna Berry Newton.

For person-centred therapists, the primary aim of the therapist is, through the provision of certain therapeutic conditions, to foster and support client creative emergence. Wood (2008) has called this the client's capacity for self-organising wisdom. Our aim is to elucidate this concept and to describe beginning research efforts.

We define self-organising wisdom as *a client generative process leading to the development of new and more adaptive solutions to life problems, and to more wise, balanced and grounded ways of being in the world.* Self-organising wisdom is different although related to the idea that there is some 'wisdom' in psychopathology – a view held by a number of writers (e.g. Boukydis, 1984; Linehan, 1997). Self-organising wisdom is also somewhat different from wisdom *per se*.

We have been influenced by two views of wisdom. The first is Sternberg's (1998) theory, which describes wisdom as a matter of balance: for instance, balancing what is good for the self with what is good for others. The second view is that of Baltes and Staudinger (2000), who define wisdom as 'expert-level performance in the fundamental pragmatics of life' (Staudinger et al., 1994). They have developed scoring systems both for wisdom *per se* and for 'self-related wisdom'. Their research involves giving participants a dilemma and having them think aloud. Below we reproduce their five components of wisdom (Staudinger et al., 1994):

1. Rich factual knowledge about the fundamental pragmatics of life
2. Rich procedural knowledge about dealing with the fundamental pragmatics of life
3. Life-span contextualism – understanding of life contexts and their temporal (developmental) relations
4. Value-relativism – knowledge about the differences in values and life goals
5. Uncertainty – knowledge about the relative uncertainty of life and its management. (pp.4–5)

Their scale for self-related wisdom is similar.

Through our initial investigations of wisdom in therapy, we have come to believe that self-organising wisdom differs from wisdom *per se*. If we take Baltes and Staudinger's (2000) definition of wisdom as expert knowledge in the fundamental pragmatics of life, then almost by definition a client in therapy is not going to be showing wisdom at the start. Rather, it is towards wisdom that they are hopefully evolving.

Self-organising wisdom is therefore a generative *process*. Following Carl Rogers, we assume it is a natural property of the organism that can be mobilised under certain conditions. This does not imply that the person will always, or even usually, act wisely. Under the right conditions, the person will begin to think and process information in such a way as to move in a wiser direction. The person will a) move towards balancing various competing factors in their life, and b) intuitively use the dimensions of wisdom as described by Baltes and Staudinger as best they can. They may not yet have expert knowledge about the fundamental pragmatics of life, but as they explore their knowledge, they enrich and deepen their understanding of it. They may not yet think in contextual terms, but they move towards that as they begin to stand back and view their lives in context. As they do that, they also begin to move away from rigid either/or thinking. They begin to evaluate values. Finally, as they engage in this contextualising, exploring and balancing process, they recognise the relative uncertainty of life and the fact that there is risk inherent in most choices.

Self-organising wisdom is construed as both a creative and a grounding process. It is creative in the sense that new, emergent solutions arise as the individual is able to think openly and escape from pre-formed ideas. However, it is more than creativity, in that creativity can be used in the service of evil (Bohart, 2013), whereas wisdom involves a balancing of self-interests with the interests of others. Self-organising wisdom is grounding in the sense that the person *locates* themselves more clearly in the matrices of their lives. They become clearer about 'who they are', what they value, and how they balance one value off against another. Accordingly, they may come to 'own' values or choices that they previously had not owned. They may come to more clearly identify what is 'my' voice.

Self-organising wisdom is a process by which the organism comes to a wiser state of self-organisation. A wise state of self-organisation is not, *per se*, knowledge. It is a state where the person exhibits signs of being more balanced, more integrated, more contextualised, more grounded and more aware, and accepting of the fundamental uncertainty of life. Experientially, the person's emotions might become more modulated and balanced. Cognitions move towards being more richly differentiated, clarified and balanced. Behaviours become more balanced with values as well as with the needs of the situation: i.e. they become more sensitively contextualised. Self-organising wisdom may be a conscious process, but it also happens in unconscious ways. Gendlin has said:

> Roger's method brought it home that the decisions a person must make are inherently that person's own. No book knowledge enables another person to decide for anyone. That goes for life decisions and life-style as well as, moment by moment, what to talk about, feel into, struggle with. Another person might make a guess, but ultimately personal growth is from the inside outward. *A process of change begins and moves in ways even the person's own mind cannot direct, let alone another person's mind.* (Gendlin, 1984, p.297, italics added)

Our conception of self-organising wisdom is that it is a creative process of synthesising and balancing. It involves the enriching and deepening of the understanding of personal knowledge, including cultural aspects, through exploring; the enriching and deepening of the understanding of personal values through exploring them, and the developing of an enriched contextual perspective on one's experience by standing back and examining things. It also includes a recognition of the fundamental uncertainty of knowledge and therefore the existence of risk in whatever choices one makes. It is fuelled by adopting an open, exploratory stance in which one moves towards a position of holding constructs tentatively. Therefore, the most fundamental sign of it is that a person openly explores, questions, evaluates, looks at things in context, and tries to understand how things fit together and balance with one another. This conception integrates ideas from Baltes and Staudinger, from Sternberg and from Rogers' views of the nature of effective therapeutic process with the conditions that foster creativity.

This process is not necessarily one of logically and linearly analysing a problem. It is not uncommon for clients to jump from one topic to another, and to recycle through topics as they compare and contrast each element to see how they balance with one another. As they do this, each part of the contextualised knowledge helps the person understand other parts. As this process happens, new aspects form and emerge, often spontaneously. A deeper understanding of each component's place in the 'net' may develop. This may lead to shifts in the nature of the components, as well as to whole Gestalt shifts. The metaphor of a 'neural net' is relevant to understanding the process (Caspar & Berger, 2012).

If the person is engaging in a wisdom-making process, we should then expect to see signs of creative *emergence*. Emergence involves the appearance of new steps in ways that may not strictly and logically be dictated by what has come before. It may be a person's suddenly realising that they have made a decision, or that they now know what to do, without necessarily engaging in the conscious process of deciding. It may occur as a sign that the person is moving towards reaching some degree of closure or resolution on a given issue. It may appear as the emergence of a new solution, or a new step in the process, particularly if this happens without a clear-cut suggestion from the therapist. It may be the appearance of new experience. It may be the sudden appearance of a felt shift in perspective.

An example of a step spontaneously emerging is when 'Gloria', in the famous film with Carl Rogers (Shostrom, 1965), suddenly compares her experience with her father with her experience with Rogers. This is a spontaneous emergent (she says, 'I don't know why this occurred to me...').

Yet another way something may emerge is that the person now finds that they have the experience of *owning* something that they had previously only intellectually believed in. It is no longer just a 'should'. For instance, someone who has thought to themselves, 'I should forgive him' comes to a full, heartfelt 'I do forgive him.' Or someone who intellectually 'accepts' that a relationship has ended now suddenly finds themselves experiencing a sense of acceptance.

In the following study, we were interested in seeing if the wisdom-making process as we construed it indeed looked like it was occurring in person-centred therapy in the way that, theoretically, it should have been, and if there were signs of 'creative emergence.'

Method

We started our exploration by applying Mickler and Staudinger's (2005) self-related wisdom scale to Thomas Mackrill's (2011) case of Jane. The case was a 12-session therapy of a young woman who was an adult child of an alcoholic. The therapist was psychodynamic-existential in orientation. We found that Jane's wisdom score increased from 2 early in therapy to 4 later in therapy, on a 7-point scale. This moderate level of wisdom at the end of therapy was comparable with ratings in previous studies that Jane had achieved a moderate level of therapeutic change (Bohart et al., 2011a, 2011b).

We were specifically interested in seeing if clients showed signs of self-organising wisdom in individual sessions. In order to study this, we thought it best to look at single sessions of person-centred therapy, since it was theoretically in those sessions where we most expected self-organising wisdom to show up clearly.

We initially had two raters use the Mickler and Staudinger scale to rate the degree of wisdom in single demonstration sessions recorded by Carl Rogers. However we did not find that their scale was getting at what we wanted to know. Therefore we set out to develop our own tool for studying single sessions of therapy.

The scale we started to develop divides self-organising wisdom into the two components mentioned above: signs that the client is engaging in a wisdom-making *process*, and signs of creative *emergence*. Signs that the client is engaging in a wisdom-making process include:

- the person is exploring and questioning
- they are searching past history
- they take culture into account
- they search present and future circumstances
- they identify and evaluate relevant values
- they look at things in context
- they try to stand back to look at things in context and how they relate to one another
- they try to balance things
- they consider the risks in choices

- they move from blindly following previous learning to evaluating it
- they exhibit openness.

Signs of creative emergence include signs of the client's own generativity, as previously described above.

Two raters independently evaluated three transcripts. We, the co-authors, evaluated a transcript of Carl Rogers working with Gloria and a transcript of Carl Rogers working with Peter Ann (Rogers & Sanford, 1985). Makenna and an independent graduate student (Michelle Martin) evaluated a DVD of the noted person-centred therapist Maureen O'Hara working with a client, 'Anita'.[1] The sessions with Gloria and Peter Ann were single demonstration sessions of relatively short length. The session with Anita was one from a longer series of therapy sessions. The raters evaluating Gloria and Peter Ann were instructed to go response by response and to intensively study the transcript and evaluate it in terms of the scale. They were to write up their results and give an overall rating on a 7-point scale on two dimensions: did the client show signs of engaging in a wisdom-making process, and were there signs of emergence? The process was similar with Anita, although, because it was a DVD and not a transcript, the two raters were instructed to stop the video every now and then to write down their impressions, rather than to go response by response.

Next, the raters wrote up their observations. It was these notes that were used as 'data'. At this point in our process, we used the scale in a fundamentally qualitative, hermeneutic way, although raters did assign scale numbers at the end. Raters were not trained to make ratings by following specific criteria. Nor were they trained to try to agree on their ratings. The model was influenced by the adjudicational method I had used in other studies (e.g. Bohart et al., 2011a, 2011b), so it was more like how jurors evaluate evidence in a trial. Jurors have criteria they are supposed to follow

---

1. This is not a publicly available video. We have changed the client's name and removed other identifying information.

in evaluating evidence, but individual jurors may apply the criteria in different ways. They may, as happened in the previous research (Bohart et al., 2011b) make the same judgement or reach the same conclusion but based on somewhat different evidence. This is also similar to how journal reviewers operate. Thus, the scale was more of a *tool* for evaluating a data set, in this case transcripts and a film. Naturally occurring convergence was valued more than convergence based on training. If two raters did not agree, differences were used to understand further what was going on. As it happened, there was no substantial disagreement between the raters in any of the three cases.

Results
Gloria

The two raters (Makenna and I) moderately agreed on Gloria. On whether she engaged in a wisdom-making process, I rated her as 6 on the 7-point scale, and Makenna rated her 5. On creative emergence, I rated her 4 and Makenna rated her as 3. We believe that the agreement was reasonably good, since we did not 'train' to see things the same way.

Gloria's problem as initially stated had to do with telling her daughter about her sex life. However, as the session progressed, she confronted her own feelings about her sexuality and questions about how she could know what was best for her, and examined her relationship with her father. Looking at our respective analyses, Makenna and I agreed that Gloria did actively engage in exploring and questioning, after initially hoping that Carl Rogers would give her an answer. Although she held constructs relatively rigidly at first, she was actively open to exploration and began to question them as she went. She stood back and tried to see things in context, looking at her problems in relationship to what was good for her daughter, how it fit into her divorce and her relationship with her ex-husband, how it fit into her sex life, how it fit with her personality, and how it fit with earlier experiences with her mother. She explored her history and experience to understand the context for her current problems, and this in turn led to a richer understanding of her issues. She evaluated her values. Makenna noted that she took culture into account in terms of the issue of women talking about sex. Gloria also thought about her behaviour in terms of what was right or wrong, and in terms of how she knew what was true for her. Although she hadn't fitted all the pieces together, she had started to do that.

There were two steps of creative emergence. First, she came to some degree of closure on the issue of whether to tell her daughter about her sex life or not, 'owning' more fully her value of being honest. Second, we both identified the emergence of the issue with her father and how she could talk to Rogers in a different way than she had been able to talk to him. It emerged in an unexpected and unpredictable way from what had come before, although in retrospect it made sense.

Peter Ann

I rated Peter Ann 5.5 on wisdom-making. Makenna rated her 4.5. On creative emergence, I rated her 4.5 and Makenna rated her 5. Again, the agreement was reasonably good.

Peter Ann's conflict had to do with the fact that she had been pregnant with twins but had miscarried and lost them. She was conflicted about having children in the future, and whether she even could. Both raters saw Peter Ann engaging in an active exploring and questioning process. Both of us saw her contextualising the problem in part by exploring past and present experience. Makenna said that Peter Ann was exploring at the beginning, and at the end she was looking at what she had found. We both saw her as questioning and looking at her values but not as yet challenging them. Peter Ann looked at how she identified herself in life, how that fit in with what she valued, and what she learned from the death of her twins in terms of the fact that, in one sense, it had enriched her marriage, making her and her husband closer. She tried to understand what she wanted in the context of what her husband wanted, her parents wanted, and what was expected of her as a woman.

We agreed that Peter Ann made some small steps towards resolution. There were signs of creative emergence. However, she did not make a full shift or develop a solution to internal conflicts – she was just getting a sense of the picture and the experience of herself, seeing her self with a bit more clarity, as the session ended. She was still trying to identify what her needs were. In that sense, we saw the issue as that of struggling to balance and identify her needs in the context of her feelings for her husband and family, as well as in the context of her self-image as a person who had seen herself as a 'winner' in life, someone who normally got what she wanted, but not this time.

I identified two emergents that Makenna did not mention. I saw Peter Ann, someone who greatly valued having control in her life, as slowly but definitely moving towards realising that getting pregnant and carrying to term was a situation over which she did not have full control, that she would have to accept whatever was. I also saw her as more clearly coming to a realisation that 'I want to have a child' towards the end of the session (as opposed to having a child for her parents, for her husband, or because she was supposed to).

Anita

Makenna rated Anita 6 on wisdom-making and 7 on creative emergence. Michelle Martin rated her 7 on wisdom-making and 6 on creative emergence.

Anita was a college professor and a research psychologist who was struggling because she was not finding her work meaningful. She was thinking of changing professions. Although Makenna and Michelle differed slightly in their ratings, both saw Anita as strongly engaged in a wisdom-making process – actively questioning and exploring, and deeply evaluating her goals, career and cultural background. In comparison with both Gloria and Peter Ann, she seemed to be even more active in openly and thoroughly questioning, and in delving deeper and challenging herself, evaluating her goals and looking at things in the broader context. The one thing that both raters noted with Anita, and more so than with Gloria or Peter Ann, was a greater awareness of the risk involved in the choices she was considering.

In terms of creative emergence, both saw strong signs. Michelle noted:

> She indicates at the end of the session that she has an incredible feeling because she suddenly feels very strongly that there is an identity. She knows now where to start.

Makenna said:

> At the end of the session, Anita states 'that it took me by surprise'. That surprise is her own recognition that all of this has led to her acknowledging the 'personal me'... At the end of the session she has an experience of deep knowing, whole body shifts and gut level reaction to her new revelation.

Discussion

The goal of this initial research was to see if raters could identify something that looked like a wisdom-making process, and to see if there were signs of creative emergence. We concluded we were successfully able to use this frame to understand the activities of these three clients in terms of a process theoretically compatible with person-centred therapy. We saw three clients who actively struggled to fit all the pieces together. They openly stood back and questioned and explored their experience. They compared and contrasted different aspects of their present and past experience to enrich their understanding of it. They compared and contrasted their experience with their values in order to better understand both values and experience. They stepped back to see how things fit together in the broader context. The pieces did not completely fall into place for either Gloria or Peter Ann in the short sessions provided. Nonetheless, engaging in the process did lead to creative emergents, which were new steps appearing without directly being prodded for by the therapist. Anita was more fully able to fit the pieces together. However, she had done more work on them previously. In keeping with her being able to fit more pieces together, she had an unexpected and surprising major shift towards the end of the session.

One might ask, what is different about using the concept of self-organising wisdom versus related concepts to understand what is going on? For instance, what is new about observing that clients reflect on their experience in psychotherapy? Don't virtually all therapies ask clients to recount events in their lives? This is true. However, there is a difference between a client *recounting* information primarily at the behest of the therapist or interviewer and someone creatively *exploring* information for the purpose of creative understanding and wisdom-making. There are also differences in types of reflection. We believe that wisdom-making reflection is a somewhat different way of construing the activity of reflection – but that is another issue and, sadly, I do not have space to go into it here.

Another question that could be asked is to what degree does the therapist facilitate the self-organising wisdom process? Theoretically, from a person-centred point of view, the therapist's role is to provide an open, supportive 'space' within which the client can explore. Therapists help by clarifying with empathic understanding responses. However, our sense was that the therapist responses did more than that: they actively contributed to clients differentiating and integrating information, although they did not prompt the creative emergents that appeared. Further research on the therapist's role is needed.

Yet another question is, if there really is such a thing as self-organising wisdom, does it only appear in person-centred therapy? Based on Bohart and Tallman's (2010) review of research on clients' active agentic involvement in all types of therapy, we would expect the answer to this to be 'no'. We would expect it to play an active role in all approaches to therapy. However we expect it will be more complicated to identify its role in therapies where therapists are more actively guiding and structuring. Again, further research is needed.

6 | Some neglected insights of Carl Rogers

This is an updated version of a paper presented at the conference of the World Association of Person-Centered and Experiential Psychotherapy and Counseling in Norwich, England in 2008. The presentation was a series of short vignettes, not fleshed-out papers. I wanted to identify several of what I thought were Carl Rogers' neglected insights. By 'neglected', I meant ideas that many in mainstream psychology did not take seriously. This is not to say they were neglected by everyone. They were certainly taken seriously by many at the conference. I believe the points I make in these vignettes are still valid 12 years later, and this is one of my favourites of the papers I have written.

Insight #1: Becoming the self that one is – deep experience of the self

Carl Rogers talked about people becoming the self that they are (Rogers, 1961a). Although I do not believe that Rogers had a concept of the 'real self' versus the 'false self', as others have had, he did talk about becoming the self that one is. This concept would be meaningless at best or mystical at worst to many in current mainstream psychology. Many mainstream concepts of the self rob it of any meaning that could be related to what Rogers was talking about. For instance, in one conception, the self is nothing but an aspect that evolved to give the person an evolutionary advantage (Kurzban & Aktipis, 2007). The 'self' is basically a set of cognitive mechanisms designed for strategic manipulation of how others see one's traits, abilities and prospects. Its sole purpose is to present oneself to the world in manipulative ways that give one an evolutionary advantage. There is no 'real' self. In fact, there is no self; there are different modules of experience that operate to control the person, but the belief in a unified self is an illusion. Another popular view from social constructionist theory is that the self is nothing but a social construction (for an example of this perspective, see Harré, 1987). The very idea of the 'self' is itself culturally based (not every culture shares our construct of self), and our personal self is what we learn from the culture and the people around us.

I do not have space here to consider the virtues or drawbacks of such views. From all these points of view, there is no real self. So, Rogers' idea of 'becoming the self that one is' makes no sense. Yet I believe there is truth in it. First, I want to point out that Rogers' view does not mean there is a 'real self' inside, in the sense of a stable enduring part of the psyche, such that, if one were in touch with it, one would always know what was best for oneself. For some who talk as if there is a 'real self', this stable, enduring structure presumably gets hidden under the 'false self', which is the self imposed on one by how others want one to be.

Rather, what I think Rogers meant by 'becoming the self that one is' is becoming more personally congruent. That means, indeed, being able to shed the false self imposed by society, the shoulds that constrict us and blind us to what we may actually think and feel. But what one gets in touch with is the ongoing flow of personal experience, not a stable, fixed structure with enduring personal truths. Rather, one becomes the congruent process of listening to one's organismic experience, thinking and finding out for oneself what is true for oneself in the moment, on an ongoing basis. Becoming the self that one is is an ongoing process of a dialogue between self-reflection and organismic experiencing. The self is an ongoing forming and re-forming process, not a thing.

In becoming congruent with oneself, one can get in touch with something that is very much like a 'real self', although it is not a structure. One can get in touch with what is most deeply true for oneself in regard to some issue or another. This truth can have a stability to it. The fact that this can happen is why people talk about a 'real self' inside, and in one sense they are right. We can have the experience of finding some truth about ourselves in a deep and abiding sense. That is, we can get in touch with things that are true for ourselves and represent our 'whole selves'. In the famous 'Gloria' film (Shostrom, 1965; the transcript is also published in Rogers & Wood, 1974), there is a moment when 'Gloria' talks about her decision to leave her husband and how good it felt to just know that was the right decision for her. I would say that there is such a thing as a 'real-self' experience, and this is one example. Things finally had come into focus for her in terms of what she deeply believed and what was best for her. So there is the experience of when the sense of my self comes into a deep and clear focus — when I can say 'This is me', 'This is what I believe', 'This is who I am'.

To put it in other words, we might talk about 'finding one's own voice' as metaphor for the experience. There is something meaningful about 'finding one's own voice', and people can identify that experience, or when they know that they are 'speaking their truth' or coming from an authentic place.

Thus, whether there is a 'real self' or not, there is a 'real-self' experience. We can debate endlessly as to what that is theoretically. But experientially there is no doubt that people can have a sense of 'who one is'. The experience is one of 'that which is me' — of fitting, of knowing who you are. Other metaphors include 'coming home to oneself' and having oneself come into focus. The experience is often one of *finding*: 'That's it!' We need a phenomenology of this (see next section).

Alternatively, people can have the opposite experience: of feeling 'I am not myself' or that something is not them, does not fit them, or not knowing who they are. They can have the experience of losing themselves. I had one such experience when I had a severe anxiety attack when I was 22. For a time I lost a sense of myself. I could not tell what 'I' wanted or believed. And for me, the therapy I had (with a Jungian who practised like a

Rogerian) led to a sense of 'coming home to myself', coming into focus, in a way that I had never experienced before.

An example from literature of someone becoming the self that one is is that of Stephen Daedalus in James Joyce's *A Portrait of the Artist as a Young Man* (1948):

> 'Did you believe in it [religion] when you were at school?...'
>
> 'I did,' Stephen answered... 'I was someone else then... I mean,' said Stephen, 'that I was not myself as I am now, as I had to become.' (Joyce, 1948, p.188)

Therefore, if we forget theory and look at people's experience (at least in this culture), their experience teaches us that there is something we could call 'true-self' experience, as well as the equivalent experience of losing oneself, being out of touch with oneself, and so on. You can identify 'that which is me' and that which does not feel like me at a feeling/experiential level.

Below I give two examples. One is another example from *A Portrait of the Artist as a Young Man.* It is the passage where Stephen decides not to follow the dictates of his mother to be a priest, which he is just about to commit himself to, and instead decides to be a writer:

> So he had passed beyond the sentries who had stood as guardians of his boyhood and had sought to keep him among them that he might be subject to them and serve their ends... The end he had been born to serve yet did not see had led him to escape by an unseen path... he seemed to hear the noise of dim waves and to see a winged form flying above the waves and slowly climbing the air. What did it mean? Was it... a prophecy of the end he had been born to serve and had been following through the mists of childhood and boyhood; a symbol of the artist forging anew in his workshop out of the sluggish matter of the earth a new soaring impalpable imperishable being? (Joyce, 1948, pp.127–131)

I have only quoted a small part of the section of the book, but it is where Stephen 'finds himself', 'finds out who he is', becomes the self that he is, or however you want to put it. Another way of saying it is that it is where he 'finds his true path'.

My second example is from J.K. Rowling, author of the *Harry Potter* books. She has said:

> I was convinced that the only thing I wanted to do, ever, was to write novels… So why do I talk about the benefits of failure? Simply because failure meant a stripping away of the inessential. I stopped pretending to myself that I was anything other than what I was, and began to direct all my energy into finishing the only work that mattered to me. Had I really succeeded at anything else, I might never have found the determination to succeed in the one arena I believed I truly belonged. (Rowling, 2008)

Not only have I had experiences like this, many of my clients have as well. I have said that such experiences do not fit with some of the concepts popular in current mainstream psychology about the self. However they do relate to other concepts that occur in the humanistic and existential literature. One is the concept of 'authenticity'. There would not be such a concept if the idea of 'being true to oneself' made no sense. According to Smith (2001), the meaning of being authentic is that of 'being yourself'. She reviews the ideas of various writers and notes that, for Heidegger, authenticity meant an entity that genuinely exemplifies its Being. For Sartre, 'bad faith' was pretending to be what one is not. Authenticity also can be seen as a state of integrity between one's innermost self and external manifestations. For Sartre, good faith was grasping the deeper reality of what one truly is.

Smith defines authentic as being true to oneself. She then goes on to study person-to-person authenticity: that is, two or more people being authentic with one another, or being authentic in the presence of another. As I reflect on this, I must ask, would person-to-person authenticity make any sense of the person if we were merely a collection of modules or socially constructed selves? Would interpersonal authenticity be one module 'encountering' another module?

A criticism could be made that the examples I have given are from literature or from personal experience or from philosophy; I have not cited any empirical research. This is true. I would argue that we actually do not know much about how people *experience* the self because our field has tended to distrust studies of human phenomenology (see the next section). Yet, if we take subjective experience seriously, then many people, including myself, find the concept of deeply experiencing oneself, or finding oneself, to be a meaningful experience.

One might also argue that this is a culture-specific experience. There is some evidence that what people believe to be their 'real self' has culture-specific elements. For instance, Turner (1976) studied the 'real-self' experience in the USA and England in the 1960s and early 1970s. He found that college students in England felt they were being their real selves when they were actualising their values, while college students in the USA felt they were actualising their true selves when they were closer to acting out their feelings and when they were being open and intimate with others. While this shows there can be culture-specific aspects to the real-self experience, it does not negate the fact that people can have the *experience* of what is most true for themselves – of coming into focus.

Landrine (1992) has argued that some cultures do not even have a concept of the self as we know it. It would be interesting to study the phenomenological experience of self across cultures, foregoing the cultures' *concepts* of self. Even in cultures where there is no concept of self as we know it, is there something like that, of being personally congruent with one's deepest values, deepest aims and goals and so on? Is there the experience of finding one's true path? Is there not something akin to 'being true to oneself', or the sense of coming home to oneself? There may be equivalents across cultures – of having the *experience* of being true to oneself, even though the content of the experience may be culturally influenced.

My last point is that, for us as therapists, is there not something intrinsically moral about helping people find their own voices, of helping people be congruent with themselves? This would not be the case if one did not believe in such things. It would make therapy nothing but programming and engineering people to function 'normally'. The concept of real-self experience would not make sense if one believed the human being were nothing but a bunch of cognitive schemas, like a computer. It would be as if you were saying that a computer needed to find its own voice. Yet there are dominant approaches to therapy today that have no concept of 'helping people come home to themselves'.

In summary, one neglected insight of Carl Rogers is that there is something called a true-self experience. However, we don't know enough about this experience, because we have not done enough of the kinds of phenomenological studies of the experience to unpack it. This leads me to the next neglected insight.

Insight #2: The importance of subjective experience and phenomenology

By and large, modern psychology (at least in the USA) works from the outside in. Going back to the behaviourist revolution of the 1930s, when psychology became the study of 'observable behaviour', introspective methods have been suspect. The typical way of studying aspects of psychological functioning is to form a hypothesis about something, manipulate and measure some variables, and then use 'objective' measures to see what happens. Objective measures may include self-report scales, but these have usually been 'validated' against some kind of non-self-report criteria. Participants' subjective reports may be gathered, but this is typically seen as a secondary, imperfect form of data. In psychotherapy research, simply asking clients whether therapy helped or not is distrusted as a measure of outcome. As I have mentioned, although self-report measures are often used, they have been standardised against 'objective' indicators.

A good deal of such research has led to the proposition that people's judgement (i.e. people's subjective perceptions and opinions) is erroneous and flawed. Examples include people's eyewitness testimony, people being fooled by perceptual illusions, and numerous studies suggesting that people are not in touch with their own experience, motives or reasons for doing things. An example with emotion are studies where you ask participants to keep track of their emotions on a day-by-day basis (e.g. Thomas & Diener, 1990). At the end of a week, you ask them to say how happy they've been over the past week. Their ratings are different to the average of each day's ratings. This has been taken to imply that people don't know their own experience.

However, what researchers rarely do is in-depth interviews with their participants to explore their phenomenological experience when they made the rating of their emotions at the end of the week. Perhaps if we asked them, we might discover that what they are doing is more complex than we imagine, and makes sense. It is possible that when you ask someone to rate how their emotions were the previous week, they selectively base their decision on the most important or salient experiences, and that is what is most personally meaningful for them. That may be why the average of their scores for the week is different from their summative rating at the end of the week. That does not mean they are imperfect in their self-knowledge. It means they are answering a different question to the one the researcher is asking.

As I have said, if you listen to many mainstream psychologists, the human being is someone who misperceives reality, is fooled into seeing what they think they see, cannot be trusted to report what they think they see or the causes of their own behaviour, does not know what they are experiencing, and so on. However, by contrast, Cissna and Anderson (1994) noted the importance Carl Rogers placed on subjective experience. Not only did he take subjective experience seriously, it was an epistemological position for him. He trusted subjective experience. I want to argue that, like Carl Rogers, we should take phenomenology more seriously.

In fact, there is evidence that the mainstream views that emphasise us not knowing ourselves, that we cannot trust subjective experience, may be overdrawn, as the philosopher C.A.J. Coady (1992) has shown in his book *Testimony*. J.J. Gibson, the perceptual psychologist, noted that, when perceptual psychologists focus on illusions as evidence that human perception is not veridical, they miss the fact that most perception is veridical, and that illusions exist because of inadequate information (de Wit et al., 2015). For instance, in the well-known illusion of the old woman/young woman, in real life you could shift your perspective, look at her from a different angle, perhaps even walk around her, and the illusion would vanish. You would see what was 'really there'. Daniel Kahneman (e.g. Kahneman & Klein, 2009), who has studied the flaws in human judgement, has also noted that human intuition is frequently correct. It could be argued that, if human judgement were as bad as some psychologists make it out to be, it is a miracle humans have survived at all.

I would like to argue that, along with Rogers, we should pay more attention to subjective experience, and take it more seriously than we do.[1] This is true both in therapy and in psychological theory and research. When we do pay attention to subjective experience, we may discover things that do not fit with what some mainstream psychologists are saying. We discover, for instance, that, as I pointed out in the previous section, there is something genuine about the real-self experience, even if it does not fit with many mainstream conceptions of the self in academic psychology. We need a science of phenomenology as much as we need a science of behaviour. We should more carefully study the experience of people and then map that onto our more traditional psychology.

To use an example, consider the literature that holds that we cannot know ourselves very well through introspection (e.g. Wilson & Dunn, 2004). Nisbett and Ross (1980) report research studies that suggest that people do not know why they might prefer some thing over another. When asked, they do not have access to their own experiential reasons. Rather, they make up a plausible theory for their preferences. I will not go over how

---

1. This is happening somewhat more now, with the increased acceptance of qualitative research, which is often based on interview data. But even here, there is still a tendency to take the results of such data as merely about what participants are experiencing, rather than about anything 'real'.

the research is done. But what the researchers did not do, as I have previously indicated, is conduct a careful phenomenological exploration of the person's experience of the situation when they are answering questions as to why they preferred what they did. Perhaps if we did, we would find that they know more than they have reported. Or perhaps we would find that there is some 'wisdom' in their answer.

A key part of the Rogerian point of view is that, if carefully attended to and given the chance to spell out their thinking and feelings, what clients do or feel generally makes sense. That is why we can introspect in therapy and find the underlying wisdom. This is not a matter of creating a narrative about the self in order to make sense out of one's experience. This may indeed happen. Therapists may 'coach' clients into construing their experience in a certain way. That is why, as others have noted, Freudians get Freudian insights and Jungians get Jungian insights. Spence (1982) has argued that the past that we get in touch with in therapy is a reconstruction, a 'narrative truth', but not a historical truth.

However, as Gendlin (1997) has argued, that does not mean that, as one gets in touch with one's felt meanings and experience, rather than trying to reconstruct intellectually some causal narrative, what emerges or what one gets in touch with has no genuine personal reality, but rather is based on narrative constructs imported from outside. In this regard, Gendlin and Johnson (2004) have argued for a 'first-person science', based on the idea of studying how internal experience relates to a variety of other variables. The fact of the matter is that it is possible that many of the research findings showing a lack of self-awareness are based on the kinds of questions that are asked, the lack of intensive listening and exploration on the part of the researcher, and the fact that we humans are probably far more inexperienced at looking within than we are at looking without. What if we were to teach people how to listen to their own experience in the same way that we teach them to be better observers of their physical environments? We need to create expert observers of their own experience (this may be what person-centred therapy does and in fact what the Experiencing Scale measures (Hendricks, 2002)). As I have suggested above, I believe there is much to be learned by taking the exploration of our phenomenology seriously.

Similarly, this is a key way that therapy can work. We can talk about therapy in terms of how much the therapist works from the inside out, in contrast to working from the outside in – or, to put it another way, how much the client's subjectivity is co-ordinated into therapy. Person-centred therapy works from subjectivity outward. It provides a platform for clients to be able to be in touch with their inner experience in a friendly way, and then learn to elaborate, deepen and enrich it by going deeper into it and articulating it in words and other symbols. Person-centred therapists work from inner to outer. Through this process, we trust clients to bring the inner into alignment with the outer. And that is what happens.

By contrast, many other points of view work primarily from outer to inner. That is most clear with cognitive therapy. Cognitive therapists look at the client from the outside and 'objectively' assess the existence of dysfunctional patterns of behaviour, thinking and feeling. These are based in clients' subjective experience – their dysfunctional thinking, experience of transference and so on. However, subjectivity is viewed as distorted, and the goal then becomes to bring subjectivity in line with the more objective point of view, in line with supposed objective reality. This is also true, at least to some extent, of traditional psychodynamic therapy. Although psychodynamic therapy does indeed help clients plumb subjective experience, it is done in the belief that subjective experience can be distorted and untrustworthy. Psychodynamic therapists also look at the client from outside and diagnose their experience in terms such as transference, defensiveness or resistance, and then try to objectively 'correct' it with insights provided from outside.

There is nothing wrong with this. It works and there are many clients who like it. However, person-centred therapy works literally by deepening subjectivity and by trusting it. We believe that, as clients become more deeply subjective, they paradoxically become more deeply objective. In discovering internal wisdom and internal resources within, they open up to co-ordinating their subjectivity with objectivity and find wiser ways of integrating the two.

Insight #3: The intrinsic value of empathic listening and witnessing

I want to talk about the intrinsic value of what I have come to believe is best called 'empathic witnessing'. In contrast to a view of empathy as a form of interactive responding (that is, empathic following responses or 'reflections'), I see empathic witnessing as a fundamental way of pure listening and appreciating the experience of another person, of 'witnessing' their struggle, their experience, their pain, their triumphs and who they are. The concept of witnessing does not imply that anything has to be *done*. It is not an instrumental concept. One is not empathically listening *in order to* give advice, solve problems or provide a new perspective. It is also not to facilitate experiential exploration, help access feelings, deepen experience, provide mirroring, lead to acceptance or further understanding, make the client feel safe or any of the other functions that have been postulated to happen as a function of empathic responding. It is not even to relieve someone's pain. One is, rather, simply empathically *witnessing* their struggle in order to share it with them, or to 'be with' them in their struggle.

This does not mean the witness is merely a silent observer. They may respond with empathic following responses, to try to understand what the other is saying. They may respond non-verbally, showing they understand and appreciate the struggle the person is going through (or, if they are witnessing a triumph, show they understand and appreciate what it feels like to have triumphed), or they may respond in other ways to show that they recognise and appreciate what the person is feeling/experiencing or undergoing. They may simply hold the person's hand. Or they could ask questions, but with the purpose of being with the person, not to gather information. Or they could express sympathy, but again, to be with them, not to try to talk them out of their pain.

This is a concept that does not fit well into our instrumental psychotherapy culture. Can you imagine manualising empathic witnessing? We would be pressed to operationalise it and explain how it 'worked' to change clients' behaviour. Our goal would become to be able to *operate on* clients' experience, emotions, behaviour and cognitions in order to facilitate their growth, or correct them, with empathic witnessing. To simply witness does not sit well, unless it can be operationalised. We want to dissect witnessing, to find out how it works so that we can more efficiently produce the 'effects' it is purported to produce. I submit that the very spirit of such dissecting is contrary to the power of empathic witnessing.

I give the example of empathic witnessing from Arthur Kleinman (1988b):

> During the early 1970s… I encountered several patients whose powerful experiences… fixed my interest on the intimate and manifold ways by which illness comes to affect our lives.
>
> The first patient was a pathetic seven-year-old girl who had been badly burned over most of her body. She had to undergo a daily ordeal of a whirlpool bath, during which the burnt flesh was tweezered away from her raw, open wounds. This experience was horribly painful to her. She screamed and moaned and begged the medical team, whose efforts she stubbornly fought off, not to hurt her anymore. My job as a neophyte clinical student was to hold her uninjured hand, as much to reassure her and calm her as to enable the surgical resident to quickly pull away the dead, infected tissue in the pool of swirling water, which rapidly turned pinkish, then bloody red… I tried to distract this little patient from her traumatic daily confrontation with terrible pain. I tried talking to her about her home, her family, her school… I could barely tolerate the daily horror: her screams, dead tissue floating in the blood-stained water… Then, one day, I made contact. At wit's end… uncertain what to do besides clutching the small hand, and in despair over her unrelenting anguish, I found myself asking her to tell me how she tolerated it, what the feeling was like of being so badly burned and having to experience the

awful surgical ritual, day after day after day. She stopped, quite surprised, and looked at me from a face so disfigured it was difficult to read the expression; then, in terms direct and simple, she told me. While she spoke, she grasped my hand harder and neither screamed nor fought off the surgeon or the nurse. Each day from then on, her trust established, she tried to give me a feeling of what she was experiencing. By the time my training took me off this rehabilitation unit, the little burned patient seemed noticeably better able to tolerate her debridement... She taught me a grand lesson... about the actual experience of illness, and that witnessing and helping to order that experience can be of therapeutic value. (pp.xi–xii)

Another example of empathic witnessing would be if one were to sit with someone dying and listen to them share whatever they have to say, and just dialogue with them and keep them company. I have often used this as a role-play exercise with my students, as a way of helping them explore the experience of empathically following and being with another person without trying to 'solve' anything or make anything happen.

I take the value of empathic witnessing to be a truth of Carl Rogers, because Rogers recognised the intrinsic value of listening and, in my language, bearing witness with the other. In the Rogers-Buber dialogue (Cissna & Anderson, 1994), Rogers says that therapy is a meeting of persons and help is a by-product of that. This is very close to what I am saying here: there is intrinsic therapeutic value in empathic witnessing, or simple empathic listening.

In a culture where it is believed that people must be 'done to' in order for change to occur, it has been forgotten, or perhaps never even noticed, that simple empathic listening and witnessing is a powerful personal experience that can precipitate change. Because the therapist is not 'doing anything', this tends not to be believed. Indeed, it is just the opposite. Those who believe that things must be 'done to' clients cannot believe this and find ways of discounting it. I will not cite anyone here, but both psychodynamic and cognitive therapist writers have argued that simple empathic witnessing could 'reinforce' dysfunctional behaviour. From their perspective, the therapist needs to provide 'objective' feedback.

Yet, over and over, listening to people, giving people a chance to tell their stories seems to help, all by itself in many cases. I recall three clients who were seriously depressed, yet, after one session of empathic listening and witnessing, within which I did nothing but be with them in their experience, there was significant alleviation of the depression. In one session! I am not saying this has happened with all the depressed people I've worked with (it hasn't). But the point is that it can happen. It is a real phenomenon. This is now becoming important in medicine, where some doctors are now including the idea of narrative medicine in their practice (Charon, 2008).

I think one reason our culture has a hard time believing this is because we don't believe in the active, constructive efforts of the person. Gendlin (1990) pointed out that this culture believes that if something is to 'get inside' a person, such as having a good sense of self, it must be instilled from without. We simply cannot imagine that a person telling their story can work through and assimilate emotional trauma, get rid of distorted thoughts and expand ways of seeing, figure out ways of overcoming problems like drinking or anxiety or depression, or discover useful new solutions. We do not believe there is such a thing as an ongoing generative, organismic process.

Being heard is 'person-enhancing', *but not as a technique*. In fact, if it were a technique, rather than a genuine, heartfelt sharing-with the client, and the client caught on, it would very likely backfire (have you ever tried to empathically reflect with someone who knows what you are doing, and have them say, 'Don't do that to me!'? I have).

There is no smoking-gun evidence of the kind that those who believe therapy must be an instrumental 'doing to' would accept to prove that empathic witnessing is valuable. However, construing evidence another way, there is evidence that supports the importance of just listening. If we consider that empathic witnessing includes empathic listening and acceptance, there are many studies where clients are asked what was important to them about therapy. Over and over, they report that the most important thing – or one of the most important things – is to be listened to, heard, to have someone to talk to or to be understood. Cullari (2000) reviewed six studies that found this. Cullari also reported his own finding that the two most important things were the therapist's ability to understand the client's problem and the therapist's willingness to listen. The 'perfect therapist' was someone who was a good listener. Similarly, Phillips (1984) found that what was important for clients was having a time and place where they could focus on themselves and talk.

None of this research supports the intrinsic value of empathic listening and witnessing all by itself. The fact that clients repeatedly refer to listening and understanding as central qualities of therapy does not mean they necessarily believe that these are the only thing that helps. Nonetheless, the fact that these are so often listed as the most important things is compatible with the idea that there is something intrinsically helpful about listening and understanding.

We also know that Eugene Gendlin's technique of focusing has empirical support as a useful technique (Hendricks, 2002). Therapists who use focusing often have the client engage in the focusing process while they sit nearby. The process is going on entirely internally. Yet Gendlin (1996) has said that focusing works better when another person keeps you company. Another example is research done by Smith (2001) with the aim to understand the structure of authentic experiences. She intensively interviewed people about their person-to-person authentic experiences. Some of the people reported that the experience of being interviewed was more therapeutic than talking to a therapist. If this were to be more formally studied, it would be good evidence for the existence of empathic witnessing: being interviewed (empathically) by an interviewer for a research project where the interviewer does not attempt to 'solve problems', 'help them get in touch with feelings', 'help them change their dysfunctional cognitions' and so on, and yet the person experiences it as therapeutic! Parenthetically, I suspect this may have happened *because neither they nor Smith were trying to be therapeutic.*

The basic idea is of doing something non-instrumental, of doing something that can be helpful without trying to be helpful. I was thinking about the difference between listening to understand and listening (and empathically responding) in order to make something happen, like deepening processing, heightening experiencing, focusing on the future and so forth. Perhaps I'm creating a dichotomy here, but think of a parent reading to a child. I have a vivid and poignant memory of my parents sitting at the dining room table reading to me from the new book on real cowboys they had bought me. I was probably five or six years old. I was really into cowboys. They used to read to me all the time. I know they did it because they enjoyed it and they knew I enjoyed it. This new book on real cowboys was like something precious and magical (I still have it).

Now, we also know that reading to children is good for them. It helps them learn language and grammar, learn about the world, learn about story structure. It helps them learn to read. It helps cognitive development in terms of depth of information processing. And it probably models other good things – that books can be interesting, for example. (I was about to say 'That learning is good' but I doubt it models that – learning often doesn't sound like fun, even though learning for a kid can be incredibly fun, as long as they don't think they are learning.) But if your parents read to you in order to make all these things happen, unless they get seduced into the fun of it and *forget* all these things, I doubt a child would enjoy it so much.

It's the same with having someone listen to you in order to understand. What if you knew that the therapist was listening to you in order to point you at experience, heighten experience; that they were responding deliberately to heighten processing, or even empathically reflecting so you reflect on your own experience or take responsibility for yourself? How much would the zest and life be sucked out of it? The therapist too needs to get sucked into the real flow of it and enjoy listening to understand. You want someone to be there, really understanding you, not 'doing' this or that.

Insight #4: Life is discovery

This is a short vignette from Dave Mearns (Mearns, 2006, p.131) about his experience of being supervised by Carl Rogers:

> One of the hospital patients I was working with was profoundly traumatized – very closed off to communication – indeed mute… The dialogue with Carl [Rogers] went as follows:
>
> Carl: Do you know what you are doing with him (the patient)?
>
> Dave: Not a bloody clue, Carl.
>
> Carl: That's alright, then.

The way we are extolled to live nowadays is that we are supposed to be very planful about it. We are endlessly instructed to set concrete goals, the more specific the better. And then we have to develop specific plans to achieve those goals. This is a mantra I've encountered in writings about therapy, living and in education. For instance, the university I worked for, in order to maintain its accreditation, had been told to set specific, observable and measurable goals for each class, for each programme and for the university. Not only that, it was suggested that each student should identify specific goals when they entered the university and then each year assess how well they were moving towards achieving them.

Along with setting goals, one is supposed to design a plan for achieving the goal. So, for instance, at college, when you write a paper, you are taught to develop an outline in advance, and then write to the outline. You can revise the outline as you go, but the idea is to start out with a specific plan as to how to achieve your goal of a finished paper saying X on topic Y. In some of the high schools in the USA, you have to hand in your outline with your finished paper (I always did my outline after I'd finished the paper). According to people who work this way, setting specific goals that are observable and measurable helps answer the question, 'How will you know when you have achieved your goal?' Having a specific plan supposedly helps you know when you are going off course. That is, you have to compare your progress to some *external* criterion to know if you're going off course. As a metaphor, it is as if I, who live in Northern California, set a goal of going to Southern California. However, Southern California is too vague and non-specific. So I must specify it. So I say, okay, my goal is to go to Los Angeles. How will I know when I get there? I have to have something *observable*: I will know when I get there when I see signs saying 'Los Angeles, California'. Then I develop a specific plan to get there: 'I will leave my home in El Cerrito, drive down Barrett Avenue, get on the 80 freeway and drive to the 580 freeway. Then I will take that to the 5 freeway…' and so on. With that specific model in mind, I can chart my progress by checking off the towns I pass on the way and the mile markers and so forth.

This is fine for driving to Los Angeles. But it is not fine when the terrain is uneven and not predictable. Furthermore, note that my very goal-directedness, my focus on the goal of getting to Los Angeles, may discourage me from adopting a more exploratory attitude. I will not be tempted to stop and smell the roses along the way. I will be less tempted to take interesting side routes. I will not be tempted to seek out unexpected places to eat. I will be more likely to single-mindedly pursue my goal. I may only take side routes if I unexpectedly find the major route blocked.

However, life is not like that. Life is much more ill-defined. Life is much more like setting out in one direction and having a lot of things happen that either change your plans or block you from attaining them. So what kind of skills do I need to cope with that? According to the 'specific goals' philosophy, you are to use a kind of version of 'error-corrected feedback'. That is, when something goes wrong that knocks you off course, you use the information from that to readjust your plan in order to achieve your goal. What if, when you get knocked off course, you discover something new that changes your whole plan? But that is incidental. More likely than not, your focus on your goal will narrow your attention so you are less likely to notice anything new. So, on my route to Los Angeles, if it starts to rain and part of the road is flooded out, I may have to find an alternative route. Along the way, I may encounter a charming little town where it might be fun to stop and where I may have new experiences. But if my mindset is focused on my plan, I am less likely to consider that, even if I have the time.

As I have said, I do not believe life is like this. It is more like, you do get sidetracked and find a charming little village. You do stop and go into a diner, and you meet someone who offers you a job in the town. And you decide to take it. And it turns your whole life around. The point is that life is much more like discovery. It is really more like how the pioneers were going from the settled cities of the east coast to the unexplored wilderness of the west. They had a vague idea of where they were going, but they did not know what it would look like when they got there. They were going to find out. In one sense, they were going to find themselves. What kind of skills does that take? It doesn't take planning skills (although they are certainly useful). More so, it takes 'openness to new feedback', receptivity, ability to listen and open attention skills. It takes more of a discovery orientation than a planning orientation.

I am here to speak in praise of either having no goals or having poorly defined goals. I prefer to keep my goals vague and poorly defined. I do not want to define my goals too specifically in advance because I do not want to limit my openness to discovery. I want to flesh out my goals as I go along. As I learn new things, my goals become clearer, but that is through a process of discovery. It is not something I decide on in advance. I continually find new things along the way and they continually shape me.

So how do I know when I have achieved my goals if they are vague and ill-defined? How do I know if I'm in Southern California if I do not have a specifically defined marker of that? The answer is that it is not a matter of achieving a *pre-defined* goal. Rather, I set out to see Southern California, but along the way I learn a lot about myself and that goal. I realise that it was not Southern California *per se* that I was seeking. I was seeking out more wide open spaces. And I know I have found it when I recognise that I am there, even if I did not know that was what I was seeking. It is when I *see* it that I know I am there. Not from external observable indicators decided on in advance, but when my phenomenology tells me. I don't need a cognitive match with objective indicators. I know when I have achieved an *internal* sense of fitting.

It is like writing a poem. I do not have a predefined idea of what the poem will look like. Rather, I write a draft, and then, when I look at it, the *poem* tells me what I am trying to achieve. And then I modify it. And then I modify it again, and it may not even look that much like what I thought it would look like when I started out. But eventually, after several revisions, I will know I am 'there', although I didn't know where 'there' was when I started.

The point is that these are two very fundamentally different visions of how to live life, how to make decisions, how to proceed. One is almost entirely left-brain and logic driven. The other relies on unconscious guidance, intuition, exploring, discovering and finding out. One vision holds that you need to spell out everything explicitly in advance. You may make adjustments as you move towards your goal, but they are based on your perception of deviation from your path, or 'error-corrected feedback'. As I've said, this narrows your attention in that, although you are getting feedback, you are focusing on aspects of the feedback relevant to your plan. Everything is defined in terms of your goal. You may miss unexpectedly new and interesting parts of the feedback. If you have a vague goal, your attention is more open. You are more likely to notice new ideas, new information, new possibilities that have nothing to do with the plan you have set or the goal you are pursuing. You are more likely to discover.

So my vision starts out intuitively, with the idea that you don't know explicitly where you're going. You are guided by a kind of unconscious, non-explicit prompting in a certain direction. You are discovering yourself and your direction as you go. You take a step into the unknown and something opens up new possibilities or insights. You take another step and yet another new thing presents itself. You may revise or even abandon your whole starting point.

I want to return to the Dave Mearns story that I started with, where Carl Rogers asks Dave if he knows what he is doing with a client. Dave says, 'Not a bloody clue.' Rogers says, 'That's all right then.' What is Carl talking about? I presume that Carl is happy that Dave is open to discovering what works with the client, open to receiving the client, open to the encounter as he and the client struggle together, rather than having a 'plan' and a 'goal' that he is trying to achieve.

How does this fit with Carl Rogers' ideas in general? Other than the Mearns quote above, I'm not sure that he ever explicitly talked about possible dangers in setting goals. However, I believe it is in the spirit of his process orientation. It is clear from his many writings that he viewed the good life as a process of discovery, of being open to the new and unexpected, of not being bound by rigid preconceptions.

I will close with two other examples. Katey Sagal was an actress on the hit American television show *Married... with Children*. In an interview, in answer to a question asking her for career advice, she said:

> The biggest lesson is learning how not to have rigid plans. If I'd come up with a plan and stuck to it, none of this would have happened. So staying open is the best thing you can do. (Craig, 2007, p.1)

In a book called *Goal-free Living*, the author Stephen Shapiro (2006) recounts stories of people he encountered. One is Cristine Traugott, a fifth-grade teacher at Valley Elementary School in Jefferson, Maryland. She said the following:

> Many teachers are required to post their classroom objectives daily. In this fresh culture of 'accountability', we are required to publically defend what we are teaching and why it's important. This amuses me because I imagine today in class, my curriculum-based objectives could have shared valuable chalkboard real estate with the following:
>
> > Today students will enjoy a book for reasons other than taking a test in March.

Today students will enjoy an impromptu lesson about spiders in order to debunk the myth that they are brain-eating creatures running under Zach's desk.

You certainly won't find these objectives tested in the spring; however, my students' development was unmistakably enriched by these moments. Lesson plans are tentative and fickle, as the teaching profession is an unpredictable roller-coaster ride filled with steep climbs, unexpected loops and breathtaking drops.

This is what I'm talking about.

7 | Becoming the self that one is: an implicational view of personal change

This chapter is based on my presentation titled 'Implicational view of self-healing, self-actualization, and personal change', which I gave as part of a symposium on 'Self-healing and Self-Actualization' at the Convention of the American Psychological Association, Boston, August 1999.

In this paper I will theoretically explore the nature of change in psychotherapy, focusing primarily on personality change.[1] What is personality change? The client-centred perspective is committed to the view of the person as ever-changing. People are continually self-actualis*ing* (they never reach a state where they are self-actualis*ed*). Yet both psychodynamic and trait approaches (McCrae & Costa, 1990) assert that personality is largely fixed and that change is difficult. Even recent cognitive approaches have talked about core schemas that underlie experience and remain relatively unchanged (Mahoney, 1991).

Congruent with psychoanalytic approaches is the 'foundational' model of personality, in which it is asserted that the 'foundations' of personality are set down in early childhood. These then constrain, shape and determine later personality formation. Development, from such a perspective, can be represented pictorially as a pyramid, with the most important

---

1. I will not cover 'memory reconsolidation' (Alberini & LeDoux, 2013), a recent perspective on change that, applied to psychotherapy, has focused on remediating memories of emotionally traumatic incidents.

foundational things happening in early childhood, at the bottom of the pyramid. Age becomes progressively less and less important in shaping personality over time.

Yet client-centred theory is committed to a view of the person as ever-changing. How can these two views be reconciled? First, it is worth noting that change is the norm in human affairs if viewed at a societal level. Since I was a boy, I have seen significant changes in norms about sex, marriage, raising children and what the good life is. I have seen significant change (though not significant enough) in how women, people of colour and people whose sexual orientations are not heterosexual are viewed. Clothing styles and musical fads change every year. Conditions in international relations change almost as frequently. In the arts, there is continual evolution and change. If anything, it may seem odd that we believe in permanence, given the constant change in human affairs.

However, those who believe in the fixity of personality could argue that the above kinds of changes do not mean that *personality* changes. Such views tend to include unspoken mechanistic metaphors that portray personality in terms of structures such as traits, egos and schemas. While the metaphors are never entirely spelled out, all of them are described as if they were structural components 'in' and 'of' the person that then determine behaviour. Core schemas operate like programmes to drive behaviour; traits are fixed-action dispositions that shape and constrain behaviour.

If one conceives of personality change in this form, then change must indeed be changing traits, core schemas and ego structures. Change becomes a difficult and messy business.[2] Significant change becomes a matter of 'second-order change' (Watzlawick et al., 1974). Watzlawick and colleagues have distinguished between change of the first order, which he has often labelled as 'doing more of the same', and change of the second order. Second-order change is essentially a paradigm shift (Kuhn, 1962), where the fundamental dimensions of understanding, the

---

2. Although, again, those who are proponents of memory reconsolidation argue that it can happen more quickly and profoundly than we had previously believed.

premises, are themselves finally questioned, and a whole new way of 'seeing' emerges. On this line, first-order changes *within* a pre-existing framework are not even seen as significant.

On this view then, significant personality change may indeed be rare and not achieved by most therapies (Alvin Mahrer, personal communication, August, 1991; see also Mahrer, 1993).

However, there is another way of looking at change. I believe this kind of change is what client-centred therapy is 'built' to facilitate (although client-centred therapy may also facilitate second-order change). This kind of change takes seriously the idea of first-order change and considers that it can be significant. Put another way, it does not emphasise paradigm *revolution* so much as paradigm *evolution*. This view of change does not even hold that changing traits, core schemas and the like is necessary in order that significant change can take place in therapy. Rather, important change can occur even if traits and core schemas stay 'the same'.

In this kind of change, pre-existing frameworks, the overarching edifices of experience, may stay the same. Yet *within* these frameworks, significant evolution may take place. An analogy is what Kuhn (1962) calls periods of 'normal science'. During such periods, scientists work under the framework of a given paradigm. They solve problems within that framework. Examples of this include biology under evolutionary theory and physics under the framework of quantum mechanics. Clearly, the kinds of first-order changes that have taken place in physics and biology over the years could not be considered insignificant just because they are more 'first-order' than 'second-order'.

Similar changes take place within the thought of individuals. Freud's work continually evolved over the course of his lifespan. Nevertheless, it was within his 'Freudian' paradigm. Carl Rogers' ideas also evolved over time, yet he remained a 'Rogerian'. The work of many novelists may evolve and change, yet they may be working and reworking the same themes over and over, and their general 'style' may loosely remain the same.

Social change is often of this type. For instance, law and government have both evolved and changed in the USA since the Constitution was ratified in the late 1700s. The 'core schema', or 'character structure' of the US government has remained 'the same' in a general sense for 200 years, yet significant change has also taken place.

While basic abstract guiding frameworks may remain the same, significant change can occur in the form of 'fleshing out' and the evolving of these frameworks. In a like manner, personality can change in personally significant ways even if one's 'traits' or 'core beliefs' remain the same (Cantor, 1990; Mahrer, 1978). As an example, consider Farley's (1990) concept of 'risk-taking' as a personality characteristic. He points out that a person can be a high risk-taker in a positive sense or in a negative sense. Therapy may not change the individual's propensity to take risks, but it may alter how this propensity is manifested, 'fleshed out', or operationalised, from negative to positive.

It is this kind of change that is the stuff of everyday life. In writing this article, I am not radically changing my beliefs, but I am *developing* and evolving them. In a similar manner, I have found ways of evolving my basically 'shy' and 'introverted' personality so that I am more productively 'shy' and 'introverted'. In my 20s, I fought against my shyness and was very critical of it. My shyness therefore worked against me. Now I am more accepting of my shyness and know better how to let it work for me.

This leads to a fundamentally different view of therapy. The goal of therapy is not so much to *change* personality as it is to *evolve* it. The assumption is that an individual's guiding framework of traits, core schemas and the like can be evolved in productive directions from within. Aggression can be accepted, listened to and differentiated so that it can evolve into a productive aspect of the personality instead of a destructive one – for instance, in terms of taking productive action. Even self-criticism can be productively evolved so that it is not a dysfunctional part of personality (Bohart et al., 1991).

Furthermore, from an ecological, contextual or narrative view of personal ways of knowing and interacting with the world, the *meaning* of any given trait, idea or construct is not a fixed, invariant property of itself alone. Rather, it exists in a context of other relationships. The meaning of a trait partially depends on how it is organised and integrated into a structure of other traits, goals, values and the like. As we grow, our organisations of goals, values, traits and the like expand, becoming more differentiated and integrated. In this respect, personal evolution resembles the process of evolution of life from amoebas into more differentiated life forms. Thus, development from this perspective could be represented as an inverted pyramid. Earlier elements indeed form the building blocks of later experience but can be incorporated into progressively more and more expansive, complex, organised and overarching organisations of experience. Thus, the meaning of a trait or core schema is coloured by its place in a network of relationships, which shifts over time.

However, there is something more fundamental about human knowing. The key idea is the *process* nature of knowledge. Knowledge is not fixed. When we talk about traits and core schemas as if they are somehow monadic, encapsulated little units or programmes, we miss the organic nature of knowledge. Human knowing is *recursive*. What this means is that later learning, knowing and experiencing feeds back to re-configure earlier learnings. Even if core schemas persist from early childhood, their *meaning* may shift, although sometimes perhaps only in subtle ways.

An example here is the US Constitution. There are continuing battles over its 'original meaning', with even a recent conservative Supreme Court appointee admitting that the actual original meaning was undecidable. Clearly, while the 'core schemas' of the governmental structure of the USA have remained 'unchanged' (in some sense) over 200 years, at the same time they have changed in how they are interpreted, understood and used.

Knowing, and therefore change, is implicational

This brings me to the last but perhaps most important point that I want to make. It is that knowing and knowledge have a fundamentally implicational nature. What I mean by this, following Gendlin (1984, 1990), is that any act of knowing, any formulation of knowledge, any organised schema has built into it the potential for an implicit 'next'. The recognition that much of knowing is tacit and implicit is now widespread (Mahoney, 1991). But in most accounts of tacit knowing, its tacitness is attributed to its automaticity and its non-conscious nature. In other words, certain knowings are learned so automatically that they 'run' at a non-conscious level.

None of this handles the fact that what is tacit about knowing and knowledge is that it contains *implications for a next step* (Gendlin, 1990). The tacitness of knowledge is not merely due to a stamped-in automatic nature. Tacit knowing is fundamentally rich in its implications for *new knowing*. There is therefore a fundamentally creative aspect to tacit knowing that is not captured in concepts like the concepts used in modern cognitive science of 'controlled' versus 'automatic' processing.

This was brought home to me most forcefully by my experience as an undergraduate. My major was mathematics. In mathematics, theoreticians set up a set of postulates. From that set, they derive a number of theorems. Often, the theorems are already known, and the formalisation of the system is merely to organise the derivations into a logical and consistent form. The interesting thing, however, is that *from that same set of postulates, new, unexpected theorems can be derived*. One of the most famous cases of this was Gödel's demonstration from attempts to formalise proofs in number theory that a system with sufficient complexity could not be shown to be both complete and consistent at the same time (Hofstadter, 1979).

So, even in the most logical and formal of disciplines, the encoding of ideas in some kind of language seems to 'allow' that there may be more implicit in them than is known. Thus, knowledge by its very nature is not fixed, but contains a potential for 'more'.

That knowledge (of sufficient complexity) is always incomplete has been known for a long time (see Kuhn, 1962). However, this is usually explained by pointing out that any time one draws a 'map', it will necessarily be less complete than the territory it is describing. On such a view, the incompleteness of knowledge is due to the fact that any encoded system will of necessity be less complex than what it is describing. However,

I am arguing something fundamentally different. I am arguing that any encoding of knowledge is incomplete because it contains implications for new, unexpected ways of seeing things that are not obvious at the time of formulation. If anything, I am arguing that any formulation of knowledge contains more potential complexity than we are aware of.

Thus, knowing is inherently incomplete and unfinished, not simply because any theory or map of reality will be limited in its ability to represent reality (Kuhn, 1962), but because knowing itself always seems to imply a 'more'. Freyd (1987), in this regard, has noted that all perception fundamentally includes a quality of 'momentum', which is an implicit 'next step'.

A theory of why this may be so can be derived from the work of Gendlin. Gendlin (1968) notes that the function of therapeutic responses is to 'point' towards implicit experiencing. The exact words do not matter so much. The function of words is to explore experience, rather than to somehow 'copy' it into words. If we think of verbal formulations as attempts to 'copy' reality, then it is unclear how a formulation could have an implicit 'next' built into it. However, if we think of words, concepts and ideas as 'tools' or 'prostheses' (Shotter, 1990) to be used to explore reality, then it is easier to understand how an idea has built into it the potential for discovery. Imagine an idea or a concept to be metaphorically like a stick. The shape of the stick will influence what one discovers anew about reality as one probes it with the stick. If ideas are hypotheses to be used for exploration and new learning – i.e. things to probe reality with – then each formulation is tentative and has the potential to uncover further, richer understanding.

This leads to a view of knowing as a kind of 'unfolding' (Gilligan et al., 1990) or discovering of new potential in what was already known. Early formulations of self and world are simple, superficial, vague and abstract. Yet they include in themselves enormous potential for unfolding a more richly differentiated understanding of self and world. Early formulations, like the amoeba, can be unfolded and differentiated into more complex and sophisticated 'forms' of living. They need not be 'fixed', replaced or overthrown.

In fact, I believe that the process of 'working through' is precisely the unfolding of implicit positive perspectives and usages embedded in even the most negative of experiences. The unfolding process is inherently interactional and takes place in reference to a life context. Humans are interactional creatures. Their personalities are always in dialogue with their life-worlds. Different potentials will be discovered and evolved depending on the particular life-contexts the person encounters. This unfolding can occur in either a positive or a negative direction. It is the goal of therapy to bring out implicit positive potential, and, further, to help individuals learn how to continue to self-evolve in a positive fashion (Bohart, 1992).

Unfoldings, then, are discoveries of new meaning, or new implications concealed, or implicit, in old frameworks. As such, they are a 'carrying forward' (Gendlin, 1968) of old constructs and ideas. The old constructs are not lost so much as new aspects of their meaning are discovered: certain directions or implications in them are differentiated, elaborated, spelled out and carried forward. Each carrying forward will itself contain implicit new directions for further development. In this sense, knowledge could be said to be 'restless', and as 'alive' as life itself.

I have emphasised the unfolding process as a within-paradigm elaboration. I believe that is most often the kind of continual but significant personal change that takes place on an everyday basis. I also believe that this is frequently the kind of change that therapists facilitate. At the same time, there will be occasions when personal knowing systems are unable to accommodate some new life problem within the general outlines of the old frameworks. At such times, second-order changes, paradigm shifts or leaps to new and more inclusive frameworks for understanding and knowing may occur (Mahoney, 1991). However, even these are in some sense an 'unfolding' of the potential within the old framework. Furthermore, the new framework does not replace the old one so much as it reframes things so that the old one is retained and incorporated. The reframing creates new meaning. Thus, even here personality change is more like expansion than transformation from one thing into another.

Implications for therapy

From a client-centred perspective, the goal of therapy is to help the self 'become who one is'. This sounds paradoxical: isn't everyone already the self who they are? If we view therapy traditionally, then we might assume, along the lines of object relations theory, that there is a 'false self' overlaid on a 'true self'. The goal of therapy is to somehow free the true self from the false self. One then changes in therapy from 'not being oneself' to 'being oneself'. However, this concept has always bothered me. I always felt, even when I was struggling with my own problems in therapy in my 20s, that I was 'myself', though certainly a more limited self than I wanted to be. Further, as a therapist, I have found that it is therapeutic to treat my clients as if they already were 'themselves' (which is essentially what client-centred therapy does). I do not assume there is a 'real self' somewhere down there, and that I am relating to a false self on the surface confronting me. I assume I am already relating to that whole person who is a real self.

But if this is so, in what sense is it meaningful to describe therapy as a process of 'becoming oneself'? I think in the sense of therapy as an unfolding. What one is really doing is helping the client unfold the potential richness implicit in who the client already is. This potential richness may be being blocked by the client's defences, lack of self-acceptance or inability to listen and trust their own process. The client may be unfolding and actualising some aspects of themselves (perhaps needs for security), while other very important aspects may lie untouched and unevolved (perhaps needs for meaning). This means that the client's 'self' at the moment is limited in comparison with what it could be. It does not mean that it is false in comparison with what it could be. Therapy is about expanding, enriching, unfolding and bringing forth of implicit potential, rather than correcting, fixing or freeing 'true selves'. Further, because there is always more implicit potential, one is *always* 'limited' at any given moment in comparison with what one might become the next moment, and that is true of all of us.

In this sense, client-centred therapy can be seen as a 'depth psychotherapy'. If depth is the differentiation and articulation of implicit meanings, then client-centred therapy is as 'deep' as psychoanalysis, in that it helps clients unfold and differentiate the rich implicit meanings in their prior organisations of experience.

The modality of client-centred therapy is particularly suited to an 'unfolding' view of human knowledge and human nature. The basic mode of simply 'being with' the client and empathically reflecting is itself the process of unfolding the implicit meaning in personal frameworks. In many cases, this may lead to a richer and deeper organisation and incorporation of material into the self and into the life space. On occasion it will result in a second-order change.

In any case, there is no attempt to *change* the person into something other than they are. For instance, I was recently conducting a graduate class on therapy and one of the students was being self-critical because she had a propensity to give advice. She 'knew' that 'good therapists don't give advice'. Yet, as a client-centred teacher (in this respect), my goal was not to change her into a non-advice-giving therapist, but rather to help her learn how to be the best advice-giving therapist she could be. (Or, if after self-exploration she chose to become a non-advice-giver – i.e. a second-order change – that would have been all right also.) Since Robert Elliott (Elliott et al., 1985) has discovered that one need not reflect in order to convey empathy (one may convey empathy through advice), I imagined my student evolving to where she could give advice in an empathic and permission-giving manner, and tried to create a context in which she could choose which path to go in.

In sum, personal knowing always includes implications for further evolution. One need not change people into other than they are. One need not alter core schemas or personality traits. One need merely help clients tap into the implicit potential in what they already know, how they already are, and help them become 'more themselves'.

8 | Listening to subjectivity

This chapter is based on a presentation I gave to the American Psychological Association Convention, Washington, DC, August, 2014.

The main point I wish to make is that our current dominant models of psychotherapy don't take subjectivity seriously as a phenomenon in its own right, no matter what other virtues these models may have. This includes the two phenomena of authenticity and creativity.

One thing lost in the battle over evidence-based psychotherapy is that there is a fundamental difference in the nature of psychotherapy among different models. I am not talking about the usual things, such as what the therapist does. I am talking about something more fundamental. When I say the dominant cognitive-behaviour therapy (CBT) model can best be thought of as an engineering model, I mean the *theoretical* model. I am not talking about what cognitive-behaviour therapists actually do in practice.

In CBT, subjectivity is something to be engineered from without by the therapist. Client problems are based on distorted cognitions and beliefs, or on conditioned-in dysfunctional emotional responses or behaviours. The expert therapist diagnoses what is wrong and then has the know-how to 're-engineer' the client's dysfunctional cognitions, emotion schemas and behaviours so that the person can behave more effectively in the world. Thus, subjectivity, in the form of dysfunctional cognitions and emotions, is changed from *without*. There is no concept of internal *generativity* from within the subjectivity of the person in CBT. Nor is there any kind of concept of discovering the *authenticity* within. In fact, there is no concept of authenticity in these theories. Or even what it means to be a person. And, in that sense, to be true to oneself, or to find oneself, is not a goal of CBT.

What that means is that the CBT theoretical model of mind does not include a subjective agent in there – a person. In practice, CBT works by enlisting the aid of that subjective agent, and certainly good CBT therapists treat clients as persons. Nonetheless, the *model* is more like a computer metaphor, with cognitive and emotion schemas that 'run' the person and need to be reprogrammed by the therapist. The person *is* those schemas.

By contrast, person-centred therapy holds that the subjective world is much more than a repository of functional and dysfunctional thoughts, schemas or conditioned emotions. The subjective world is dynamic and generative. Subjective experience is the fundamental support for personhood and agency. To know oneself as an agent *is* a subjective experience.

It is through the therapist's listening to that subjectivity and taking it seriously that therapeutic change comes about. The goal is not to re-engineer cognitions, although that might happen; nor is it to extinguish or modify emotions, although that might happen; nor even learn about oneself, although that does happen. Rather, it is the *process* of subjective self-exploration itself that is the key change event. It is the 'listening to subjectivity' that generates the change. The person becomes different through this process, and it is not a top-down cognitively generated change. It is through the experience of two persons doing this together that change occurs. It is from the whole person who is the client encountering the whole person who is the therapist.

One thing that this does is strengthen agency. We could say that, by treating the client as an authentic agent, the therapist helps them become an authentic agent. However, this has too much of a 'programming' feel to it. The therapist is not trying to reinforce client agency. Rather, it is through the shared journey together, two people working on a life and a set of problems, that change occurs.

This becomes a context for agency. The sharing allows clients to become more agentic. And that helps the person learn to listen to themselves and use their subjectivity productively. Through listening, they differentiate out their experience, they see things they have missed before, they get new perspectives on things. Their subjective life becomes richer and more differentiated.

Moreover, through this, the person discovers what it means to be a person. People who have rarely or never been listened to in the way that a person-centred therapist listens may never, or rarely, have had the experience of what it means to feel like they have an authentic centre, a 'me'. They have trouble locating themselves 'inside'. To experience oneself as a person is to experience oneself as the subjective centre of one's experience – to paraphrase Leslie Greenberg, to experience oneself as the authentic centre of one's own experience (Bohart & Greenberg, 1997). That is what it means to have a sense of a centre. To be able to locate that centre within, that sense of an 'I' that one comes from. And that is the fundamental change event. It is not only *what* the client learns about themselves; it is the *process* of taking one's subjectivity seriously, exploring it, encoding it in words, and listening to oneself as one does it.

This implies that therapy is inherently a *moral* enterprise. What does morality have to do with subjectivity? By moral, here I mean that the person must deal with basic value-decisions about how they want to be in the world. The client, in some sense, becomes a moral philosopher, sorting through their values, evaluating them in terms of the situations of their life, and then finding moral ground to stand on. That is a subjective process. That is the process of finding what really, truly fits for you. To find the subjective truth in your values.

These value-issues inevitably manifest themselves as the person listens to their subjectivity. This is another area where there is a clear conceptual difference between person-centred therapy and CBT. For CBT, a person who is troubled by traumatic memories from being on active service in a war presents as an engineering problem: how to change dysfunctional cognitions and extinguish traumatic memories and emotions.

From a humanistic-existential/person-centred point of view, it is a matter of the person, as an authentic centre of their own experience, confronting their own actions and struggling with the moral issues involved. It is the *struggle* that is therapeutic. It is not re-engineering in order to make the problem go away. This means listening to and exploring one's subjectivity.

Clients must confront issues of basic value: what is the right way to be in the world? What are the right values to adopt? This is not positive psychology where one 'engineers' forgiveness through little rituals. This is where one must struggle with and explore the issues involved, face a moral crisis, in order to come to terms with what one might have done, and give oneself forgiveness. Therapy could be ultimately seen as dealing with a moral crisis in this sense.

I will give two examples. First, consider someone suffering from post-traumatic stress disorder because, in a war zone, he had to kill children in order to kill the enemy. Enemy soldiers were holed up in a house, firing on him and his comrades. Children were in the house. What was he to do? Should he throw a grenade into the house, knowing that children might be harmed? His choice was either kill the enemy and the children or for him and his comrades to be killed. He comes to therapy wracked with guilt and self-blame. He feels like a bad, worthless person. He is bothered by repetitive memories he cannot get rid of – the faces of the dead children he saw when he finally was able to enter the house. Over and over, he has told himself that he did the right thing. His comrades have told him that too. But he still has flashbacks and periods of feeling intense guilt.

A cognitive therapist might challenge his self-condemnation. The therapist might even point out that others in the same situation would have acted as he did. Would he condemn them? Or would he forgive them? This might even work, but this is 'engineering' the person and the problem from a predetermined outside view that global self-blame (I am a bad person) is irrational. By contrast, I could view this as a real moral dilemma. On the one hand, the man was acting as a soldier in a war. He was doing what he was supposed to do. On the other hand, in order to carry out his mission (and preserve his own life and the lives of others), he had to kill children. This is a genuine moral dilemma: when is it okay to take the lives of children? Is it okay to do that in order to save one's own life? Is it okay because you are carrying out your mission? Is it okay because you are simultaneously ridding the world of an enemy who himself has killed others? Framed this way, this is a true moral dilemma.

A person-centred therapist might work with this client by staying with him while he explores all sides of the dilemma. Through that, the man may re-experience the fear he felt at the thought of losing his own life; he may re-experience the fear he experienced at the thought of hurting the children; he may re-experience the tangled sense of conflict he felt for a moment before he threw the hand-grenade, and he will re-experience the regret and conflict he has had over it ever since. He will 'hear his conflicting voices' – the voices saying he did the right thing, which may include the voices of his comrades, his superiors, perhaps even his chaplain. And he may hear other voices telling him, 'But you killed innocent children.'

Through accessing and experiencing all these sides of the conflict, he is able to explore them in more depth, both cognitively and at a feeling level, to get a 'feel for' each. He discovers each point of view makes sense. He begins to move up a little and grapple with the fact that life is not easy; life is messy, and sometimes there are no easy answers. At some point, he may come to a kind of 'and' position. It is not either/or: it is not that either he did the right thing or he did the wrong thing. Rather, he may gain a kind of meta-perspective on it: he did both the right thing and the wrong thing. Sometimes life does not let you make clean choices. He had to make a choice and he made the best choice he could, given the double-bind situation life had placed him in. And the fact that he *feels* regret about the fact that life did not let him do better does him credit. He forgives himself.

The point is that this is an essentially moral dilemma and the answer is a more complex moral position than he had inhabited before. It is not merely a matter of changing dysfunctional cognitions.

Consider a second example, a more conventional example. The client is a woman, aged 35, who experiences anxiety attacks. She works as a college professor, a professor of economics. She is married and has one child. She is successful at her job. Yet she is suffering periodic anxiety. She reports that she never feels 'good enough'. Even though she has published and has got tenure, she feels she is not living up to her potential. She blames it on her life, in part: she has a husband and children to take care of. Yet, at the same time, she feels she is selling herself out by not doing more in her field. She also reports having a highly critical mother who was constantly belittling her and telling her she would never make much of herself. A cognitive therapist might assume that she is treating herself with rigid either/or shoulds: that she *must* be a star in her field. The therapist might get her to add up the evidence and then say: 'Now, is it fair to say that you are a failure? And what is the evidence that you must be a star?', and so forth.

By contrast, a person-centred therapist would stay with her as she unfolds the narrative of her story. The client might hop from topic to topic, starting out with a vivid memory of when one of her colleagues got an award and she didn't. That might make her think of her successful husband, with whom she also compares herself. But then she thinks of her children and the loyalty she feels to them, and for a moment she is a mother who does not want to be a great success at the expense of her children. And then, perhaps, an aspect of the problem surfaces that she has not even thought about before: some lingering resentment at her husband, perhaps not because he doesn't help with the kids (he does), but because she feels like it is discretionary that he helps, while it is a duty that she takes care of the kids, and he doesn't understand the pressures put on women to sacrifice their career for being a mother. Perhaps the problem is that, although he works hard and is nice, she doesn't feel listened to and seen by him. And, suddenly, that ties into the work problem: she feels anonymous. She doesn't feel of worth. And yes, that relates to her experiences with her mother, but it is more than that. She wants to be recognised.

And so maybe we do couples therapy and, as her husband comes to listen to her more and to appreciate her experience more, she finds her conflicts melting away. She gets a more authentic sense of where she is in life: I want my children – they make me feel valuable, and I will do the best I can in my career. And she feels grounded. And feeling grounded, she is better able to use her time. And her anxiety goes away as she stops self-criticising and 'owns' her life. And perhaps that even includes mourning that she didn't have a more supportive mother. And maybe the jealousy of others vanishes as she feels more grounded in her own life. And, as that happens, paradoxically, she balances things in her life better and achieves more.

It is not that some of these changes might not have come about through a cognitive therapist engineering her cognitions. It is that, through dipping into her subjectivity, she explores all aspects of *herself* – she is the person who values doing something important in her career; she is the person who values her children, she is the person who feels sad about her mother; she is the person who wants a better relationship with her husband. And, as she owns all that – that she is that complex being with all those feelings – as she provides a home for all that within herself, she feels more 'at home' with herself and her anxiety goes away.

Let me give you another example of 'outside in'. I have just finished teaching a graduate course in couples therapy. One of the common goals of many couples therapy approaches is to get clients to use what some have called 'soft start-ups': that is, to talk about their longings, their hurts and so on, rather than attack and criticise the partner. This 'softening' allows the partners to move towards one another and to collaborate more.

However, again, it is talked about in most theories in terms of engineering. For some CBT approaches, it is literally *trained* as a skill. Emotion-focused therapy, an approach based on person-centred counselling that I have much admiration for, does not talk about training clients in how to deal with emotions. However, they do talk about deliberately wanting to 'access' soft emotions. I know that if I were in therapy I would not like the therapist working to 'access' my soft emotions. I would feel engineered. It would be an entirely different matter if, through the therapist's attentive listening to my subjective experience, softer emotions emerged as a broadening sense of self emerged as well. But that would be a matter of authenticity.

I will briefly contrast my view with psychoanalysis as well. Psychoanalysis as a *method* can also be seen as one of expanding subjectivity (consciousness raising, as are the existential-humanistic therapies). However, *theoretically*, the subjective world, for many psychoanalytic theories, is not really the subjective world as people experience it. For Freud, there was no concept of 'self'. It was a matter of 're-engineering' the psyche so that the ego was more aware of and in charge of the super-ego and id. In many newer psychodynamic theories, there is no subjective centre, no self, no authentic source of one's own experience (although there are some theories that talk about the true self and false self). Rather, the internal world is populated by objects internalised in childhood, or 'internal working models'. The job of the therapist is to change the bad internalised objects or the dysfunctional internal working models.

I want to say some words about what I would call the experience of authenticity, or the 'real-self' experience. Intellectually there is a current fashion to doubt the existence of the self as any kind of unified entity at all, and certainly to doubt the existence of the real self. However, we have a subjective felt sense of who we are, or of what is true for us. And for humanistic therapies, particularly for person-centred therapy, the goal of therapy could be said to be that of *finding one's own voice*. Or, perhaps more accurately, finding how to find one's own voice in a given moment. And, again, if we listen to subjectivity, this is an *experience* that is unmistakeable when it happens. I refer again to the example (see Chapter 6) of Stephen Daedalus in James Joyce's novel *A Portrait of the Artist as a Young Man* (1948), when he decides not to follow the dictates of his mother to be a priest and instead decides to be a writer and runs down to the beach in joy. He has 'found himself', and it is unmistakable. The experience is of one of coming into focus, almost literally like focusing the lens of a camera. It also can feel like 'coming home to oneself'.

These are the *experiences* of these things. Intellectually, we can doubt them, contest them, find ways of explaining them away, but I contend that these are unmistakable experiences that I and my clients have had. These experiences do not exist in most psychodynamic theories, and certainly not in the CBT theories, although they may happen to clients as they participate in those psychotherapies.

I would like briefly to comment on some words commonly attributed to the playwright George Bernard Shaw: 'Life isn't about finding yourself. Life is about creating yourself.' While I get what the quote is saying and agree with some of it, fundamentally, if we listen to subjectivity, it is wrong – at least for some of us. It is literally more an experience of finding – of hearing one's voice more clearly as it emerges, of finding convergences in one's experience, of finding what one values most, and so on, although one often has to engage in a creative process of searching to find oneself.

In fact, I believe that creativity itself is more a matter of finding, seeing, noticing, happening upon, having something hit you, than it is of doing or making, although after finding then comes the making or shaping process. I think of Michelangelo, who said that the sculpture was already dormant in the stone; it merely had to be liberated. My high-school friend, the artist James Turrell, who was awarded a national medal of the arts by President Obama, used to say that his ideas 'came to him' and he would gesture vaguely near the top of his head. Keith Richards, the Rolling Stones guitarist and composer, said the same thing about the inspiration for his songs. We did a study years ago where we interviewed artists, writers and songwriters, and just about everyone reported more 'finding' or 'seeing' a work of art first, and then working on it to further create a shape for it (Loesch et al., 1996).

So I would say that, in person-centred therapy, listening to subjectivity is a fundamentally creative process that allows that which is true for oneself to shape itself and emerge. The authentic centre of one's own existence, experientially, comes more into focus and you become more grounded in yourself – again an experience that is felt and is unmistakable. The therapy is 'inside out', not 'outside in'.

9 | Of mindsets and meta-perspectives: person-centred therapy and assimilative integration

This chapter is based on an interesting observation that occurred to me and my students as we attempted to 'inhabit' the role of client in various therapy films as part of a research project. It is part of my continuing attempt to elaborate the fundamental difference between the mindset of a person-centred therapist and the mindset that accompanies most other approaches. I presented the paper on which it is based at the Conference of the Society for the Exploration of Psychotherapy Integration, Evanston, Illinois, 17–20 May 2012. I was hoping to interest therapists from other mindsets in the idea that there is this fundamental difference, or at least to get them to think about it. But, sadly, I did not feel I succeeded in that regard.

The original question that led to this presentation was: 'Can a therapist be integrative from the person-centred perspective, and how might they be an assimilative integrative therapist from this perspective?' To answer this question, I will first talk about the idea of therapists' mindsets. I will then discuss my radical person-centred mindset, and assimilative integration from that point of view. I will then briefly comment on the nature of assimilative integration itself.

To define my terms: a mindset is the set of lenses through which the person perceives and construes the nature of a phenomenon (see, for instance, Dweck, 2007). It is a 'set' to view things in a certain way. Assimilative integration (Messer, 1992) is an approach to psychotherapy integration in which the therapist identifies with one particular theoretical base, but from within that is willing to use ideas and techniques from other approaches.

I had already started to think about therapists' mindsets before I attended a recent 'think tank' conference of therapist-researchers at Pennsylvania State University on the role of the therapist in therapy. One participant presented a video clip of a relational psychodynamic therapist working with a woman who had been given a diagnosis of 'borderline personality disorder'. The group of therapists then engaged in a discussion about the film. It struck me how much their point of view determined what each therapist saw in the video clip. I don't mean how they *interpreted* things but, at a more basic level, what they *saw*. I mean how they immediately grasped and perceived the interaction, pre-influenced by their schemas for picking up and synthesising information.

I 'saw' a very different interaction to my psychodynamic colleagues. What I mean by that is that I parsed the situation differently, focused my attention on different aspects of both the client's and therapist's behaviour, and interpreted the 'flow' of what was going on – the narrative, if you will – in a different way that would have led me, had I been the therapist, to respond in a different way. I will describe this later.

Mindsets are related to but conceptually different from the therapist's theory and their meta-perspective. By meta-perspective, I primarily mean whether they view therapy through a diagnostic, pathology-oriented model, or through a non-diagnostic, growth-oriented model. Do you 'see' pathology in how your client is behaving, or do you 'see' it in a different way? Meta-perspectives can be thought of as paradigms that underlie a specific theory. For instance, therapists could hold a psychodynamic or cognitive-behavioural theory from within a diagnostic mindset, or meta-perspective.

Therapists' mindsets can be said to consist of (at least) the following inter-locking influences: their theory, their underlying meta-perspective (embedded in their theory), their cultural background and assumptions, their personal history and folk psychology belief, and their personal issues (countertransference).

These feed into one another and shape where therapists look in therapy, how they follow the flow, what information they pick up, how they interpret that information and how they subsequently react. A lot of this happens nonconsciously.

As one example of a mindset, think of the invisible gorilla (Chabris & Simons, 2011) experiment. This experiment and its follow-ups consist of asking someone to watch a video of two groups of people playing basketball, and instructing them to count the number of passes. In the middle of the video, a person in a gorilla suit walks through the basketball players, and even stops for a moment. Approximately half the people viewing the video do not notice the gorilla. A mindset oriented towards focusing on the players and counting their passes influences what they see.

The mindset idea can also be illustrated by thinking of a therapy film – say, 'Gloria' working with Carl Rogers (Shostrom, 1965). Gloria's presenting problem is that she has lied about her sex life to her daughter. Imagine that you are watching and listening to Rogers as Gloria's therapist. I see Rogers as a therapist trying to help her by facilitating her in exploring her experience. I see the interaction through the 'therapy' lens of her trying to work towards a resolution of her conflicts and come to her own 'personal truth'. Now imagine that Rogers is Gloria's minister. If I imagine Rogers as a minister, what comes to the fore for me is that I might see Rogers' communications as sounding absolving or forgiving, and I am led to wonder if Gloria is experiencing a sense of being forgiven by him.

The existence of therapists' mindsets can be inferred from the research on how therapists and clients perceive the therapy environment. Many studies have shown that therapists and clients live in different worlds. Castonguay and colleagues (2010) found there was little overlap in the types of activities reported as helpful by therapists and clients. One study (Altimir et al., 2010) found that clients identified a more differentiated set of events as helpful in therapy than did their therapists, indicating that clients may be more tuned into what they find helpful than are their therapists. The fact that clients pick up on more change processes may mean that therapists' pre-existing schemas for what counts as helpful are less comprehensive . This suggests that therapists may benefit from paying closer attention to clients' more nuanced perceptions. Levitt and Rennie (2004) found that, when clients and therapists looked at tapes of their interactions, there was only partial overlap in what they saw as going on and what was helpful. These studies of therapist and client differences have shown that not infrequently clients will identify events as helpful that are trivial or unimportant from the therapist's point of view, probably because they do not fit the therapist's theory or the measures researchers have developed for what researchers think are significant events.

In studies we did several years ago and reported at meetings of the Society for Psychotherapy Research (e.g. Byock et al., 2005), I and my graduate students 'simulated' being clients in therapy films. We went through films and transcripts and tried, response by response, to imagine ourselves into the client's role. How would each of us interpret what the therapist was saying? What we were interested in was getting insights into how clients might use and interpret what therapists offer. What we found was that different 'clients' (each of us) did interpret and 'use' therapists' responses in different ways.

However, there was an unexpected finding. What was most interesting to me was how much my perspective on the therapy interaction *changed* when I was vicariously in the role of the client. After having done this exercise with more than 20 graduate students, I can say that I was not alone in this. What I realised is that, when I normally watch a film of a therapist, I primarily do it from the perspective of the therapist. I watch the client carefully *as* a therapist, and judge what the therapist in the video is doing from my vantage point as a therapist. This is a quite different mindset from the one I discovered I held as a vicarious client. For instance, despite my having watched the film of Carl Rogers and Gloria more than 20 times, I was surprised to find that, when I put myself in Gloria's shoes systematically, for the whole session, I saw Rogers as missing considerably more in his empathy responses than I had when watching the film as a person-centred therapist watching Rogers.

Therapists' mindsets interest me because they have the capacity to both enhance and block effective therapist responding. They enhance in that they can allow quick and fast identification of what is going on, and then responding from that. New college quarterbacks in the game of football talk about how it takes a while to get comfortable with what they're doing because, at first, the game is so much 'faster' than in high school. As they practise, it gradually 'slows down'. What they are doing is learning to 'read' the situation. Therapists do the same thing. They learn to read the evolving 'text' of the interaction quickly and to respond quickly. There is some reason to believe that therapists, and other experts, often do not 'think' (Rosenbaum & Bohart, 1993). Perhaps they 'think' when things are not going well. However, this is both a blessing and a curse, in that the same mindset that can lead to rapid identification of what is going on from the therapist's point of view can also lead therapists to miss important things that may not fit their mindsets, just like people can miss the invisible gorilla.

Let me now move to the person-centred therapist mindset and how one might practise in an assimilative, integrative way from such a mindset. Put another way, how might a therapist integrate ideas and procedures from other points of view? This is particularly challenging from a person-centred mindset because it is so radically different from any other mindset that I know of, including other humanistic mindsets such as that of existentialism.

The person-centred mindset, the genuine, traditional, non-directive person-centred mindset, as exemplified by Barbara Brodley (Moon et al., 2013), is significantly different from the 'dominant' mindset of the current field. It is different on two of the dimensions I previously mentioned: first, the theoretical level, and second, the meta-theoretical or meta-perspective level.

On the meta-theoretical level, the person-centred mindset is first of all non-pathology-oriented. As an example, consider the film I previously mentioned that was shown at the Pennsylvania State University conference. In that film, the client with the diagnosis of borderline personality disorder showed a lot of fluctuation between alternately condemning and devaluing her therapist and liking and prizing him. Psychodynamic therapists in the room identified this as splitting. Splitting is seen as pathological, as a primitive mental carry-over from childhood.

By contrast, the person-centred therapist's mindset is one of listening to the client *as if* the client makes sense, no matter what. It did not enter my mind to see the client as splitting. Instead, I would have been interested in empathically understanding the 'wisdom' behind what the client was saying in this moment and the next. That in one moment they might be attacking me and in the next moment praising me would not matter. In either case, I would be trying to empathically respond to the client to understand their point of view, in that moment, as I would with any human being making sense of their journey through the world. I would be looking for, in essence, the wisdom, the sense, in what they were saying right now. It is very much like Marsha Linehan's (1997) fifth stage of validation—the idea that whatever the client is 'pathologically' doing in the moment has some wisdom in it. Thus, I would be literally 'seeing' the client in a different way than, I think, my psychodynamic or cognitive-behavioural colleagues, and perhaps even my existential and Gestalt colleagues, who might choose to 'confront' the client's 'inconsistency'.

Overall, the person-centred mindset is set to focus on two things: empathic understanding, and holding unconditional positive regard towards the client – or, more deeply, relating to the client as an authentic source of their own experience (Bohart & Greenberg, 1997). The focus in the term 'empathic understanding' is on the word *understanding*. The therapist is trying to empathically follow the client. But 'following' here does not mean 'follow' as in follow versus leading. Rather, 'follow' here means to try to follow in the sense that one tries to follow and make sense out of an argument that one reads, trying to empathically inhabit it, or trying to follow a novel or a story. Unconditional positive regard means seeing the client as a person worthy of respect and of being listened to and treated with dignity. It means taking them *seriously,* as *persons* worthy of respect, no matter how 'pathological' their behaviour might seem – and then trying to make sense out of what they are saying.

The goal of the person-centred therapist is to do this and nothing more. The person-centred therapist is not there to 'help'. In fact, Lisbeth Sommerbeck, a person-centred therapist in Denmark, likes to have person-centred therapists sign a pledge not to try to 'help' in any way. Person-centred therapists' goals are only for themselves: to listen and understand as best they can, and to be with the other person in a respectful, authentic way. They are not there to help or to heal. They do not empathically respond because empathic responding helps clients get in touch with feelings, helps them process information, or any of those things, although those things might happen. They empathically listen and respond because their goal is to test their understanding and try to grasp and understand the client's experience and journey as best they can. It is not unlike reading a novel.

This is, in one key sense, a kind of Zen mindset. You help by not trying to help. You promote healing by not trying to promote healing.

This is frequently surprising for people from other perspectives to hear because it is so different from almost every other mindset. Person-centred therapists hope to help too, of course, but paradoxically they help by focusing not on helping but on meeting the other in a face-to-face, person-to-person relationship. It is so different that, when I was trying to explain this on the American Psychological Association's Division of Humanistic Psychology listserve to some existential therapists, I was told that what I was saying was unethical and I had better not be teaching it to students. If the Board of Psychology found out they'd take away my licence, according to these therapists.

Now, the original question I was going to answer was: Can a therapist be integrative from the person-centred perspective, and how might they be an assimilative integrative therapist from this perspective? That is, how might I use ideas and techniques from other points of view while coming from this mindset? Parenthetically, there are person-centred therapists who deny that you can. However, I do not agree. The answer is that one can be an integrative therapist, but from a very different mindset than from the dominant diagnosis-treatment mindset. There is nothing in the radical person-centred mindset to preclude suggesting or bringing up the possible use of various techniques to your client, or offering your perspective, such as even a psychodynamic interpretation. *But it is done from a very different mindset.*

Let us think in terms of how that mindset is going to shape how I pick up information and how I respond. First of all, the determinant of whether an idea that arises in me to offer to the client is useful or not is the client and client experience in the moment, not research and not theory, even person-centred theory. Second, it must be in *response* to the client. The direction of therapy, as Peter Schmid (2004) has said, is 'thou–I' rather than 'I–thou'. My number one job is receptive listening, and my responses arise out of that. I am most primarily a receiver; I receive and clarify as best I can. If I hear well enough, if I am in tune with the client and something occurs to me in resonance with their narrative flow, then, in a therapeutically responsive way, I may say it or offer it. But the overarching goal is to preserve the 'frame' of the therapy, which is to empathically follow them and react to them with regard and respect. Within that frame, I could responsively offer things. I can particularly do this if the client initiates it. Then, the final arbiter of whether it is useful or not is the client's own experience of it. The frame of therapy becomes much more dialogical. In other words, I place my knowledge at the service of the client, but ultimately the primary goal, the prime directive, is not to interfere with their culture, so to speak, but to be in it like a good anthropologist – to understand it. Ideas and techniques can be offered and used as forms of resonant understanding.

In conclusion, what this shows is that, when one integrates ideas and theories from other points of view, the mindset you are coming from makes a huge difference. I would submit that all therapists come from mindsets. Their mindsets may not be specifically as theoretically driven as I have just portrayed. In fact, their mindset may be a mix or even a mishmash of theories. However, they are still coming from implicit assumptions that influence how they pick up information and how they respond.

And that will determine *how* they assimilate ideas integratively from other theories and perspectives.

10 | Listening as being: an alternative to hope

The theme of the Conference of the World Association of Person-Centered and Experiential Psychotherapists and Counseling in Vienna, Austria, in July 2018, had to do with facilitating hope. I was invited to give a semi-plenary address. Being somewhat of a pessimist (despite my belief in human potential), I decided to present my negative thoughts about hope, and to provide an alternative. I expected my talk to be roundly rejected. I was surprised how many people came up to me at the coffee break and said they agreed with me!

> Hope is not for the wise… Wise men hope for nothing. (Robinson Jeffers, *Hope is not for the Wise: an unpublished poem*)
>
> All human wisdom is contained in the two words – 'wait' and 'hope'. (Alexandre Dumas, *The Count of Monte Cristo*)
>
> I said to my soul, be still, and wait without hope. For hope would be hope for the wrong thing. (T.S. Eliot, *Four Quartets*)
>
> Hope… is an openness, a curiosity, a receptivity, and an optimism about how things are going to reveal themselves. (A.H. Almaas, *Facets of Unity: the enneagram of holy ideas*)

The theme of this conference has to do with hope. However, what I'm going to discuss today is basically the downside of hope and an alternative to facilitating hope. This probably comes out of my personality. I tend to be a pessimist. In fact, I'm affiliated to a group of thinkers in the USA who call themselves the Negateers. One of them, Barbara Held, is a well-known philosophical psychologist who has been outspoken in her criticism of positive psychology and its focus on optimism. She has written a book called *Stop Smiling and Start Kvetching* (2001). Another is the journalist Barbara Ehrenreich, who wrote *Brightsided* (2010).

I am what the psychologist Julie Norem (2002) calls a 'defensive pessimist'. Defensive pessimists are people who predict the worst and then use that to motivate themselves to take action, work hard and try to make things come out positively. Her research shows that this works. Defensive pessimists don't approach things with hope or optimism. They actually approach things with fear and catastrophising predictions. However, what they don't do is give into despair and do nothing. I'm in that camp. So I want to give a view of hope that may be somewhat different from what others might say at this conference.

I basically have not lived my life relying on hope. I started losing hope back in the 1970s. I went through a rough time. I got fired (unfairly, in my view) from my first academic job. My wife's best friend was murdered by her estranged husband in our house, as I tried to fight him off but failed. My best friend at work died of a brain tumour aged 33. I then went through a year and a half of looking for another job. I got turned down time after time before landing the last possible job available at the last possible moment at the end of the hiring season. By then I had stopped hoping. I subsequently came to the conclusion that the idea that we have control over life or over our fates was a myth. I had always had the belief that, if you worked hard and did the right things, you could relatively control your fate. I came out of those experiences believing this wasn't true, that basically we don't have any control over life.

For quite a while, I adopted a pessimistic mindset. But I kept on going. I kept on trying to make my life work and do constructive things, despite the fact that I did not feel I had control over whether it would work out or not, or what would happen to me. How did I do that? I did it in part by relying on two of the quotes above. The Robinson Jeffers quote, 'Hope is not for the wise', I found reassuring and reinforcing: you could keep on keeping on without having hope. I also found reassuring the quote from Dumas: 'All human wisdom is contained in the two words "wait" and "hope".' Now that sounds contradictory, since it does have the word 'hope' in it, but the way I interpreted that was to focus on hope in the context of the word 'wait'. What I took that to mean was, 'Wait and stay open to possibility. Don't preoccupy yourself with hoping. Do what you can, but keep an open mind because you never know what will happen in the future.' 'Wait' here does not mean passive waiting. It is a mental attitude of being prepared, ready, as one moves on in life, doing what one can do. And that is the philosophy I've always lived by since. Mostly I don't hope things will turn out right. I'm definitely not an optimist. I do not look on the bright side or expect things to turn out okay. So that is basically the idea I'm going to elaborate on today.

I'm going to start with the fact that I'm in another pessimistic period today.

I am very pessimistic about what is happening in the USA under our current president – Donald Trump.[1] I'm also pessimistic about what I see going on in the world at large. That has led me to become more pessimistic about human nature and its capacity to act wisely on its own behalf. That fits with a good deal of pessimism I have about our chances of survival as a species. On top of that, I'm pessimistic about what is happening in my profession of psychology.

It is particularly the Trump administration and what is happening to my country that has caused me to feel much more frightened and pessimistic about the future than I have ever felt. More important than that, it is the damage this has done to my beliefs about humanity and our ability to make wise decisions.

---

1. I have not altered the wording since I presented this in 2018. By the time this is published, yes, the Democrats won the 2020 election and Donald Trump is no longer the president of the United States. But, even now he has been defeated, that has not changed the things that made me pessimistic when I gave this talk – namely, that he was supported by such a large percentage of the US population.

Carl Rogers once said (I don't recall precisely where) that he was not naïve; he was vividly aware of how cruel humans could be to one another. But he said he had seen that there was a fundamentally constructive tendency within us that came out in therapy, when a person was treated as a person and listened to with empathic understanding and unconditional positive regard. He said that, under those conditions, people grew not only in the direction of actualisation of the self, but towards being more caring towards others (see Schmid, 2013, pp.42–43). Or perhaps it is better to say that positive actualisation of the self *includes* becoming more open, supportive and caring towards others. Beyond that, I believed that there was and is a core of wisdom in people. Under the conditions of therapy, I have seen people move from being defensive, constricted and rigidly either/or in the way they treated themselves and the world, to being more wise, inclusive and balanced in terms of their judgements and perceptions – more conscious, in a sense.

However, while I still believe that constructive tendency is there, I no longer have much faith that it comes out enough in everyday life to mitigate our seemingly almost equal capacity for narrow-mindedness, blindness, insensitivity, lack of caring and compassion, lack of wisdom and judgement and even cruelty.

So what is happening in the USA? I feel like I am living in a kind of Kafka nightmare. It is because of what is happening primarily with the Republican party, which is the party of Trump. Many of my friends are as dumbfounded and bewildered as I am. In a recent poll commissioned by former president George W. Bush and former vice president Joe Biden, it was found that 50% of the population is afraid that democracy is being destroyed and we are sliding into an authoritarian state.

What is so dumbfounding is not that Donald Trump is doing what he is doing. He is a self-aggrandising, principle-less, amoral person, who openly believes that life is a matter of the strong dominating the weak, and that the only 'sin' is to be weak. He has dictatorial tendencies. He shows no respect for democratic traditions. He attacks the integrity of our court system. He attacks law enforcement. He has threatened the freedom of the press and has actively undermined it. He is a master propagandist and regularly bends and distorts the truth to suit his purposes, shamelessly lying and completely contradicting himself when it suits his purposes. He has no moral fidelity to anyone or anything. It is simply a matter of win-lose for him.

In the meantime, he has obstructed justice; he has praised Nazis and white nationalists; he has spewed racist insults; he has made fun of disabled people; he has insulted war heroes; he has bragged about sexually harassing women (and he has a history of sexually abusing women, as well as of sexually profligate behaviour). He has taken the USA out of the international treaty on climate change. He has insulted our friends while befriending dictators, and so on.

Beyond all this, his administration has done cruel things. He has cut back on environmental protections; he has reduced aid for food for poor people; he has reduced aid for the poor and elderly for things like paying rent and heating their houses in the winter. He has torn families apart at the border and has taken children as young as four months old away from their parents and is housing them and other children in what can only be described as concentration camps.

Yet, and here is the part that is so mind-boggling, more than 40% of the population has continually supported him. And, within the Republican party, one of the two major political parties in the USA, his popularity has grown stronger and stronger. It now stands at 90%, and interviews with many Republican voters about his policy of separating families found that, basically, they simply didn't care. It wasn't a big deal as far as they were concerned. And yet the Republican Party has trumpeted itself as the party of family values. His popularity is now higher among Republican party members than that of Ronald Reagan, who is one of the all-time Republican heroes. And that is what is so crazy-making. As he does one horrible thing after another, he gets more and more popular, at least with the Republicans, and some other segments of the population. It boggles the mind. It makes one wonder how truly wise and intelligent people really are.

What is so maddening is how easy it is for people to completely abrogate their principles to support and follow an authoritarian leader. I used to think that authoritarians got into power through the use of force, or through other illegitimate means. I never imagined that nearly half the US populace would support an authoritarian, although there is evidence that, when there is economic inequality, people seek out a strong leader who has authoritarian tendencies (Sprong et al., 2019).

So what bothers me the most is the complete and utter abandonment of principles by those who support him. That has done damage to my image of humanity. I simply cannot believe how *easily* this happened. I still believe that, in therapy, people do rise to their higher moral potential. They do move in the direction of wisdom. But I now wonder how easy it is for us to hang onto and be that part of ourselves in everyday life. Not only can people be cruel themselves; they can support and approve of others who are cruel. For instance, the research has shown that bullies are not infrequently the most popular kids in school.

There is a quote from the film critic Mick LaSalle, reviewing a recent *Jurassic Park* movie, that says what I am feeling: 'There's a sense that there's no problem [in the movie] that couldn't be solved by compassion, common sense and a spirit of generosity, and that there's no chance of humanity ever summoning those virtues *en masse*, even when its survival is at stake' (LaSalle, 2018). And that is what is worrying me.

This situation in the USA is far from anomalous. I know things like that are going on in other countries. I also think of what happened in Rwanda about 25 years ago, when the Hutu government started a genocide against the Tutsis. Hutu people turned, practically overnight, against their Tutsi neighbours, with whom they had previously lived in peace, and began slaughtering them. There is research that shows how easily people obey when instructed to become cruel to one another. I think of the Milgram (1963) experiment and the Stanford Prison experiment (Haney et al., 1973) as two examples. So what happened to our constructive tendencies?

Of course, you could point out that in the USA, the fact that 44% support Trump means that 56% don't. That is true. There are many people who are appalled, and there are many people who are resisting. But 44% is a large number. It is nearly half of the population.

And in the meantime, we continue to destroy the planet. Stephen Hawking predicted several times that within the next 100 years, humanity would destroy itself, whether through global warming, through other forms of environmental assault, through overpopulation or through nuclear war. It is hard to argue that, *en masse*, we are a very wise species.

So I have become pessimistic about humanity. And I am pessimistic about my profession as well. If you look at the history of mental health care, there has been a persistent tendency to minimise and denigrate the healing aspects of human caring and empathy in favour of more impersonal treatments. Currently, the dominant treatments in the USA are drugs and cognitive-behaviour therapy. I have nothing against either one. I do have something against the marginalisation of the personal caring and relationship-based approaches like person-centred therapy. This marginalisation started before the 1990s but really picked up steam with the evidence-based therapy movement. In many states and governmental agencies, you only get paid for doing so-called evidence-based therapies, and in many cases they are exclusively cognitive-behavioural and engineering-oriented. Now, despite the fact that person-centred therapy and emotion-focused therapy are as evidence-based as anything else, they are still marginalised. Worse, prominent writers deride and dismiss the idea that the relationship could be healing. When Professor John Norcross managed to get empirically supported relationships (Norcross, 2011) added into the US governmental database on evidence-based practices, some of these critics howled in outrage. They strongly protested and tried to get the decision reversed.

I do not understand why it is so hard for humans to accept and believe that human caring, empathic relating, meeting people as people, and listening to them, can be a major, if not the major, healing element. There is a long history of this, especially in the treatment of those we label schizophrenic, going back to the dismissal of 'moral therapy' in the 19th century in favour of more cruel physical approaches, eventually leading to things like lobotomies. Nowadays, if you argue that empathic listening can help people with schizophrenic experiences, there are some who will call you foolish and naïve. Again, why is it so hard for us to be human with one another?

So I've been asked to give a talk on facilitating hope. But I'm not sure I feel much hope at the present time. I want to talk about that. But in order to do that, I want to first discuss hope and then take a detour to person-centred therapy.

....

So what is wrong with hope? Why would Robinson Jeffers say, 'Hope is not for the wise… wise men hope for nothing,' and T.S. Eliot advise us, 'Wait without hope, for hope would be hope for the wrong thing'? First, I should say what I believe hope typically means, at least in the USA. It is different from optimism, as Peter Schmid has pointed out (2018). For me, optimism is looking on the bright side of things; it is expecting the best. An optimist looks towards the future with the expectation that the positive is going to happen. Hope is somewhat different. One meaning of hope seems to be that it is something one wishes for. I was not sure that I'd be able to come to this conference because of medical problems, but I *hoped* I could, meaning that I wanted to, or wished that it would happen. The other meaning is to have hope. That means, I think, that there is at least some probability that something positive will happen. I have hope that my friend will survive his cancer. I have hope that the Democrats may win the 2020 election.

So, what is wrong with having hope? In one sense, nothing. Hope can be motivating. To feel hopeless in a way that leads one to fall into despair so that one gives up is not a good thing. When people say hope is good, I think what they mean is that it is better than feeling so demoralised and discouraged that one stops trying. However, there is an alternative, which is to give up the hope dimension altogether and think neither in terms of hope nor in terms of hopelessness. Think in terms of what needs to be done. That is what I am going to focus on today.

There are problems with hope. One problem is that there are situations where there may be no discernable hope. To give hope in such situations may be to give false hope. Second, to look at the T.S. Eliot quote, what if hope is hope for the wrong thing? If you get what you hope for, you may be disappointed. I'm sure I'm not the only one who has been madly in love with someone who ignored me. You keep hoping and hoping. Meanwhile, sitting near, is someone who would be better for you, but you ignore them because of your hoping for the other. Then, eventually, the other shows interest. You kiss. You both turn into frogs – you are not right for each other. In the meantime, the one who would have been right has gone. Hope can lead to despair sometimes.

More fundamentally, I think what those quotes are getting at is the idea of narrowed attention. The problem with hope or optimism is that it can narrow your attention. I am going to give a case below of a woman with cancer. Trying to give her hope in the ways many people might narrows her attention. That is what I think T.S. Eliot was getting at by saying hope may be for the wrong thing. Waiting without hope means to be open to what is, what will happen, to wait without expectation either way – to neither dwell on the positive (optimism) nor on the negative (pessimism). This the same as what Dumas' Count of Monte Cristo says. As I have said, hope, in the context of 'wait and hope', means, I believe, to keep an open mind as opposed to narrowing one's attention by hoping for this or that. Be open to and notice possibilities that do exist and that may present themselves.

Does person-centred therapy facilitate hope? It certainly can. But if it does, I think it is a by-product. Should person-centred therapy facilitate hope? That is not a goal for me. This is particularly true since person-centred therapists do not typically have goals for their clients.

Consider the following case. This is a fictional case, based on a real one, but with things added in so that I can illustrate the points I am making. The client – I'll call her Astrid - comes to therapy because she is feeling suicidal. She is 60 years old. Her husband died a couple of years before. She lives alone. She has no close relatives. She has a daughter, but they are estranged from one another. She works, but in a low-level job that brings her enough income to scrape by but does not provide personally meaningful occupation. She is not a social isolate, but she has few friends. She spends most of her time doing her job, then coming home and watching television. She has been content with that life until, just a week ago, she discovered that she has cancer that is probably terminal.

She says, 'I'm going to die and I've never lived. I might as well kill myself and get it over with.'

Based on a video I have seen of a cognitive therapist working with a somewhat similar case, I have an idea of what *some* cognitive therapists might do. One such therapist might challenge the client's 'dysfunctional' cognition that she is going to die – dysfunctional because she does not know that yet. He might also challenge the dysfunctional cognition that she has 'never lived', and ask her to come up with evidence to dispute that belief. A positive psychologist, who believes that the research shows that optimism is mentally healthy, might encourage her to look on the bright side – or at least to have hope. They might say she does not know for sure that it is terminal; there are always treatments that may delay its course; there are still things she can do to make her life meaningful. She might, for instance, make up with her daughter. Perhaps she could volunteer to help people, and so on.

But, as a person-centred therapist, I would not do any of these things. In this particular case, they would function to dismiss her feelings and she might experience them as such. What I do is empathically listen and witness her experience. What emerges is that it isn't the cancer *per se* that is bothering her. It is that it has led her to re-evaluate her whole life, and she is in despair over it. She does not want to sugar-coat the choices she has made. She does not want hope. She wants to face the future unflinchingly. So I just stay with her. As I do that, several things happen. The main process that she initiates and carries through I would call 'coming to terms with her life'. Components of that include coming to accept what is and what has been, as well as the possibility that she faces a constricted future ahead. Another component is making new meaning: she explores the reasons for her choices in life and comes to terms with them. What she does not do is try to come up with alternatives in order to try to give herself hope. She is not future-focused. She does not develop a plan to make up with her daughter in order to make her last days meaningful. She does not decide to go on one last vacation, or write a book about her experience, or join a church, or volunteer, or work out her bucket list, or all the things some other therapists might have suggested to her as a way of making her final days meaningful.

However, as she comes to terms with her life, she gets over feeling pessimistic and suicidal. What she develops is courage to face the unknown. And that leads her to make greater peace with the moment. That leads to her being able to be more open in the moment. It is a receptive kind of openness, a kind of 'abide with the moment' openness – a listening and seeing kind of openness that enables her to move more easily through life. It is, in a funny kind of way, a giving up, but in a positive sense of acceptance, of living with, of not trying to force things, not thinking in terms of what she should do or should have done. It is coming to a place where she is riding the waves of life.

As that happens, she notices possibilities that she might have missed had she stayed despairing, or even if she had been focused on hoping. There is a stray cat that hangs around her apartment building. She has noticed it before but has been so wrapped up in her life that she has ignored it. Now, one day, she notices burrs in its fur. She takes them out. She starts to feed it, not to give herself hope but because she finds herself caring for it in the moment. It becomes a companion. At one point she decides to take it to the veterinarian to get shots. There she sees a flyer for an animal shelter that is looking for volunteers. She decides to volunteer. She gets involved in helping animals. But she does this not *in order* to give her final days meaning, but because she discovers that it is intrinsically rewarding to work with animals.

And then, one day, after helping an animal, she decides to drop her daughter a card saying how she regrets their estrangement.

The thought to do this comes out of nowhere. It just 'bubbles up'. She says that she can understand if her daughter does not want to communicate with her. She does not ask to make up. She has no expectation that the daughter will respond, it is done mostly 'without hope', out of her own moral sense of making amends. To her surprise, the daughter responds, possibly because she senses that there are no expectations or demands. They have a meeting and begin to rebuild their relationship. In all this, it is not that Astrid has developed hope. Hope is future-oriented. These things spontaneously occur because she has developed the capacity for greater openness to the present. And, finally, I want to emphasise her courage – courage to face whatever is to come. I think that the opposite of despair is courage, not hope.

What did I facilitate? I facilitated acceptance, a coming to terms with her life, meaning-making, her creativity, her courage and her agency, and being more open to the present. I would say, overall, what I did was facilitate her abiding with the present, but not particularly hope.

I did not do that by trying to intervene. Interventionist models are often based on some model of positing a good future state and then trying to change the person in the direction of that future state. They are based in some sense on planning and trying to control the future.

You do not have to have hope in order not to give up. It is like a football game. Suppose you fall way behind in the score. In a sense, hope does you no good. What you have to focus on is the moment, and doing your best, one moment to the next. Hoping may actually distract you.

I think of a story about the therapist Milton Erickson (Feldman, 1985). He was working with a depressed woman who was supposed to go on a vacation but was hesitating. Erickson encouraged her to go and made a prediction that, on the vacation, she would see an unexpected burst of colour. I don't think she was hoping to see this. But what his intervention did was prime her to begin looking. And, although she did eventually see an unexpected burst of colour – a woodpecker – more important than that, with her eyes open, she saw a bunch of other things that helped lift her depression. But it was not through Erickson facilitating hope.

....

Let me use that example to talk about myself. I'm feeling pessimistic about humankind at the moment. Am I going to give up in despair and do nothing? No. I'm going to keep on keeping on. I'm going to try to take care as best I can of my own little corner of the world. That means that I am going to keep speaking out on the things I believe. I'm going to try to inspire my students as best I can. I will donate to the political causes I support. I may volunteer to help like I did a few years ago during the Obama campaign for president. This is not because I have any hope that I individually am going to make a difference in the world. I do not do it for the sake of hope. I do it to tend to the world as best I can. And, through doing that, some doors might open up to do some good for someone or something. You never know.

I can take action, but ultimately I do not have control over what happens. All I can do is what I do, as in therapy, where I do not have control over my client. I do not have control over if I have any impact or not. It is not helpful to think about whether I can or cannot make a difference. And that is where hope can be derailing. If I start hoping that I can make a difference, I may actually feel discouraged. I may start thinking about how I can control things, and that may distract me from what I can do.

Let me go back to the quote from Dumas: 'All human wisdom is contained in the two words – "wait" and "hope".' As I've said, I have taken that to mean: 'Keep on living your life, and always be open to possibility. Do not close off possibility, but do not have expectations either.' It is not hope as I think we typically understand it. I think it is more like hope in the quote from Almaas: 'Hope… is an openness, a curiosity, a receptivity, and an optimism about how things are going to reveal themselves.' Only I would probably take out the part about optimism and say, 'Hope… is an openness, a curiosity, a receptivity… about how things are going to reveal themselves.' So this brings us back to the idea of staying open in the moment, and listening as a way of being and as a way of living.

It is the same manner of staying open that a person-centred therapist values – that is, it is a form of receptive listening. Can we generalise this to how we live? What would it look like to be a person-centred therapist with life?

When I am working with my clients, when I am at my best, my full attention is on them and their experience. I am not trying to accept them. It is not a matter of acceptance or non-acceptance. Similarly, I am not focusing on hope or non-hope. I am trying to hear and receive them. When I am like that, it increases my odds of being – as Bill Stiles calls it , appropriately responsive (e.g. Stiles & Horvath, 2017). I find things bubbling up inside in resonant response to the client – appropriate and helpful things. What if I could be in similar dialogue with the world? Receptive listening does not mean I could not take action. Appropriate responsiveness to the situation might include organising a demonstration, or running for office. It might even, in some cases, mean fighting back.

I would like to contrast it with an alternative way of being – the way of being that is most prized by our Western technological society. This is a control way of being. This pits us against the world, in some sense, as a basic stance. You can see it clearly in some interventionist models of therapy that try to modify and change clients' ways of being.

What I am advocating is different from a planning philosophy of life. In the West we are particularly enamoured of a plan-and-control, interventionist way of living, in contrast to a more receptive, listening, dialogical, live-in-appropriate-responsiveness way of living. We try to impose our will on things and engineer them. If we have a problem, we do a left-brain analysis and, based on that, try to control it. What we don't do is wait, listen and stay open – borrowing from Leonard Cohen, we don't look for the cracks where the light can come in. We try to force things. The paradox is that actually trying to control problems sometimes makes them worse. Sometimes it is better to wait until reality presents some kind of opening, or do something else rather than persevere with something that may not be working. This implies a discovery-oriented way of living. This is not a passive way of living. You're still actively interacting, but interacting in a more dialogical way.

The idea that trying to intellectually analyse and control a personal problem can backfire, or be useless, is an insight that psychotherapists have had since Freud. Paradoxically, our left-brain way of solving things doesn't usually work with personal problems. Gendlin (1970) has been most clear in mapping this out, with his taxonomy of the ways we think at ourselves and then try to control or engineer ourselves, and how that doesn't work. And what is Gendlin's answer? Receptive listening. His focusing technique is listening. This does not preclude thinking. But it is a different kind of thinking. It is a thinking that emerges from listening, in dialogue with ourselves, as opposed to being directed at us from above.

Our typical way of thinking is outline thinking. In school, we're taught how to write a paper by preparing an outline and then filling it in. That is how we are expected to live life too: set a goal and then develop a plan for achieving it. There is nothing wrong with that. However, it is limited. The problem is that life is much more unpredictable than that. I believe the best way to cope with life is to be able to ride the waves, like a surfer. It is moment-to-moment listening, just as we do with our clients. It is a kind of responsive dialogue with the world, moment to moment, and often times, when we don't have a plan, or our plans are failing, solutions emerge in harmony with the world, if we listen.

This may sound like the serenity prayer:

> God, grant me the serenity
> To accept the things I cannot change,
> Courage to change the things that I can,
> And the wisdom to know the difference.

However, the serenity prayer is oddly pessimistic. There is something depressing about having to 'accept the things I cannot change'. In fact, while what I am talking about sounds like acceptance, it isn't exactly acceptance either. Have you ever *tried* to tell yourself to accept something? It doesn't work. Acceptance is a by-product of a change in listening, a change in attention. It is more a difference in mindset. It is a shift towards an open-attention, hearing and noticing mindset – *wait and hope*.

This does not mean one cannot take action, that one must always wait until an opening presents itself. It does not mean one cannot speak out against injustice, fight for what is right, and so on. However, listening is still the best way to go, even when you're doing that. If you are really attuned to the rhythms in life, you will be better able to find ways to work with that to change things. As I have said, it is through taking steps, moving forward, taking action, looking, that opportunity presents itself. But one can do that without hope; one can do it by focusing on what one sees and hears.

There is nothing wrong with planning. Planning can be a good thing. But why? There is a wonderful quote from Dwight Eisenhower, the former US president. He was apparently quoting what is US Army lore: 'Plans are worthless. But planning is everything.' Planning helps you be prepared to respond to whatever presents itself in the moment. Therefore, planning is useful. But plans themselves may be worthless. I believe it was Bismarck, the first German chancellor, who said that, in a war, plans go out the window when the first bullets are fired. They may set you going, but they can narrow your attention too much. The value of planning is in the preparation. You learn the terrain. Then you can be open to adjust to the moment as you travel. This is like Carl Rogers' idea of holding constructs tentatively (Rogers, 1961b).

I have a good friend from high school, Jim Turrell, who has become a famous artist. You may know him as James Turrell. Jim knew practically right from high school that he wanted to be an artist. He did a lot of planning. Yet his life has taken many twists and turns, and he had to make much of it up as he went along. His big life-work project is turning an extinct volcano, Rodin Crater in Arizona, into a huge, natural work of art. Some have said it may be the major work of art of the 20th and 21st centuries. When he started on it more than 20 years ago, he never envisioned it as a life work, but that is what it has become, as new ideas presented themselves, obstacles presented themselves, and so on. That is how life is. Most of the people I've talked to, their lives have been like that. They started out one way and ended up somewhere else. Life is a series of unexpected encounters. And a lot of it is adjusting on the fly, making it up as we go along, seizing the moment when it presents itself.

So life is a form of travelling. And the best way to travel, at least for me, especially in dark times, when things are not clear, has been to wait and hope, or wait without hope, which means to be open to discovery, and that means to be able to listen and to see. To bring it full circle – that is what I want to facilitate for my clients; that is what I want to facilitate for my students.

Can I offer you hope for the future of humankind, hope for the future of my profession? No. I have no hope, but nor, in a sense, do I feel hopeless, as long as I focus on what is open in the moment to do, and do what needs to be done.

11 | The pernicious idea of avoidance

This chapter is based on a talk I gave at the World Association for Person-Centered and Experiential Psychotherapy and Counseling, Antwerp, 2012. I knew I would be attacking a 'sacred cow' – the belief that many of people's problems are based on avoiding feelings, and that they avoid feelings because they don't want to experience pain. In contrast to the reaction I got to my talk on hope (see Chapter 10), this paper was controversial. I could tell that I had unsettled a number of people! Still, I believe it is important to emphasise the courage of our clients.

In this chapter, I attack one of the biggest sacred cows in the field of psychotherapy: the idea that various kinds of psychopathology are based on avoidance of feelings, and that people avoid feelings because, in one form or the other, to face up to them is too painful. Recently this concept has been proposed as an explanation for anxiety disorders. It has been held that anxiety, which is a painful feeling in itself, is a defence against other feelings that the person is avoiding. In other words, people make themselves miserable, incapacitatingly so in many cases, in order to avoid feeling miserable.

I believe this idea is both wrong and pernicious. I do not believe people for the most part avoid feelings because they are painful *per se*, although this can happen. On the contrary, the clients I have known have been adept at facing a great deal of pain and continuing to live as best they can, despite feeling miserable. Why would they then avoid pain? The answer most often given is that the feelings being avoided are even more painful than the feelings generated by avoiding them. This puts the client in the position of the flagellants of the Middle Ages, who whipped themselves in order to avoid the even worse punishment of going to hell or getting the plague. This is, in my view, a 'blame-the-victim' view of psychopathology.

This idea also frames how therapists talk about therapy. Therapy becomes a matter of making people – who presumably are so fragile that they are shaking in their boots with fear about confronting unpleasant reality – feel safe so that they can face up to their pain and then take risks. The function of empathic responses in early sessions, for instance, has been portrayed as making people feel safe, as if the function of empathy is somehow to calm people's fears. I do not believe this is primarily how empathy or therapy operates, although providing safety is of course one important aspect that helps make therapy work. But even there, I do not believe the function of safety is necessarily to make clients feel safe so they are able to face up to their fears, although this, too, can happen.

I believe that the idea of avoidance is malicious. It negatively stereotypes clients. The message, although not intended, is that they are cowards or wimps. Their problems are due to the fact that *they* are afraid to face up to pain or the truth. Thus, clients who already had one problem – that of the anxiety or the eating disorder or the depression – now have two. Not only are they anxious, depressed, drinking too much or starving themselves, but they are also people who cannot face up to painful truths about themselves, or to painful experiences.

I know many would object to my framing it that way. They would say they aren't really accusing clients of being wimps or cowards. After all, they are sympathetic. They 'understand' their clients' pain and can empathise with it. It is normal and human to avoid pain. This does not make it better. The implication is still that clients' problems are based on their fear and that the answer is for them to overcome their fear and to 'face up', no matter how gently and empathically therapists believe they relate to clients in order to help them do this. So, yes, whether they mean to or not, I believe therapists are implicitly accusing clients of being cowardly. And I know that some clients, including me some years ago, have interpreted such ideas that way.

I will give my own example. I had a severe anxiety disorder in my early 20s. It started when I was on the verge of graduating from college. I was so anxious, I had both experiences of depersonalisation and almost complete alienation from my body. I had no sense inside of what I wanted, who I was, or what I thought about anything, because I was so chaotic inside. I totally lost any inner sense of anything I could identify as 'me'. It is accurate to say that I had totally lost myself. I was a broken person. I had to run myself consciously for a while. I had to consciously say 'Now I have to do my term paper', or 'Now I have to eat', because I felt so anxious inside I could not find any inner sense of direction. Although the intensity waxed and waned somewhat, overall, this lasted for about three years.

For two years I saw a psychoanalyst. We probed my childhood and tried to unearth things that I must have been avoiding. Not only do I not remember finding any important things that I was avoiding, but the act of looking for this made my problem worse. The idea that I was avoiding was itself a major source of my pain and anxiety. It fed into my tendency to self-criticise, which was actually the source of my anxiety. Finally, I switched to a Jungian therapist who practised as a Rogerian. Within five months, the anxiety suddenly went away. To this day, I do not know exactly what made it go away the day it did. What I do know is that I cannot think of any feeling that I was supposedly avoiding that I had gotten in touch with. Nor can I think of any memory or truth about myself that I was supposedly avoiding and had gotten in touch with. What helped was a shift in attitude towards myself, from being very self-watching and self-critical, *thinking* myself to be an avoiding wimp, to being much more self-empathic and self-respecting and affirming myself the way I was. How that shift happened when it happened, I do not specifically know. But I do know that it had to do with my therapist, who listened to me, took me seriously, and supported my positive growth towards the future rather than focusing on unearthing feelings and hidden truths and the like. And it wasn't so much that his empathy made me feel *safe* as that his empathically understanding listening made me feel *sensible* and *understood, or understandable*. It made me feel more *intelligent and intelligible*. I think of Gendlin (1967), who says he assumes that there is a sensible person inside and talks to the sensible person. That is what my therapist did. He didn't sooth me much at all, as far as I can remember. Nor did he treat me as fragile, although I certainly could have seemed that way to him. What he did was listen intently and take me seriously.

I am not alone in thinking that the idea of avoidance creates pathology. Dan Wile (1981), a couples therapist whose ideas I deeply admire, has pointed out that many of our ideas about what is wrong with people are themselves pathology-creating, including the idea that we are avoiding things we should be facing up to. Marsha Linehan (1989) has made a similar point: that people we label 'borderline' are often accusing themselves of the very things that therapists accuse them of, and it is the accusations that are a significant source of their problem. In my case, it was precisely the idea that I was avoiding something that was one of the major culprits in my pain. I was certain that I was deeply flawed because I was not facing up to something about myself. So not only did I feel bad about myself because I was anxious; I blamed myself for my anxiety and that made it even worse. It was when I stopped worrying about this and started trusting myself that the storm of anxiety went away. That was 45 years ago and, so far, it has never come back.

Why do individuals inflict pain on themselves, particularly in the form of self-criticism? They inflict it on themselves because they are legitimately trying to find a way to cure their problems, to shape themselves up, to find a way to live in a world they find problematic and conflictual. They are trying to find a way of keeping themselves on the planet. Anxiety is a *signal,* or what Wile calls a clue, that something is wrong. Something is askew. It is a call to try to set things right. It is not a defence. Rather, it is an 'offence', in the sense that it is a proactive attempt by the organism to move forward.[1]

Then the self-criticism becomes an attempt to solve whatever is wrong and creates more anxiety. People self-criticise in order to try to set their lives right. It just so happens that, in so doing, they may inadvertently make things worse. As Gendlin (1964) pointed out long ago, there are productive and unproductive ways of relating to oneself when one is stuck. People pay attention to themselves in the wrong way, although it comes out of a proactive attempt to set things right. These ways of solving problems represent the self-defeating vicious circles people get into. What is needed is to provide people with a space where they can step back, see themselves and their lives in perspective, begin to *hear* their inner voice over the din of the self-criticism and the criticism of others and the everyday bustle of life, and find a path forward. That is what therapy does: help people find a path forward.

In my experience, for the most part, clients do not have problems facing up to painful truths. Not only are my clients able to face up to painful truth, they are adept at generating painful truths to face up to that aren't even true. They are convinced they are bad, evil, wrong and so on. They *look for* painful truths to face up to. Hardly do they avoid them. Why? Because they are trying to find the truth, figure out why they are stuck, right the ship, keep their lives on track and find a place on this planet. They hurt themselves by trying so hard to be honest with themselves.

This does not mean that people do not unearth things in psychotherapy, have new insights and access previously unexperienced feelings that they weren't aware of. I take it as established by research that accessing previously unexperienced feelings is a useful part of the therapeutic process. That does not mean the feelings were avoided in the first place because they were painful. Nor does it mean that the non-awareness of the feelings is the cause of the problem. That unearthing and experiencing feelings is therapeutic does not mean previous lack

---

1. People with anxiety disorders may be said to be suffering from trying too hard.

of awareness of the feelings is a cause of the person's problems, any more than the fact that aspirin cures headaches means that it was the avoidance of aspirin that caused the headache.

So, I am not entirely denying that people avoid or, as I would prefer to say, neglect or fail to pay attention to certain emotions, thoughts and experiences in their lives. Nor am I denying that getting in touch with them is often a helpful part of the therapeutic process. But why do they 'avoid', for want of a better word? Is it mainly because they cannot face up to pain? As I've shown already, that cannot be true. People are adept at facing up to great amounts of pain. No matter how bad, fragile and suicidal they feel, they are almost always continuing to fight to carve out a place on the planet. Despite how awful I felt, I graduated from college, was a successful graduate student, and was rated as one of the better graduate student therapists by my supervisor.

I am not alone in this. Many deeply troubled people keep on going and maintain a life. They not only endure, they often prevail. They are much stronger than our theories give them credit for. However, they are too busy surviving, keeping their lives together, coping with difficult and often unlivable circumstances to dwell on painful feelings or experiences that they do not believe they can do much about. They do not have the time, space or luxury of dwelling on feelings that they won't be able to understand or process under the circumstances. Consider the complexity of processing the kinds of feelings clients often process in therapy. Imagine, for instance, a client who was sexually abused by her father. Imagine the tangle of feelings. How is someone who is living with danger going to process such feelings on their own in everyday life? They have no one to help them. They do not know how (we do not teach people how to process feelings as they grow up).

Furthermore, people are often *taught* to avoid feelings: that dwelling on feelings is wrong or useless, that one needs to be logical. By not focusing on feelings, they are acting in good faith, trying to solve their problems as they have been taught.

To reiterate, often they simply do not have the time or space. They have other, more important things to do, like take care of the kids, deal with their relationships, pay bills and work. I think of Jack Youngblood, a defensive end for the Los Angeles Rams, who played the entire second half of a championship football game with a broken leg, 'avoiding', if you will, the pain, because he had something more important to do.

For many of my clients, it has proven useless in their personal experience to dwell on certain feelings. It is hard to 'face up' to feelings and experience when one can do nothing about them. I imagine many of you reading this text have dwelled on feelings without that leading to anything productive at all. In fact, it often makes people feel worse. People know all too well how painful and useless it can be to feel feelings unless you are lucky enough to have someone to talk with who can help you process them. Otherwise, if you pay attention to them, they just lie there like painful dead weights or dead lumps. No wonder people 'avoid' them.

I submit that we avoid things that we perceive to be harmful and damaging to our wellbeing. In addition, we avoid something when it seems to us to be unsolvable or unmasterable.[2] We do *not* avoid painful and risky situations if there is sufficient reason for trying to face up to them *or* if we feel we have some chance of mastering them. You can see this everywhere. You see children falling off their bikes and getting back on again. Even if it hurts, they get back on their bikes. If people see no reason for confronting a dangerous or challenging situation, or think they can do nothing to change it, they may then 'avoid' it. Thus, if I perceive myself as stuck in a bad job and I cannot get out, for whatever reasons, I may 'avoid' dwelling on my pain about it. But that makes perfect sense. In fact, we psychologists recommend it. The serenity prayer, in essence, says to focus your attention on what you can do something about and not to dwell on what you cannot. People intuitively know this and act on it.

Why should a child who has an abusive father, for instance, focus her attention on how bad he is, how unloved she feels or

---

2. People feel vulnerable and that is what leads them to be defensively oriented. Vulnerability happens because they feel they cannot cope and protect themselves. So they particularly look out for pain and danger.

how hurt she feels, when there is nothing she can do about it? The little girl must carefully arrange her life structure to both protect herself and promote her life as best she can. Of course, she carries that into adulthood. And there is certainly no one she can talk to about it to productively process it. Is it not sane and rational to focus your attention elsewhere, on the things you *can* control? She is *conserving resources and devoting her resources to things she can control.* This is intelligent behaviour. In other words, what we call avoidance is in most cases a proactive coping strategy. I remember reading in the news of Dylan McDermott, an American actor, whose mother died in traumatic circumstances. When, some time after, he 'came out' about it, he said he had to wait until his life was in the right place so he could deal with it. We 'avoid' to maintain momentum, like Jack Youngblood in the Super Bowl.

I prefer the unfinished business metaphor used by the emotion-focused therapy people. That is, it is not so much the avoidance that is the problem as that the working through of the problem is unfinished. This may happen whether the person avoids feelings or not. However, I am not convinced that we always need to deal with unfinished business either, as I will describe shortly.

I want to move on to give my own personal view of psychopathology from my person-centred point of view. It is based on the idea that the person is stuck in their life-forward process. There is nothing new in what I'm going to say. It is pure Carl Rogers and Eugene Gendlin. Following those two, I believe that people are built to have the potential to be always moving forward, to be 'self-correcting' organisms. That means we are constantly interacting with the world and with ourselves, processing information, working to deal with situations and integrate new information while preserving our own integrity. We *are* dialogues, to quote Peter Schmid (2006). Psychopathology happens when we get stuck going forward. We struggle and struggle to get out of the trap, but the more we struggle, often the more stuck we become, and our behaviour deteriorates. We begin to behave, think and feel in more desperate and less functional ways. Psychopathology is not *in* people, it is *between* people and situations.

What leads to this vicious circle? I believe it is mismatches between the environment and ourselves – mismatches we have trouble coping with. There may be many reasons we are having trouble coping, but basically problems are based on threats to the integrity of our life structures. It is when our life-forward process is being threatened that we have the potential to get stuck. Some of this may happen because we are having trouble establishing a workable 'fit' between ourselves and our environment. Prominent among the causes of this are conditions of worth. I will include as a subset of this issues like bad childhoods and early trauma and so on, which create feelings of inadequacy and vulnerability. But conditions of worth do not happen just in childhood. They are omnipresent. Human beings are very good at judging one another and making others feel bad about the way they are. I would say I've never dealt with a client where conditions of worth in the here and now were not a contributor, and frequently an important contributor, to their problem.[3]

So we get stuck. And then we try to dig ourselves out. We have this natural self-correcting ability for moving forward towards the future. Under normal circumstances, we do it all the time, in countless, everyday, creative ways. We evolve our life structures. We do not massively change them but we evolve them. If we are lucky, we become better and better at 'being ourselves'. However, we all run into glitches.

Serious psychological problems arise from living with intense contradictions in one's life structure. And then, along with the problem, the self-correcting process gets interfered with. This can be partly situational. People often do not have the space, time, a listening ear or whatever would be needed for them to pay effective attention. In order for self-organising wisdom to operate, one must be able to be effectively, receptively open to oneself. And that is hard when one is feeling threatened, defensive or stressed out. In addition, under threat, we often react to our

---

3. We get traumatised for being who we are.

problems with less than optimal problem-solving strategies, such as self-criticism, which make things worse. The more it doesn't work, the more we try to solve the problem by doing 'more of the same', as the strategic therapists pointed out long ago (Watzlawick et al., 1974). And we dig ourselves in and get more stuck. As that happens, we feel more hopeless, and as we feel more hopeless, we react in further ways to make the situation worse.

From a Rogerian point of view, therapy is less to correct the problems as it is to help the person's own natural, self-correcting, life-forward process to operate. Accordingly, therapy works by providing a time and a space where people can 'dwell with' their problems and pay productive attention to them. Indeed, people often come to therapy because they feel hopeless, defeated and vulnerable. But it is not only the reassuring aspects of therapy that are helpful. It is also the *understanding* aspects, which help people begin to trust themselves, listen to themselves in fruitful ways and begin to access and trust their own ability to use their own creative, problem-solving potential to solve their problems. As people do this, they also develop more confidence. As this happens, feelings and experiences may surface that the organism intuitively knows need to be dealt with. The interesting thing, though, is that this happens because the person has already changed. However, people do not always have to explicitly focus on and finish unfinished business, or deal with what was presumably avoided. As the organismic system evolves and becomes more open, integrative and effective in its interactions with the world, it may naturally metabolise some of these unaccessed experiences, without the conscious person ever having to deal with them. I know this sounds odd, but if you think of traditional Chinese medicine, which focuses on mobilising health rather than curing disease, you might imagine how mobilising the organism's overall natural health-maintaining processes might cure a disorder that the person doesn't even know they have.

In conclusion, I believe clients are much stronger than we, or they themselves, give them credit for. Most of them are able to face up to a great deal of pain and chaos, carve out some semi-functional life structure, no matter how bad they feel, and keep on going. I see them as heroic. To accuse them of avoiding is to add insult to injury and can be a pathology-creating idea in its own right. I believe psychopathology largely has to do with intense mismatches between person and life situation, where the person's reason for being on the planet gets threatened and, in trying to keep a place on the planet, they develop some dysfunctional ways of acting and feeling, including anxiety, which is a signal that something needs to be attended to. What is therapeutic is less about soothing – although soothing can help – and more about respecting, trusting and listening to the sensible person inside.

12 | Working with the internal critic

This is a slightly modified and updated version of a paper presented at the Annual Conference of The Society for the Exploration of Psychotherapy Integration, in July 1991, in London. It is not specifically about person-centred therapy. Rather, it reflects my 'other hat', as someone interested in psychotherapy integration. Still, self-criticism is seen by person-centred therapists as a major contributor to psychological problems, in the form of a response to conditions of worth. So I hope readers of this volume will find something of worth in this chapter! The presentation was a part of a symposium that included three of the authors whose work is included in the paper: Leslie Greenberg, Richard Wessler and Richard Driscoll.

Introduction

It is probably lucky for us that Hamlet didn't see a therapist. If he had, it is possible that he might have worked through all his conflicts about revenging his father and his mother's hasty marriage, taken decisive action one way or the other, married Ophelia and lived happily ever after. We might only have heard about him in a book of some 17th-century healer's case histories.

Hamlet was adept at self-criticism. At one point he says, 'Oh what a rogue and peasant slave am I.' It is interesting to imagine him being treated by different psychotherapists. Leslie Greenberg (Greenberg et al., 1993), working from an emotion-focused point of view, would have this accusing side of Hamlet confront the 'experiencing' (his reluctant-to-act) side in a Gestalt two-chair experiment. By giving the experiencing side a voice, we might actually find the emotions and reasons underlying Hamlet's resistance, thereby making centuries of Shakespearean criticism superfluous. We might find, for instance, that Hamlet really wants to return to Wittenberg to be a poet, to be the Baudelaire or Jim Morrison of his age, rather than go around avenging injustice.

The rational-emotive therapist Albert Ellis (1984) might confront the underlying absolutistic self-condemnation in 'Oh what a rogue and peasant slave am I', and point out that, while Hamlet might prefer not to be a rogue and peasant slave, where is it written that he must not be a rogue and peasant slave? Ellis would then work on other implicit 'shoulds', such as that Hamlet should take revenge, or that it was awful his mother married Claudius so soon after her husband's death.

The cognitive therapist Aaron Beck (1987) might get Hamlet to consider the evidence *pro* and *con*, and collaboratively help him realise that, in fact, he is not a rogue and peasant slave but, rather, a prince of Denmark. Beck might then go on to help Hamlet see how he is over-generalising: just because he is failing to do this one little thing (take revenge against his uncle) does not mean that in general he is a rogue and peasant slave.

Traditional psychoanalysts would assume that Hamlet's self-criticism is actually a defence against his unconscious Oedipal feelings, which have been activated by the fact that Claudius has done what Hamlet himself unconsciously wished to do – murder his father and marry his mother (Freud, 1938). After many years on the couch (by which time Claudius would have died of alcoholism), Hamlet would come to resolve his ambivalence and find ways of sublimating his vengeful and erotic wishes, perhaps by becoming a poet and writing stormy tragedies filled with loss of love. Or, perhaps, Hamlet would come to identify with Claudius and become his devoted stepson.

Object relations theorists might assume that Hamlet's real problem is with his mother. He has split her into good and bad and is feeling depressed and abandoned as he confronts her as a 'bad object' who has dishonoured his father and himself by remarrying too quickly. This activates Hamlet's 'bad self' or 'internal saboteur' (St. Clair, 1986). Object relations therapists might expect that Hamlet will similarly criticise himself in therapy by breaking into long-winded soliloquies whenever he fails at some therapeutic task. They would hope that, through therapy, Hamlet will internalise the therapist as a model of a whole, integrated human being, which of course is what we therapists all are.

Carl Rogers (1961) might attempt to relate to Hamlet in a warm, non-judgemental way by reflecting his feelings and meanings. He might, in an empathic tone of voice, say something like, 'You're feeling like you're a big piece of crap.' By such an empathic response, Rogers would hope to make Hamlet feel deeply understood and accepted and imply that he is worth appreciating even if he is a rogue and peasant slave.

The notion that Hamlet needs to access his rage towards his uncle and his mother would run through a variety of therapeutic approaches. It would be assumed that Hamlet is criticising himself instead of expressing his rage. In the safety of the therapy room, various therapists might get Hamlet to pretend that Claudius and Gertrude are pillows, and then let him reduce the pillows to their component parts. Through this Hamlet might be able to 'let go' of his anger, come to a peaceful acceptance of 'what is', turn his attention to writing poetry and forget that his uncle murdered his father.

A behaviourist might want Hamlet to learn to express his feelings in an appropriate, problem-solving fashion. He might be taught effective assertion and communication skills, so that, instead of threatening Claudius through veiled, poetic allusions, as Hamlet does throughout the play, he can directly confront Claudius in a collaborative, problem-solving way. The play would be less interesting, but it would at least teach effective communication skills to children, instead of modelling the use of violent solutions to problems.

Richard Wessler (Wessler & Hankin-Wessler, 1986, 1989), using his own version of cognitive therapy, might also assume that Hamlet's guilt is anger directed towards the self because Hamlet is violating his own nonconscious personal rules for living. In addition, Hamlet may have been criticised a lot as a child and may actually feel more secure in his identity when he is picking on himself. Therefore, he can't take revenge because he would begin to feel that he 'wasn't himself' anymore. After all, if he did take revenge, how could he then return to Wittenberg and write depressing poetry about the futility of life?

Richard Driscoll (1984, 1989) would want to identify the underlying purposes behind Hamlet's self-criticism. Perhaps Hamlet is criticising himself to affirm his moral character. Even though he isn't doing anything, at least he is sufficiently moral to be aware that he isn't doing anything. After all, people with the character of a rogue and peasant slave can't be expected to go around acting nobly by avenging injustice.

Or perhaps Hamlet is trying to set low expectations for himself as a defence against a big let-down if he does try to exact revenge and fails. Perhaps he worries that, if he tries to stab Claudius, he'll miss and look like a fool. So he prepares himself by accusing himself of being a rogue and peasant slave. Then, if he does succeed, he can be pleasantly surprised.

Paul Watzlawick (1984), from a strategic therapy point of view, might assume that the problem is the way Hamlet is defining the problem: either he must take action, or he is a rogue and peasant slave. He needs a second-order change, and Watzlawick might be tempted to use reframing. Hamlet would be congratulated on his self-effacing humility, and on the rigour of his searching self-examination. He might especially be congratulated on 'facing up to an issue most of us avoid' in talking about whether 'to be or not to be'.

Family systems theorists might want to have the whole family come in: Claudius, Gertrude and Hamlet. Possibly they might even hire in a clairvoyant and have Hamlet's father's ghost join the therapy session. It might be pointed out that Hamlet is triangulating his problems with Claudius by focusing on his mother. Maybe Hamlet's ambivalence is a systemic way of keeping the family together. One can only wonder at what kind of systemic meaning might be attributed to Claudius' murder of Hamlet's father in the first place.

John Bradshaw (1990) would probably assume that Hamlet's wonder child has been injured and needs to be healed. Based on the amount of drinking that Hamlet alludes to in the play, he might also recommend that Hamlet join an adult children of alcoholics group where he could learn to be less co-dependent. After all, he need not take care of a ghost!

Perspectives on self-criticism

Self-criticism, self-condemnation and their relatives form an important body of treatment issues in psychotherapy. Closely related to self-criticism are issues of low self-esteem, guilt, shame, perfectionism, the use of shoulds and oughts, self-acceptance, and the owning and disowning of actions and experience. Many theoretical concepts are involved in explaining dysfunctional self-criticism – superego, splitting, lack of separation and individuation, disowning of the true self, not listening to one's feelings or organismic wisdom (often due to conditions of worth), introjection of parental voices, the making of global characterological attributions, dysfunctional use of self-guiding strategies, dysfunctional drawing of inferences from experience, and 'musturbatory' thinking. In recent social psychological theorising, self-criticism relates to issues like self-handicapping (Jones & Berglas, 1978), self-serving biases (Miller & Porter, 1988) and positive illusions about the self (Taylor & Brown, 1988).

I want to briefly sketch out some of the different ways self-criticism is conceptualised and treated. The categories I propose below are rough. The views of the theorists involved are often more complex than my category scheme, and therefore tend to fall into more than one category.

Self-criticism as an internalised 'tape', 'voice' or habit

Self-criticism is sometimes portrayed as a kind of internalised tape, voice or programme. One assumption is that these tapes or voices are parental introjects. For instance, in object relations theory (Bollas, 1987), it is assumed that the client is sometimes 'speaking' with the voice of one or the other of their parents. As another example, transactional analysis assumes that there is a 'parental' ego state that is responsible for self-criticism. Perspectives that fall into this category in varying degrees include psychoanalysis, object relations theory and client-centred theory. Behavioural views also belong here, except that they do not use the concept of introjection. For them the tape of self-criticism may be a habitual way of self-responding learned from modelling the parent.

These perspectives assume that the negative aspects of self-criticism result from the bad feelings and avoidant behaviours elicited by these self-critical voices. Object relational and client-centred views also assume that the self-critical voices block internal integration and access to, respectively, one's 'true self' or 'organismic wisdom'.

Therapeutic interventions based on this set of perspectives consist of attempts at replacing the critical internal voices with more benign voices. Object relations theorists hope that clients will introject the therapist as a more benign internal object. Similarly, client-centred therapists hope that clients will learn how to empathically listen to and accept themselves as the therapist listens to and accepts them. Therefore, for these perspectives, treatment of self-criticism depends importantly on the therapist's provision of a certain kind of accepting, non-judgemental relationship, and the assumption is that this relationship will be modelled or internalised by the client.

Behaviourally oriented therapists would rely on more direct replacement of the self-critical self-statements with positive, useful self-guiding speech. Meichenbaum (1977) might actively model positive self-reinforcing, self-guiding speech. Lazarus's (1976) multimodal therapy might use both cognitive and imagistic methods to do this, along, perhaps, with assertion training. Clients might be trained to stand up for themselves rather than self-criticise for not defending themselves in conflict situations.

Self-criticism is dysfunctional because it is illogical and unrealistic

Mahoney (1991) has described the difference between 'rational cognitive' and constructivist approaches to therapy. For rational-cognitive approaches, such as those of Aaron Beck and Albert Ellis, what is wrong with self-critical statements is that they are in some sense inaccurate or illogical. Beck and Ellis both attack generalised self-critical statements. Both argue that evaluating one's behaviours can be rational and effective. However, generalising from specific behavioural failures to global negative self-characterisations is dysfunctional. It is dysfunctional for two reasons. First, such characterisations are in principle unverifiable. Second, such characterisations do not conform to evidence.

Rational-cognitive perspectives depend on an objectivist conception (Lakoff, 1987) of knowledge and categorisation in which a one-to-one correspondence between reality and categories can be assumed. As such, mental categories or schematisations can be said either to conform to the facts (or to possible facts), or to not conform. The goal of rational-cognitive therapies is to either directly and forcefully (Ellis) or through the use of Socratic questioning (Beck) get the client's beliefs to conform more to reality. It is assumed that when they do, dysfunctional moods and behaviours will be reduced.

For Ellis, categories of experience such as those of characterological self-blame ('I am a bad person') would be seen as essentially meaningless, since they cannot in principle refer to anything in reality. Beck assumes that a complete survey of the evidence on the self will almost invariably turn up evidence showing that such a simple, global categorisation is not supported by the facts.

The dysfunctional aspects of global negative trait attributions have also been a key part of helplessness and hopelessness theories of depression (Abramson et al., 1988). Evidence from Janoff-Bulman's (1979) work on rape victims has supported the idea that behavioural self-blame is more functional than characterological self-blame. Behavioural self-blame is more in accord with what Bandura (1986) sees as the kind of evaluations that are part of effective self-regulation. An example is, 'I shouldn't have been walking in that dangerous area,' versus a characterological self-attribution, 'I'm a bad person for putting myself in a dangerous situation.'

As a general part of his perspective, Ellis has particularly attacked the whole concept of 'shoulds', going to the extent of completely eliminating the words 'should' and 'ought' from his writing. Both Beck and Ellis also see perfectionism as a form of dysfunctional thinking.

Self-criticism is purposive

What is common to the theories in this category is an assumption that there is some underlying purposive intent to self-criticism. Therefore, the objective truthfulness of the self-criticism is less important than the function the self-criticism is serving, or failing to serve. For many therapists in this category, the purpose may not be conscious, and bringing it into awareness is an important therapeutic goal. There are three subcategories: self-criticism as defence, self-criticism as security operation and self-criticism as a proactive attempt at self-management.

Self-criticism as defence

For psychodynamic theorists, self-criticism is not merely the introjection of parental tapes or voices. In addition, such introjection serves a defensive, self-protective function. In classical analytic theory, self-criticism may be a way of binding unacceptable unconscious impulses. In object relations theory, self-criticism may be a way of preserving relationships with important objects (e.g. the mother). Self-criticism therefore represents more than merely an internalised 'tape'. It has dynamic properties in psychological functioning and is really a symptom of a more pervasive problem in psychological organisation. Treatment therefore includes the active promotion of insight, acceptance and integration of the frightening aspects of experience that are being repressed or disowned.

Driscoll's (1984, 1989) integrative 'ordinary language' perspective on self-criticism is based on the idea that it is purposive. Driscoll presents a typology of 12 different categories of purposes. Several of these are primarily defensive in nature. They include attempting to give the appearance of ineptness to avoid responsibility (self-handicapping); attempting to allay the shock of possible failure, and attempting to prevent the accusations of others. Driscoll catalogues a variety of interventions for dealing with these purposes for self-criticism.

In general, for perspectives in this category, simple attempts to logically disconfirm self-critical statements might not be expected to work, since the self-criticism is being used for a variety of defensive purposes. Having clients simply practise positive self-statements would not be expected to work for similar reasons.

Self-criticism as a 'security operation'
Wessler and Hankin-Wessler (1986, 1989) have argued that people will seek to replicate dysphoric experience if it has been associated with feelings of security in the past. Thus, if one has been criticised in one's family, one may repeat self-criticism to create a negative mood state, yet be uncannily comfortable with it. Individuals will act in ways to maintain a negative self-identity, often 'rescuing defeat from the jaws of victory'.

John Andrews' (1991) self-confirmation model makes similar assumptions. For Andrews, the particular focus is to maintain self-consistency. Self-criticism may again be part of maintaining one's negative identity. Andrews presents a model of how therapists may intervene in a variety of different ways at different points to productively alter a negative self-confirmation cycle.

Self-criticism as a proactive attempt at self-management
The distinction between 'defensive' and 'proactive' purposes can be somewhat arbitrary. However, I believe that, in theory, there is a difference between an act that is taken primarily to protect and defend oneself and an act taken to proactively pursue a goal or move one's life forward. This may reflect a psychological difference, rather than a difference at the behavioural level. For instance, one might eat primarily to 'avoid hunger' or to 'promote health and bodily integrity'.

There are two subsets of views in this category. The first consists of views arising from the behavioural tradition, such as those of Meichenbaum (1977) and Bandura (1986). For both, self-criticism falls under the general rubric of self-reinforcement/

self-management. What is dysfunctional about it is when it is not used in a viable self-managing way. It is not the truthfulness of the self-criticism that is at issue, but how well self-criticism helps in self-regulation. In general, use of positive self-reinforcing statements contingent on successful performance and statements used to identify dysfunctional behaviours or specific performance deficits is seen as useful. General, global self-attributions are not effective self-regulatory strategies. Bandura and Meichenbaum use teaching and modelling to help clients acquire effective self-reinforcement/self-regulatory strategies in place of unproductive self-critical ones.

The second subset of views assumes there is an underlying 'positive thrust' (Gendlin, 1968) or 'sense' in the client's behaviour in general, and self-critical behaviour in particular. Self-criticism is seen as an attempt by the person to get themselves to live and behave better. Similarly, the 'personal rules for living' (Wessler & Hankin-Wessler, 1986, 1989), premises (Driscoll, 1984), or implicit felt purposes underlying the client's behaviour are also seen as having some positive, proactive sense.

Wile (1981), from an ego-analytic perspective, has particularly emphasised that self-criticism is an attempt at self-management that backfires. The individual is usually criticising themselves for feelings and wishes that are understandable adult human needs and desires, even though they may appear to be unrealistic. While self-criticism is an understandable attempt to cope, Wile encourages a full, acceptant owning and incorporation of the criticised wishes and desires and a suspension of self-criticism.

The perspectives in this subcategory would generally be compatible with constructivistic and 'postrational' cognitive perspectives (Mahoney, 1991; Watzlawick, 1984). Constructivistic perspectives assume that there is no simple, decidable relationship between a concept and 'truth'. Kruglanski and Jaffe (1988), for instance, have argued that all inference is arbitrary, and all abstraction (in contrast to Aaron Beck's view that selective abstraction is dysfunctional) is selective. Concepts cannot even be falsified, let alone verified. Therefore, one cannot talk about beliefs or concepts as 'true', 'false', 'rational' or 'irrational'. Concepts are more like 'tools' (Bohart, 1990; Bruner, 1986) for doing things in the world, and the issue is how well they are doing the job. In other words, the criterion for a belief or concept is its viability or usefulness, rather than its veridicality. This suggests that 'should' statements are not inherently dysfunctional. Nor are global self-attributions. Nor are other forms of self-criticism.

The functionality of different kinds of belief statements may vary from situation to situation and person to person. Reality is personal and multiple. This has important therapeutic implications. It means that the therapist is not in a position to know in any *a priori* sense (independent of the client and of their circumstances) whether or not a client's beliefs are dysfunctional. Therefore the therapist cannot simply set out to correct the client's way of thinking, either through direct confrontation (Ellis), or through collaborative, Socratic questioning (Beck). Instead, the therapist must adopt more of an exploratory stance. An important therapeutic strategy is to help the client explore the structure of their personal reality and to help him or her evaluate how well it is working. This is compatible with person-centred philosophy.

Driscoll's (1984, 1989) integrative 'ordinary language' model of psychotherapy is generally based on this premise. Driscoll does not inform the client of the dysfunctionality of a client's act of self-criticism. Rather, Driscoll helps the client identify the underlying, often nonconscious premises driving the self-criticism and then helps them explore how useful they are. For Driscoll, perfectionism is not inherently dysfunctional. To the contrary, it can often be functional.

For Driscoll, there are several possible proactive motives for self-criticism. For instance, self-criticism may be an attempt at accurate self-appraisal: i.e. 'to be honest with oneself'. It also may be an attempt to mobilise the self, in a manner similar to how football coaches such as Vince Lombardi have used criticism to motivate their players to perform better.

There is some evidence to support Driscoll's views that self-criticism can be functional. Norem (1989) has found that 'defensive pessimism' – i.e. using catastrophising self-statements to mobilise performance in exams – can be a useful test-taking strategy for some people. The person predicts doom, but then uses that to mobilise themselves to study harder. Similarly, Markus and Nurius (1987) have found that healthy functioning involves having a balance between positive, optimistic, possible-future self-images and negative, catastrophic ones.

Wessler and Hankin-Wessler's (1986, 1989) cognitive appraisal therapy is based on the premise that people guide their lives with nonconscious 'personal rules for living'. Some of these personal rules are of the moral/prescriptive variety. Wessler and Hankin-Wessler do not assume that shoulds are inherently dysfunctional, or that any personal rules for living can be said to be dysfunctional in and of themselves. Instead, it is often the rigidity and inflexibility with which personal rules for living (PRLs) are employed that determines their dysfunctionality. Therapy consists of making the PRLs conscious, and then helping the client explore their usefulness and applicability. A variety of techniques, both cognitive and experiential, may be used to do this.

Client-centred therapists believe people learn shoulds and oughts from their parents and use them to disown their own experience. However, disowning is not only for defensive purposes (i.e. to avoid loss of parental approval); it is also a proactive attempt to positively self-organise. For instance, a person may learn a value that one 'should never get angry', and be self-critical if they do feel angry. However, the person is doing this because they have learned from their parents that 'good people don't get angry', or 'emotions are to be distrusted when decision-making'. Thus, by denying or self-criticising anger, the person is actively trying to make themselves a better person, although it backfires because feelings are a crucial part of effective organismic self-regulation.

This perspective is congruent with Greenberg's (1984) experiential approach. Greenberg's research on the two-chair technique has found that the 'top dog' or critical side of the self is trying to help the whole self prevail and cope. For Greenberg, shoulds are not automatically dysfunctional. They are only dysfunctional if they are used in such a way that they create splits in experiencing that inhibit the person's organismic self-regulatory capacities.

In particular, shoulds that are not 'owned' or chosen as personally meaningful are likely to create splits in experience. Shoulds simply adopted and conformed to unquestioningly are more likely to be dysfunctional. I would suggest that there may be a parallel here between the 'conformist' use of shoulds and Kohlberg's (1976) conventional stage in moral development. The 'owning' of shoulds may parallel Kohlberg's post-conventional morality stage, where morality is based on deeply held and thought-through values.

There is a significant theoretical difference between Greenberg's experiential approach (and other humanistic approaches) and rational-cognitive approaches to self-criticism. I (Bohart, 1982) have previously noted that, while both cognitive and humanistic approaches attempt to reduce the rigid use of self-critical thoughts, humanists believe that this modification does more than merely reduce the negative effects of self-criticism. In addition, it allows the person's inherent 'organismic wisdom' to operate and facilitate creative adaptation. It is not necessary to replace dysfunctional ways of thinking with functional ways because humans have their own inherent order-making and order-generating capacities (Gendlin, 1990). Reduction of self-criticism based on external, unowned shoulds facilitates the emergence of this experientially-based organismic capacity for creative personal growth and advancement. Creative functioning is dependent on having full integrative access to organismic information (Greenberg & Safran, 1987; Rogers, 1961), which is often what 'shouldistic' self-criticism is blocking.

The experiential/humanistic therapist is therefore more interested in promoting the individual's use of this experiential, organismic creative process than they are in reducing dysfunctional self-criticism *per se*. Therefore, the experiential/humanistic therapist, perhaps even more than Driscoll or Wessler, has as a priority setting up therapy so that it is the client who does the evaluating and processing of the dysfunctional shoulds and self-criticism. This means supporting and promoting the client's own process of experiential assimilation.

It is therefore no joke that Carl Rogers might actively empathise with how badly a client is putting themself down (by perhaps saying, 'You're really feeling hopeless about yourself at the moment'). Rice and Greenberg (1991) have recently identified a 'vulnerability' marker at the point where the therapist promotes a full 'staying with' client experience, even if the client is deeply experiencing a negative, critical view of the self. The belief is that fully allowing and empathising with such negative self-experience facilitates the client's own ability to creatively move beyond it. How this may work is demonstrated in the Rice and Greenberg article.

In the Gestalt two-chair technique, Greenberg (1984) promotes contact between different sides of the self. He is 'process-directive' and 'content-non-directive'. It is believed that, by creating contact, awareness and dialogue between the critical side of the self and the 'experiencing' side, a productive integration takes place. Shoulds and criticisms are not eliminated so much as they are incorporated into a more productive, 'organismically wise' approach to the problem.

Humanistic therapists also encourage clients to temporarily suspend their dysfunctional self-evaluative activities – as do many cognitive and psychodynamic therapists. I have called this the use of the 'phenomenological method', and have claimed that it is a therapeutic commonality (Bohart & Todd, 1988). Safran and Segal (1990) have identified a similar process, which they call 'decentering'. An example of its use is in Rice and Saperia's (1984) work with 'problem-reaction points'. Clients are encouraged to suspend their self-critical reactions to their own behaviour in a given situation in order to return to a step-by-step 'sensory' examination of that situation. This usually leads to an unearthing of the implicit positive or proactive 'wisdom' underlying whatever behaviour the client has been criticising themselves for.

Reframing

I will briefly note how two other approaches might treat self-criticism. Both strategic and solution-focused therapists might use reframing. For instance, de Shazer (1985) congratulates a young woman who is criticising herself for being shy around others, having learned one of the most important skills of interpersonal interaction – that of listening. It is unclear how reframing works – possibly by validating the person in such a way that they take performance pressure off themselves. After all, if you enter a social situation already criticising yourself for not being socially fluent, that will get in the way of your attempts to be more socially fluent.

An integrative process perspective

I'd like to briefly present my views of self-criticism based on my integrative process model of psychotherapy (Bohart, 1992). There is an emerging interest in psychology in viewing humans as ongoing processes, rather than as receptacles containing internalised structures. This can be found in recent developments in personality research, as summarised by Cantor (1990) and Cantor and Zirkel (1990), and in cognitive theory – for instance, in the work of Tulving (1983). Tulving notes that the analogy of the memory system as a machine-like structure has not been useful, and that memory research is switching from a focus on structure to a focus on activity and function. He says that he will:

> ... adopt the orientation in which mental activity plays a central role and in which constructs implying stationary states – such as 'engram' and 'recollective experience' – serve simply as labels for dispositions, or processes held in abeyance, or as indicants that some processes have been completed and others have not yet begun. (p.132)

The process emphasis is also compatible with an emerging interest in viewing the human being as a purposive, future-oriented, goal-directed organism (Cantor & Zirkel, 1990; Driscoll, 1984; Howard, 1986; Markus & Nurius, 1987; Rychlak, 1991), and the idea of understanding people through the metaphor of narrative (Bruner, 1986; Howard, 1991; Sarbin, 1990; Wessler & Hankin-Wessler, 1986).

From a process perspective, it has been argued by Bruner (1986) that concepts, schemas and the like should be seen as tools or prosthetic devices used by the active organism to cope with and explore its world. Their 'truthfulness' is less of an issue than their usefulness. Tools can be used for the right job in the wrong way, or used for the wrong job. A hammer, for instance, is an excellent tool, but probably not for trying to kill a fly.

If a person is trying to solve a problem with a tool and it is not working, they need to be able to relate productively to the information they receive back from that failure and change tools, modify the tool, or modify the way they are using it. Psychopathology is not so much the misuse of the tool as the failure to productively learn from feedback that the tool is not working and adapt accordingly. Psychopathology, therefore, lies neither in dysfunctional schemas nor in dysfunctional behaviour, but in the failure to productively use failure feedback to modify schemas and behaviour when they are leading to dysfunctional or 'failure' outcomes (see also Seligman, 1991). All humans from time to time misperceive and fail to use effective coping strategies. This becomes 'pathological' only if they then fail to learn from failure feedback and persist in their dysfunctional uses.

Therefore, compatible with many of the perspectives above, the use of self-criticism and shoulds is not by itself dysfunctional. Rather, it depends on how, when, and where one is using them.

More importantly, it relates to the issue of what one does when one's use of self-criticism or shoulds leads to experiences of failure, blocks in one's life-stream, dysphoric experiences and the like. What is needed when one's use of a tool is not working is the adoption of what I would call a productive, task-oriented, mastery-oriented approach to the problem, patterned after the work of Dweck and Leggett (1988). What one needs to be able to do in such situations is explore, hypothesis-test, back off from the problem ('decenter', to use Safran and Segal's (1990) term), and attend to all possible useful information.

The idea of 'decentering' includes disengaging from one's problem in order to be able to get a better perspective on it. I believe that most therapies operate by helping the client develop their ability to 'move up a level' to a 'metacognitive' perspective (Carmin & Dowd, 1988; Flavell, 1979), although I would wish to broaden the concept to include 'meta-experiential' (experiencing how one is experiencing) and 'meta-perceptual' (perceiving how one is perceiving) perspectives. As an example of how a therapist may help clients with their problems by 'moving them up a level', Wile (1981) helps couples develop a 'relationship about their relationship'. Having second-order changes (Watzlawick, 1984) may not only be a content or perspective change; it may also be a shift 'up a level' in perspective-taking. In other words, learning the process skill of being able to shift up a level in order to form a productive relationship with oneself about one's problems may be an important component of therapy.

Therefore, a goal of an integrative-process approach to therapy is helping clients learn how to relate productively to their shoulds and self-criticisms. They can adopt an exploratory, hypothesis-testing attitude towards their own self-criticisms and shoulds, as they do to problems in the task environment. Why fully empathising with client self-criticism (as done by Rogers and Rice and Greenberg) may work is that it may shift the client to a 'meta-experiential level', where they come to experience and perceive themselves in the process of putting themselves down. This may lead to productive assimilation and integration.

To borrow a term from Masten and colleagues (1990), the important thing in therapy and in life is the mobilisation of the self-righting capacity of the organism. 'Pathology', or dysfunctional, self-defeating behaviour, thinking and feeling, can be said to be what happens when something goes wrong with this self-righting capacity. Parenthetically, based on their study of resilient individuals, Masten and colleagues (1990, p.438) conclude that 'studies of psychological resilience support the view that human psychological development is highly buffered and self-righting'.

One way that self-righting can go wrong is if people become primarily 'danger-oriented' in their focus (Bohart, 1990; Briere, 1989). That is, for various reasons, some environmental, some personal-historical (such as having been sexually abused as children), people become more chronically focused on avoiding potential danger in themselves and in their life situations than on exploring and looking for possibility. A danger orientation is also a product of feeling helpless or low in self-efficacy (Bandura, 1986). It leads to the adoption of a defensive, avoidant, conservative (Kahneman & Tversky, 1984) strategy towards problem-solving, rather than an exploratory, hypothesis-testing, mastery-oriented process approach. Being danger-oriented, as in states of high stress (Meichenbaum, 1985) or high need (Bruner, 1986), leads to narrowed attention, defensiveness, self-preoccupation, absolutistic thinking, and other dysfunctional ways of being (Meichenbaum, 1985). Further, it tends to polarise the client's view of a situation into 'either/or' (or what object relations theorists call 'splitting'). Therefore, it is not the presence of stress *per se*, or of failure, dysphoric affect, or dysfunctional beliefs that is the problem but, rather, how one relates to these things. Does one relate to them in a process-oriented, hypothesis-testing, exploratory manner, or does one relate to them in a defensive, avoidant, conservative, danger-oriented manner?

I suggest that self-criticism and 'shouldism' become dysfunctional when they are used in a primarily danger-oriented manner. I further suggest that being criticised in childhood may be harmful not so much because the individual 'internalises' critical voices (in fact, some may use internalised critical voices to productively mobilise themselves), but because such criticism may lead to them adopting a danger-oriented stance towards themselves and towards the world. They become much more concerned with avoiding mistakes and failure than with taking a chance on failure in order to master things.

To return to Hamlet, what is dysfunctional, from my perspective, about his self-criticism is that he is primarily danger-oriented. He is focusing far more on what may be wrong with him than he is on the task at hand, which is to engage in a productive exploration of self, values and situation, in order to discover what possibilities of creative integration or creative movement lie open to him. He is so worried about what is 'dangerous' about himself that he relates to himself in a kind of passive, helpless, low self-efficacious manner. In such a case, his self-criticism is not mobilising him in a productive, task-oriented manner, but rather creating a paralysing vicious circle.

If I were doing therapy with Hamlet, I might first work with him to clarify his goals. I might want to support him in exploring how much he wants to stand behind the 'should' that he must avenge his father. Even if he does decide he wants to stand behind it, I would help him to explore his reluctance as a positive source of information about what he also wants to do. Helping clients move out of a danger-oriented way of viewing a problem into a more possibility-oriented, exploratory modality often creates the possibility of finding 'ands' where previously the client has seen only 'either/ors'. In order to facilitate this, I might say something like, 'You would like to avenge your father and you are not sure you want to take such violent action.' I do not know what creative, life-enhancing integrative solution Hamlet might come with, since more than anything I would be trying to foster an exploratory stance towards the whole problem. I would not particularly worry about the veracity of whether or not he is a 'rogue and peasant slave'.

References

Abramson, L.Y., Metalsky, G.I. & Alloy, L.B. (1988). The hopelessness theory of depression: Does the research test the theory? In L.Y. Abramson (Ed.), *Social cognition and clinical psychology: A synthesis* (pp. 33–65). Guilford.

Andrews, J.D.W. (1991). *The active self in psychotherapy: An integration of therapeutic styles.* Allyn & Bacon.

Bandura, A. (1986). *Social foundations of thought and action: A social cognitive theory.* Prentice-Hall.

Beck, A.T. (1987). Cognitive therapy. In J. Zeig (Ed.), *The evolution of psychotherapy* (pp. 149–163). Brunner/Mazel.

Bohart, A.C. (1982). Similarities between cognitive and humanistic approaches to psychotherapy. *Cognitive Therapy and Research, 6*, 245–250.

Bohart, A.C. (1990). A cognitive client-centered perspective on borderline personality development. In G. Lietaer, J. Rombauts & R. Van Balen (Eds.), *Client-centered and experiential psychotherapy in the nineties* (pp. 599–622). Leuven University Press.

Bohart, A.C. (1992). Un modelo integrador de proceso para la psicopatologia y la psicoterapia. *Revista De Psicoterapia, 3,* 49–74.

Bohart, A.C. & Todd, J. (1988). *Foundations of clinical and counselling psychology* (1st ed). Harper Collins.

Bollas, C. (1987). *The shadow of the object.* Columbia University Press.

Bradshaw, J. (1990). *Homecoming.* Bantam.

Briere, J. (1989). *Beyond survival: Therapy for adults molested as children.* Springer.

Bruner, J. (1986). *Actual minds, possible worlds.* Harvard University Press.

Cantor, N. (1990). From thought to behavior: 'Having' and 'doing' in the study of personality and cognition. *American Psychologist, 45*(6), 735–750.

Cantor, N. & Zirkel, S. (1990). Personality, cognition, and purposive behavior. In L.A. Pervin (Ed.), *Handbook of personality: Theory and research* (pp. 135–164). Guilford.

Carmin, C.N. & Dowd, E.T. (1988). Paradigms in cognitive psychotherapy. In W. Dryden & P. Trower (Eds.), *Developments in cognitive psychotherapy* (pp. 1–22). Sage.

de Shazer, S. (1985). *Keys to solution in brief therapy.* Norton.

Driscoll, R. (1984). *Pragmatic psychotherapy.* Van Nostrand Reinhold.

Driscoll, R. (1989). Self-condemnation: A comprehensive framework for assessment and treatment. *Psychotherapy: Theory, Research, Practice, Training, 26*(1), 104–111.

Dweck, C.S. & Leggett, E.L. (1988). A social-cognitive approach to motivation and personality. *Psychological Review, 95*(2), 256–273.

Ellis, A. (1984). Rational-emotive therapy. In R. Corsini (Ed.), *Current psychotherapies* (3rd ed.) (pp.196–238). Peacock.

Flavell, J.H. (1979). Metaconition and cognitive monitoring: A new area of cognitive-developmental inquiry. *American Psychologist, 34*(10), 906–911.

Freud, S. (1938). The interpretation of dreams. In A.A. Brill (Ed.), *The basic writings of Sigmund Freud.* Random House.

Gendlin, E.T. (1968). The experiential response. In E.F. Hammer (Ed.), *Use of interpretation in treatment* (pp.208–227). Grune & Stratton.

Gendlin, E.T. (1990). The small steps of the therapy process: How they come and how to help them come. In G. Lietaer, J. Rombauts & R. Van Balen (Eds.), *Client-centered and experiential psychotherapy in the nineties* (pp. 205–224). Leuven University Press.

Greenberg, L.S. (1984). Task analysis of interpersonal conflict resolution. In L.S. Greenberg & L.N. Rice (Eds.), *Patterns of change* (pp. 67–123). Guilford.

Greenberg, L.S., Rice, L.N. & Elliott, R. (1993). *Facilitating emotional change*. Guilford.

Greenberg, L.S. & Safran, J.D. (1987). *Emotion in psychotherapy*. Guilford.

Howard, G.S. (1986). *Dare we develop a human science?* Academic Publications.

Howard, G.S. (1991). Culture tales: A narrative approach to thinking, cross-cultural psychology, and psychotherapy. *American Psychologist, 46*(3), 187–197.

Janoff-Bulman, R. (1979). Characterological versus behavioral self-blame: Inquiries into depression and rape. *Journal of Personality and Social Psychology, 37*(10), 1798–1809.

Jones, E.E. & Berglas, S. (1978). Control of attributions about the self through self-handicapping strategies: The appeal of alcohol and the role of under-achievement. *Personality and Social Psychology Bulletin,* 4(2), 200–206.

Kahneman, D. & Tversky, A. (1984). Choices, values, and frames. *American Psychologist, 39*(4), 341–350.

Kohlberg, L. (1976). Moral stages and moralization: The cognitive-developmental approach. In T. Lickona (Ed.), *Moral development and behavior: Theory. research and social issues* (pp.31–53). Holt, Rinehart & Winston.

Kruglanski, A.W. & Jaffe, Y. (1988). Curing by knowing: The epistemic approach to cognitive therapy. In L.Y. Abramson (Ed.), *Social cognition and clinical psychology: A synthesis* (pp. 254–294). Guilford.

Lakoff, G. (1987). *Women, fire, and dangerous things: What categories reveal about the mind*. University of Chicago Press.

Lazarus, A.A. (1976). *Multimodal behavior therapy*. Springer.

Mahoney, M.J. (1991). *Human change processes: The scientific foundations of psychotherapy*. Basic Books.

Markus, H. & Nurius, P. (1987). Possible selves: The interface between motivation and the self-concept. In K. Yardley & T. Honess (Eds.), *Self and identity: Psychosocial perspectives* (pp. 157–172). Wiley.

Masten, A.S., Best, K.M. & Garmezy, N. (1990). Resilience and development: Contributions from the study of children who overcome adversity. *Development and Psychopathology, 2*(4), 425–444.

Meichenbaum, D. (1977). *Cognitive behavior modification*. Plenum.

Meichenbaum, D. (1985). *Stress inoculation training*. Pergamon.

Miller, D.T. & Porter, C.A. (1988). Errors and biases in the attribution process. In L.Y. Abramson (Ed.), *Social cognition and clinical psychology: A synthesis* (pp. 3–32). Guilford.

Norem, J.K. (1989). Cognitive strategies as personality: Effectiveness, specificity, flexibility, and change. In D.M. Buss & N. Cantor (Eds.), *Personality psychology: Recent trends and emerging directions* (pp. 45–60). Springer-Verlag.

Rice, L.N. & Greenberg, L.S. (1991). Two affective change events in client-centered therapy. In J.D. Safran & L.S. Greenberg (Eds.), *Emotion, psychotherapy, and change* (pp. 197–226). Guilford.

Rice, L.N. & Saperia, E.P. (1984). Task analysis of the resolution of problematic reactions. In L.N. Rice & L.S. Greenberg (Eds.), *Patterns of change* (pp. 29–66). Guilford.

Rogers, C.R. (1961). *On becoming a person.* Houghton Mifflin.

Rychlak, J.F. (1991). *Artificial intelligence and human reason.* Columbia University Press.

Safran, J.D. & Segal, Z.V. (1990). *Interpersonal process in cognitive therapy.* Basic Books.

Sarbin, T.R. (1990). The narrative quality of action. *Theoretical and Philosophical Psychology, 10*(2), 49–65.

Seligman, M.E.P. (1991). *Learned optimism.* Vintage.

St. Clair, M. (1986). *Object relations and self psychology: An introduction.* Brooks/Cole.

Taylor, S.E. & Brown, J.D. (1988). Illusion and well-being: A social psychological perspective on mental health. *Psychological Bulletin, 103*(2), 193–210.

Tulving, E. (1983). *Elements of episodic memory.* Oxford University Press.

Watzlawick, P. (Ed.) (1984). *The invented reality.* Norton.

Wessler, R.L. & Hankin-Wessler, S.W.R. (1986). Cognitive appraisal therapy (CAT). In W. Dryden & W.L. Golden (Eds.), *Cognitive-behavioural approaches to psychotherapy* (pp. 196–223). HarperCollins.

Wessler, R.L. & Hankin-Wessler, S.W.R. (1989). Nonconscious algorithms in cognitive and affective processes. *Journal of Cognitive Psychotherapy, 3*(4), 243–254.

Wile, D.B. (1981). *Couples therapy: A nontraditional approach.* Wiley.

References (Chapters 1–11)

Alberini, C.A. & LeDoux, J.E. (2013). Memory reconsolidation. *Current Biology, 23*(17), R746–R750.

Almaas, A.H. (2012). *Facets of unity: The enneagram of holy ideas*. Shambhala.

Altimir, C., Krause, M., de la Parra, G., Dagnino, P., Tomicic, A., Valdés, N., Perez, J.C., Echávarri, O. & Vilches, O. (2010). Clients', therapists', and observers' agreement on the amount, temporal location, and content of psychotherapeutic change and its relation to outcome. *Psychotherapy Research, 20*(4), 472–487.

Anderson, R. & Cissna, K.N. (1997). *The Martin Buber-Carl Rogers dialogue: A new transcript with commentary*. State University of New York Press.

Anonymous (September 18, 2016). *The Berlin wisdom paradigm: An expert knowledge system*. [Blog.] www.evidencebasedwisdom.com

Baltes, P.B. & Staudinger, U.M. (2000). Wisdom: A metaheuristic (pragmatic) to orchestrate mind and virtue toward excellence. *American Psychologist, 55*(1), 122–136.

Bavelas, J.B., Coates, L. & Johnson, T. (2000). Listeners as co-narrators. *Journal of Personality and Social Psychology, 79*(6), 941–952.

Belenky, M.F., Clinchy, B.M., Goldberger, N.R. & Tarule, J. (1986). *Women's ways of knowing: The development of self, voice, and mind*. Basic Books.

Bohart, A.C. (1992). Un modelo integrador de proceso para la psicopatología y la psicoterapia. *Revista De Psicoterapia, 3*(9), 49–74.

Bohart, A.C. (2001). A meditation on the nature of self-healing and personality change in psychotherapy based on Gendlin's theory of experiencing. *The Humanistic Psychologist, 29*(1–3), 249–279.

Bohart, A.C. (2006, August). *The category 'psychotherapy' is a 'granfaloon of practices'*. [Paper presentation]. APA Symposium on 'What Revolution Would You Like to See in Psychotherapy?' American Psychological Association Convention, New Orleans.

Bohart, A.C. (2007). Taking steps along a path: Full functioning, openness, and personal creativity. *Person-Centered & Experiential Psychotherapies, 6*(1), 14–29.

Bohart, A.C. (2008). How clients self-heal in psychotherapy. In B. Levitt (Ed.), *Reflections on human potential* (pp. 175–186). PCCS Books.

Bohart, A.C. (2012). Can you be integrative and person-centered at the same time? *Person-Centered & Experiential Psychotherapies, 11*(1), 1–13.

Bohart, A.C. (2013). Darth Vader, Carl Rogers, and self-organizing wisdom. In A.C. Bohart, B. Held, E. Mendelowitz & K. Schneider (Eds.), *Humanity's dark side* (pp. 57–76). American Psychological Association.

Bohart, A.C. (2018, July). *Person-centred therapy: A radical vision*. Presentation to the Conference of the World Association of Person-Centered and Experiential Psychotherapy and Counseling, Vienna, Austria.

Bohart, A.C. & Berry, M.C. (2011, June/July). *Self-organizing wisdom in psychotherapy: Theoretical conception and beginning empirical investigations*. Presentation at the Conference of the Society for Psychotherapy Research, Bern, Switzerland.

Bohart, A.C., Berry, M.C. & Wicks, C.L. (2011a). Developing a systematic framework for utilizing discrete types of qualitative data as therapy research evidence. *Pragmatic Case Studies in Psychotherapy, 7*(1), 145–155. http://pcsp.libraries.rutgers.edu

Bohart, A.C. & Byock, G. (2005). Experiencing Carl Rogers from the client's point of view: A vicarious ethnographic investigation. I. Extraction and perception of meaning. *The Humanistic Psychologist, 33*(3), 187–212.

Bohart, A.C. & Greenberg, L.S. (1997). Empathy: Where are we and where do we go from here? In A.C. Bohart & L.S. Greenberg (Eds.), *Empathy reconsidered: New directions in psychotherapy* (pp. 419–450). American Psychological Association.

Bohart, A.C., Greenberg, L.S., Driscoll, R. & Wessler, R.L. (1991, July). *Working with the internal critic: A therapeutic commonality*. Symposium presented at the conference of the Society for the Exploration of Psychotherapy Integration, London.

Bohart, A.C. & Henschel, D. (1984). *Framework for a cognitive-developmental theory of psychopathology*. Paper presented at the Conference on Piagetian Theory and the Helping Professions, University of Southern California.

Bohart, A.C., O'Hara, M., & Leitner, L.M. (1998). Empirically violated treatments: Disenfranchisement of humanistic and other psychotherapies. *Psychotherapy Research, 8*(2), 141–157.

Bohart, A.C., Stacy, J., Shenefiel, L., Peng, Y. & Stelly, A. (2016, June). *Therapists' (and clients') mindsets*. Paper presented at the conference of the Society for the Exploration of Psychotherapy Integration, Dublin, Ireland.

Bohart, A.C. & Tallman, K. (1999). *How clients make therapy work: The process of active self-healing*. American Psychological Association.

Bohart, A.C. & Tallman, K. (2010). Clients as active self-healers: Implications for the person-centered approach. In M. Cooper, J.C. Watson & D. Hölldampf (Eds.), *Person-centered and experiential therapies work: A review of the research on counseling, psychotherapy and related practices* (pp. 91–133). PCCS Books.

Bohart, A.C., Tallman, K., Byock, G. & Mackrill, T. (2011b). The 'research jury method': The application of the jury trial model to evaluating the validity of descriptive and causal statements about psychotherapy process and outcome. *Pragmatic Case Studies in Psychotherapy, 7*(1), 101–144. http://pcsp.libraries.rutgers.edu

Bohart, A.C., Wickes, C. & Berry, M. (2010). *Self-organizing wisdom in person-centered therapy: Theoretical and empirical analyses*. Paper presented as part of a symposium 'Studying clinical wisdom: research on therapists and clients' wisdom-related processes'. American Psychological Association Convention, San Diego, CA.

Boukydis, K.M. (1984). Changes: Peer-counseling supportive communities as a model for community mental health. In D. Larson (Ed.), *Teaching psychological skills: Models for giving psychology away* (pp. 306–317). Brooks/Cole.

Byock, G., Bekele, A. & Bohart, A. (2005). *A vicarious empathic-hermeneutic ethnographic examination of goal negotiation from the client's point of view.* Paper presented at the International Meeting of the Society for Psychotherapy Research, Montreal, Quebec.

Cantor, N. (1990). From thought to behavior: 'Having' and 'doing' in the study of personality and cognition. *American Psychologist, 45*(6), 735–750.

Caspar, F. & Berger, T. (2012). Corrective experience and models of cognitive-emotional regulation. In L. Castonguay & C. Hill (Eds.), *Transformation in psychotherapy: Corrective experiences across cognitive behavioral, humanistic, and psychodynamic approaches* (pp. 141–157). American Psychological Association.

Castonguay, L.G., Boswell, J.F., Zack, S.E., Baker, S., Boutselis, M., Chiswick, N.R., Damer, D.D., Hemmelstein, M.A., Jackson, J.S., Morford, M., Ragusea, S.A., Gowen Roper, J., Spayd, C., Weiszer, T., Borkovec, T.D. & Grosse Holtforth, M. (2010). Helpful and hindering events in psychotherapy: A practice research network study. *Psychotherapy: Theory, Research, Practice, and Training, 47*(3), 327–344.

Chabris, C. & Simons, D. (2011). *The invisible gorilla: How our intuitions deceive us.* Harmony Press.

Cham, J. (2009, January 26). Brain on a stick (cartoon). *Piled higher and deeper by Jorge Cham.* http://phdcomics.com/comics/archive_print.php?comicid=1126

Charon, R. (2008). *Narrative medicine: Honoring the stories of illness.* Oxford University Press.

Cissna, K.N. & Anderson, R. (1994). The 1957 Martin Buber-Carl Rogers dialogue, as dialogue. *Journal of Humanistic Psychology, 34*(1), 11–45.

Clark, H.H. & Brennen, S.E. (1991). Grounding in communication. In L.B. Resnick, J.M. Levine & S.D. Teasley (Eds.), *Perspectives on socially shared cognition* (pp. 127–149). American Psychological Association.

Cleary, T. (1990). *Book of serenity: One hundred Zen dialogues*. (T. Cleary, Trans.). Lindisfarne Press.

Coady, C.A.J. (1992). *Testimony: A philosophical study.* Clarendon Press.

Cornelius-White, J.H.D., Kanamori, Y., Murphy, D. & Tickle, E. (2018). Mutuality in psychotherapy: A meta-analysis and meta-synthesis. *Journal of Psychotherapy Integration, 28*(4), 489–504.

Cowan, P.A. (1978). *Piaget: With feeling.* Holt, Rinehart & Winston.

Craig, P. (2007, September 3). Sagal makes a full circle back to music. *West County Times,* TimeOut section C, 1–2.

Cullari, S. (2000). *Counseling and psychotherapy.* Allyn & Bacon.

de Wit, M.M., van der Kamp, J. & Withagen, R. (2015). Visual illusions and direct perception: Elaborating on Gibson's insights. *New Ideas in Psychology, 36*, 1–9.

Diener, E. (1979). Deindividuation, self-awareness, and disinhibition. *Journal of Personality and Social Psychology, 37*(7), 1160–1171.

Dumas, A. (2012). *The Count of Monte Christo.* Penguin. (Originally published 1944).

Duncan, B.L., Solovey, A.D. & Rusk, G.S. (1992). *Changing the rules: A client-directed approach to therapy.* Guilford.

Dweck, C. (2007). *Mindset: The new psychology of success.* Ballentine.

Ehrenreich, B. (2010). *Brightsided: How positive thinking is undermining America.* Picador.

Eliot, T.S. (1941). *Four Quartets.* Harcourt.

Elliott, R., James, E., Reimschuessel, C., Cislo, D. & Sack, N. (1985). Significant events and the analysis of immediate therapeutic impacts. *Psychotherapy: Theory, Research, Practice, Training, 22*(3), 620–630.

Elliott, R., Watson, J.C., Goldman, R.N. & Greenberg, L.S. (2004). *Learning emotion-focused therapy: The process-experiential approach to change.* American Psychological Association.

Farley, F. (1990). Type T behavior and families: Introduction to a new theory. *The Family Psychologist, 6*(4), 24–25.

Feldman, J.B. (1985). The work of Milton Erickson: A multisystem model of eclectic therapy. *Psychotherapy, 22*(2), 154–162.

Finke, J. (2017). Beyond and on the side of orthodox client-centredness – on balancing the conceptual framework of PCT. *Person-Centered & Experiential Psychotherapies, 17*(1), 19–36.

Freyd, J. (1987). Dynamic mental representations. *Psychological Review, 94*(4), 427–436.

Gendlin, E.T. (1964). A theory of personality change. In P. Worchel & D. Byme (Eds.), *Personality change*. Wiley.

Gendlin, E.T. (1967). Therapeutic procedures in dealing with schizophrenics. In C.R. Rogers, E.T. Gendlin, D.J. Kiesler & C.B. Truax (Eds.), *The therapeutic relationship and its impact* (pp. 369–400). University of Wisconsin Press.

Gendlin, E.T. (1968). The experiential response. In E. Hammer (Ed.), *Use of interpretation in treatment* (pp. 208–227). Grune & Stratton.

Gendlin, E.T. (1970). A theory of personality change. In J.T. Hart & T.M. Tomlinson (Eds.), *New directions in client-centered therapy* (pp. 129–174). Houghton Mifflin.

Gendlin, E.T. (1984). The politics of giving therapy away: Listening and focusing. In D. Larson (Ed.), *Teaching psychological skills: Models for giving psychology away* (pp. 287–305). Brooks/Cole.

Gendlin, E.T. (1990). The small steps of the therapy process; How they come and how to help them come. In G. Lietaer, J. Rombauts & R. Van Balen (Eds.), *Client-centered and experiential psychotherapy in the nineties* (pp. 205–224). University of Leuven Press.

Gendlin, E.T. (1996) *Focusing-oriented psychotherapy: A manual of the experiential method*. Guilford.

Gendlin, E.T. (1997). How philosophy cannot appeal to experience, and how it can. In D.M. Levin (Ed.), *Language beyond postmodernism: Saying and thinking in Gendlin's philosophy* (pp. 3–41). Northwestern University Press.

Gendlin, E.T. & Johnson, D.H. (2004). *Proposal for an international group for a first-person science*. The Focusing Institute. http://previous.focusing.org/gendlin/docs/gol_2184.html

Gilligan, C., Brown, L.M. & Rogers, A.G. (1990). Psyche embedded: A place for body, relationships, and culture in personality theory. In A.J. Rabin, R.A. Zucker, R.A. Emmons & S. Frank (Eds.), *Studying persons and lives* (pp. 86-147). Springer Publishing.

Gold, J. & Stricker, G. (2020). Integrative approaches to psychotherapy. In S.B. Messer & N.J. Kaslow (Eds.), *Essential psychotherapies* (pp. 443–480). Guilford Press.

Goldberg, J. (2018, April 27). When will machine-like thinking prompt moral panic? *San Francisco Chronicle*. www.sfchronicle.com/opinion/article/When-will-machine-like-thinking-prompt-moral-12867935.php

Gopnik, A. (2016). *The gardener and the carpenter: What the new science of child development tells us about the relationship between parents and children*. Macmillan.

Greenberg, L.S., Rice, L.N. & Elliott, R. (1993). *Facilitating emotional change: The moment-by-moment process*. Guilford Press.

Haney, C., Banks, W.C. & Zimbardo, P.G. (1973). Interpersonal dynamics in a simulated prison. *International Journal of Criminology and Penology*, 1, 69–97.

Harré, R. (1987). The social construction of selves. In K. Yardley & T. Honess (Eds.), *Self and identity: Psychosocial perspectives* (pp. 41–52). John Wiley.

Hart, J.T. & Tomlinson, T.M. (Eds.). (1970). *New directions in client-centered therapy*. Houghton Mifflin.

Hedges, C. (2003) *War is a force that gives us meaning*. Anchor.

Heidegger, M. (1971/2001). On the origin of the work of art. In (A. Hofstadter, Trans.), (1st ed.) *Poetry, language, thought*. Perennial Classics.

Heidegger, M. (1927/2008). *Being and time*. Harper Perennial.

Held, B. (2001). *Stop smiling and start kvetching: A five-step guide to creative complaining*. St. Martin's Press.

Hendricks, M. (2002). Focusing-oriented/experiential psychotherapy. In D. Cain (Ed.), *Humanistic psychotherapies: Handbook of research and practice* (pp. 221–251). American Psychological Association.

Hofstadter, D. (1979). *Gödel, Escher, Bach: An eternal golden braid*. Basic Books.

Holland, S., Bresler, J., Cohen, J. & Bohart, A.C. (2018, June). *The case of Sam: Integrative technique to address core relational schemas*. Plenary symposium at the Conference of The Society for the Exploration of Psychotherapy Integration, New York, NY.

Holton, G. (1971). On trying to understand scientific genius. *The American Scholar, 41*(1), 98–99.

Jeffers, R. (1937). *Hope is not for the wise: An unpublished poem*. Quercus Press.

Joyce, J. (1948). *A portrait of the artist as a young man*. New American Library. (Original work published 1916).

Kahneman, D. & Klein, G. (2009). Conditions for intuitive experience: A failure to disagree. *American Psychologist, 64*(6), 515–526.

Kleinman, A. (1988a). *Rethinking psychiatry: From cultural category to personal experience*. Free Press.

Kleinman, A. (1988b). *The illness narratives*. Basic Books.

Kohlberg, L. & Hersh, R.H. (1997). Moral development: A review of the theory. *Theory into Practice, 16*(2), 53–59.

Kuhn, T.S. (1962). *The structure of scientific revolutions*. University of Chicago Press.

Kurzban, R. & Aktipis, C.A. (2007). Modularity and the social mind: Are psychologists too self-ish? *Personality and Social Psychology Review, 11*(2), 131–149.

Landrine, H. (1992). Clinical implications of cultural differences: The referential versus the indexical self. *Clinical Psychology Review, 12*(4), 401–415.

LaSalle, M. (2018, June 21). 'Jurassic World' has dinosaur thrills and a little extra bite. *San Francisco Chronicle*. www.sfchronicle.com/movies/article/Jurassic-World-has-dinosaur-thrills-and-a-13012161.php

Leicester, G. & O'Hara, M. (2009). *Ten things to do in a conceptual emergency.* Triarchy Press.

Le Texier, T. (2019). Debunking the Stanford Prison Experiment. *American Psychologist, 74*(7), 823–839.

Levitt, H.M. & Rennie, D.L. (2004). Narrative activity: Clients' and therapists' intentions in the process of narration. In L.E. Angus & J. McLeod (Eds.), *The handbook of narrative and psychotherapy* (pp. 299–314). Sage.

Linehan, M.M. (1989, April). *Untitled presentation.* Presentation as part of a symposium on 'What is support in psychotherapy and is it good or bad?' Conference of the Society for the Exploration of Psychotherapy Integration, Berkeley, California.

Linehan, M.M. (1997). Validation and psychotherapy. In A.C. Bohart & L.S. Greenberg (Eds.), *Empathy reconsidered: New directions in psychotherapy* (pp. 353–392). American Psychological Association.

Loesch, M., Hamilton, H., Seferian, L., Rush, S. & Bohart A. (1996). Research project 3. In A.C. Bohart & Associates, 'Experiencing, knowing, and change'. In R. Hutterer, G. Pawlowsky, P.F. Schmid & R. Stipsits (Eds.), *Client-centered and experiential psychotherapy: A paradigm in motion* (pp. 199–212). Peter Lang.

Luyten, P., Campbell, C., Allison, E. & Fonagy, P. (2020). The mentalizing approach to psychopathology: State of the art and future directions. *Annual Review of Clinical Psychology, 16,* 297–325.

Mackrill, T. (2011). A diary-based, cross-contextual case study methodology: Background for the case of 'Jane and Joe'. *Pragmatic Case Studies in Psychotherapy, 7*(1), 156–186. http://pcsp.libraries.rutgers.edu

Mahoney, M.J. (1991). *Human change processes.* Basic Books.

Mahrer, A.R. (1978). *Experiencing: A humanistic theory of psychology and psychiatry.* Brunner/Mazel.

Mahrer, A.R. (1993).Transformational psychotherapy. *Journal of Humanistic Psychology, 33*(2), 30–37.

McCrae, R.R. & Costa, P.T. (1990). *Personality in adulthood.* Guilford.

Mearns, D. (2006). Psychotherapy: The politics of liberation or collaboration? A career critically reviewed. In G. Proctor, M. Cooper, P. Sanders & B. Malcom (Eds.), *Politicizing the person-centred approach* (pp. 127–142). PCCS Books.

Messer, S.B. (1992), A critical examination of belief structures in interpretive and eclectic psychotherapy. In J.C. Norcross & M.R. Goldfried (Eds.), *Handbook of Psychotherapy Integration* (pp. 130–168). Basic Books.

Mickler, C. & Staudinger, U.M. (2005). *Manual for the assessment of self-related wisdom.* Jacobs University Bremen.

Milgram, S. (1963). Behavioral study of obedience. *Journal of Abnormal and Social Psychology, 67*(4), 371–378.

Miller, W.R. & Rollnick, S. (1991). *Motivational interviewing: Preparing people to change addictive behavior.* Guilford Press.

Miller, W.R. & Rollnick, S. (2012). *Motivational interviewing: Helping people change* (3rd ed.). Guilford Press.

Moon, K.A., Witty, M., Grant, B. & Rice, B. (2013). *Practicing client-centered therapy: Selected writings of Barbara Temaner Brodley.* PCCS Books.

Neville, B. (2018, August). *Taking Rogers seriously.* Keynote presentation at the Conference of the World Association for Person-Centered and Experiential Psychotherapy and Counseling, Vienna, Austria.

Nisbett, R.E. & Ross, L. (1980). *Human inference: Strategies and shortcomings of social judgment.* Prentice-Hall.

Norcross, J.C. (Ed.). (2011). *Psychotherapy relationships that work: Evidence-based responsiveness* (pp. 3–24). Oxford University Press.

Norem, J. (2002). *The positive power of negative thinking.* Basic Books.

O'Hara, M. (1984). Person-centered Gestalt: Toward a holistic synthesis. In R.E. Levant & J.M. Shlien (Eds.), *Client-centered therapy and the person-centered approach: New directions in theory, research, and practice* (pp. 203–221). Praeger.

O'Hara, M. (1997). Relational empathy: Beyond modernist egocentrism to postmodern holistic contextualism. In A.C. Bohart & L.S. Greenberg (Eds.), *Empathy reconsidered: New directions in psychotherapy* (pp. 295–320). American Psychological Association.

O'Hara, M. (2008). Forewords. In J.K. Wood, *Carl Rogers' person-centered approach* (pp. iii–viii). PCCS Books.

O'Hara, M. (2018, July). *Carpe diem: A transformative turn for person-centered practice?* Keynote presentation at the Conference of the World Association for Person-Centered and Experiential Psychotherapy and Counseling, Vienna, Austria.

Orlinsky, D.E., Grawe, K. & Parks, B.K. (1994). Process and outcome in psychotherapy: Noch einmal. In A.E. Bergin & S.L. Garfield (Eds.), *Handbook of psychotherapy and behavior change* (4th ed.) (pp. 270–376). Wiley.

Perry, W.G., Jr. (1970). *Forms of intellectual and ethical development in the college years: A scheme.* Holt, Rinehart, and Winston.

Phillips, J.R. (1984). Influences on personal growth as viewed by former psychotherapy patients. *Dissertation Abstracts International, 46,* 2820B.

Rogers, C.R. (1957). The necessary and sufficient conditions of therapeutic personality change. *Journal of Consulting Psychology, 21*(2), 95–103.

Rogers, C.R. (1959). A tentative scale for the measurement of process in psychotherapy. In E.A. Rubinstein & M.B. Parloff (Eds.), *Research in psychotherapy* (pp. 96–107). American Psychological Association.

Rogers, C.R. (1961a). *On becoming a person.* Houghton Mifflin.

Rogers, C.R. (1961b). The process equation of psychotherapy. *American Journal of Psychotherapy, 15,* 27–45.

Rogers C.R. (1986). Reflection of feelings. *Person-Centered Review, 1,* 375–377

Rogers C.R. & Sanford, R.C. (1985, 11–15 December). *The client-centered approach.* [Video.] Workshop presented at The Evolution of Psychotherapy Conference, 11–15 December, Arizona, USA. https://search.alexanderstreet.com/preview/work/bibliographic_entity%7Cvideo_work%7C1865902

Rogers, C.R. & Wood, J.K. (1974). Client-centered theory: Carl Rogers. In A. Burton (Ed.), *Operational theories of personality* (pp. 211–258). Brunner/Mazel.

Rosenbaum, R. & Bohart, A.C. (1993, April). *Discussion group: Thinking during therapy – should a therapist refrain?* Convention of the Society for the Exploration of Psychotherapy Integration, New York.

Rowling, J.K. (2008). The fringe benefits of failure, and the importance of imagination. *The Harvard Gazette.* https://news.harvard.edu/gazette/story/2008/06/text-of-j-k-rowling-speech/

Sabat, S.R. (2001). *The experience of Alzheimer's: Life through a tangled veil.* Wiley-Blackwell.

Schmid, P.F. (2002) Knowledge or acknowledgement? Psychotherapy as 'the art of not-knowing': Prospects on further developments of a radical paradigm. *Person-Centered & Experiential Psychotherapies, 1*(2), 56–70.

Schmid, P.F. (2003). The characteristics of a person-centered approach to therapy and counseling: Criteria for identity and coherence. *Person-Centered & Experiential Psychotherapies, 2*(2), 104–120.

Schmid, P.F. (2004). Back to the client. A phenomenological approach to the process of understanding and diagnosis. *Person-Centered & Experiential Psychotherapies, 3*(1), 36–51.

Schmid, P.F. (2006). The challenge of the other: Towards dialogical person-centered psychotherapy and counseling. *Person-Centered & Experiential Psychotherapies, 5*(4), 240–254.

Schmid, P.F. (2007). The anthropological and ethical foundations of person-centred therapy. In M. Cooper, M. O'Hara, P.F. Schmid & G. Wyatt (Eds.), *The handbook of person-centred psychotherapy and counseling* (pp. 30–46). Palgrave Macmillan.

Schmid, P.F. (2013). Whence the evil? A personalistic and dialogic perspective. In A.C. Bohart, B.S. Held, E. Mendelowitz & K.J. Schneider (Eds.), *Humanity's dark side: Evil, destructive experience, and psychotherapy* (pp. 35–56). American Psychological Association.

Schmid, P.F. (2018, July). *Hope, not optimism.* Keynote address, Conference of the World Association for Person-Centered & Experiential Psychotherapy & Counseling, Vienna, Austria.

Schmid, P.F. & Mearns, D. (2006). Being-with and being-counter: Person-centered psychotherapy as an in-depth co-creative process of personalization. *Person-Centered & Experiential Psychotherapies, 5*(3), 174–190.

Schön, D.A. (1983). *The reflective practitioner: How professionals think in action*. Basic Books.

Shapiro, F. (1995). *Eye movement desensitization and reprocessing: Basic principles, protocols, and procedures.* Guilford Press.

Shapiro, S. (2006). *Goal-free living*. Wiley.

Shostrom, E.L. (Producer). (1965). *Three approaches to psychotherapy: Carl Rogers* [Film]. Psychological Films.

Shotter, J. (1990). Getting in touch: The metamethodology of a postmodern science of mental life. *The Humanistic Psychologist, 18*(1), 7–22.

Smith, D.L. (2013). Beyond good and evil: Variations on some Freudian themes. In A.C. Bohart, B.S. Held, E. Mendelowitz & K.J. Schneider (Eds.), *Humanity's dark side: Evil, destructive experience, and psychotherapy* (pp. 193–212). American Psychological Association.

Smith, T. (2001). *A hermeneutic-phenomenological exploration of person-to-person authentic encounters*. Unpublished doctoral dissertation. Saybrook University.

Spence, D.P. (1982). *Narrative truth and historical truth*. Norton.

Sprenkle, D.H., Davis, S.D. & Lebow, J.L. (2009). *Common factors in couple and family therapy: The overlooked foundation for effective practice*. Guilford.

Sprong, S., Jetten, J., Wang, Z, Peters, K., Mols, F., Verkuyten, M., Bastian, B., Ariyanto, A., Autin, F., Ayub, N., Badea, C., Besta, T., Butera, F., Costa-Lopes, R., Cui, L., Fantini, C., Finchilescu, G., Gaertner, L., Gollwitzer, M., ... Whol, M.J.A. (2019). 'Our country needs a strong leader right now': Economic inequality enhances the wish for a strong leader. *Psychological Science, 30*(11), 1625–1637.

Staudinger, U.M. & Baltes, P.B. (1996). Interactive minds: A facilitative setting for wisdom-related performances? *Journal of Personality and Social Psychology, 71*(4), 746–762.

Staudinger, U.M., Smith, J. & Baltes, P.B. (1994). *Manual for the assessment of wisdom-related performances*. Max Planck Institute for Human Development.

Sternberg, R.J. (1998). A balance theory of wisdom. *Review of General Psychology, 2*(4), 347–365.

Sternberg, R.J. (2004). Why smart people can be so foolish. *European Psychologist, 9*(3), 145–150.

Sternberg, R.J. (2007). *Wisdom, intelligence, and creativity synthesized*. Cambridge University Press.

Stiles, W.B. & Glick, M.J. (2000). Client-centered therapy with multi-voiced clients: Empathy with whom? In J.C. Watson, R.N. Goldman & M.S. Warner (Eds.), *Client-centered and experiential psychotherapy in the 21st century: Advances in theory, research and practice* (pp. 406–414). PCCS Books.

Stiles, W.B. & Horvath, A.O. (2017). Appropriate responsiveness as a contribution to therapist effects. In L.G. Castonguay & C.E. Hill (Eds.), *How and why are some therapists better than others? Understanding therapist effects* (pp. 71–84). American Psychological Association.

Thomas, D. & Diener, E. (1990). Memory accuracy in the recall of emotions. *Journal of Personality and Social Psychology, 59*(2), 291–297.

Turner, R.H. (1976). The real self: From institution to impulse. *American Journal of Sociology, 81*(5), 989–1016.

Vonnegut K. (1963). *Cat's cradle.* Holt, Rinehart & Winston.

Watzlawick, P., Weakland, J.H. & Fisch, R. (1974). *Change: Principles of problem formation and problem resolution.* W.W. Norton.

Weitzman, S.M. (2016). A bite of the universe. In R.M. Rosenbaum & B Magid (Eds.), *What is wrong with mindfulness (and what isn't): Zen perspectives* (pp. 135–138). Wisdom Publications.

Wile, D.B. (1981). *Couples therapy: A nontraditional approach.* Wiley.

Wile, D.B. (1993). *After the fight.* Guilford Press.

Wilson, T.D. & Dunn, E.W. (2004). Self-knowledge: Its limits, value and potential for improvement. *Annual Review of Psychology, 55*(1), 493–518.

Wood, J.K. (2008). *Carl Rogers' person-centered approach: Toward an understanding of its implications.* PCCS Books.

Zilbergeld, B. & Lazarus, A.A. (1987). *Mind power: Getting what you want through mental training.* Little, Brown.

Zimring, F. (1990). Cognitive processes as a cause of psychotherapeutic change: Self-initiated processes. In G. Lietaer, J. Rombauts & R. Van Balen (Eds.), *Client-centered and experiential psychotherapy in the nineties* (pp. 361–380). Leuven University Press.

Zimring, F. (1995). A new explanation for the beneficial results of client-centered therapy: The possibility of a new paradigm. *The Person-Centered Journal, 2*(2), 36–48.

Name index

A
Abramson, L.Y. 176
Aktipis, C.A. 90
Alberini, C.A. 113
Almaas, A.H. 142, 154
Altimir, C. 135
American Psychological Association (APA) 4, 20, 113, 123, 139
Anderson, R. 10, 32, 66, 97, 103
Andrews, J.D.W. 178

B
Baltes, P.B. 40, 46, 79, 81
Bandura, A. 176, 178–179, 187
Baudelaire, C. 171
Bavelas, J.B. 40
Beck, A.T. 171, 176–177, 179, 180
Belenky, M.F. 48, 71
Berger, T. 82
Berglas, S. 174
Berry Newton, M. 12, 78, 84–88
Biden, J. 145
Bohart, A.C. 4, 11, 12, 21, 23, 25, 27, 28, 33, 36, 41, 52, 54, 59, 61–62, 65, 73, 74, 80, 83, 84–85, 89, 116, 120, 125, 137, 138, 180, 182, 183, 184, 187
Bollas, C. 174
Boukydis, K.M. 78

Bozarth, J. 5, 75
Bradshaw, J. 174
Brennen, S.E. 72
Briere, J. 187
Brodley, B. 5, 62, 137
Brown, J.D. 174
Bruner, J. 180, 185
Buber, M. 66–67, 103
Bush, G.W. 145
Byock, G. 41, 136

C
Cantor, N. 116, 184
Carmin, C.N. 186
Caspar, F. 82
Castonguay, L.G. 135
Chabris, C. 135
Cham, J. 5
Charon, R. 104
Cissna, K.N. 10, 32, 66, 97, 103
Clark, H.H. 72
Claudius 171, 173
Cleary, T. 20
Coady, C.A.J. 97
Cohen, L. 155
Cornelius-White, J.H.D. 72, 77
Costa, P.T. 113
Cowan, P.A. 47
Craig, P. 111
Cullari, S. 105

D

Davis, S.D. 48
de Shazer, S. 184
de Wit, M.M. 98
Diener, E. 39, 97
Dowd, E.T. 186
Driscoll, R. 170, 173, 177–178, 179, 180, 182, 184
Dumas, A. 142, 144, 150, 154
Duncan, B.L. 25
Dunn, E.W. 98
Dweck, C.S. 133, 185

E

Ehrenreich, B. 143
Einstein, A. 27
Eisenhower, D. 157
Eliot, T.S. 142, 149, 150
Elliott, R. 7, 58, 60, 77, 122
Ellis, A. 171, 176–177, 180
Erickson, M. 26, 153–154

F

Farley, F. 116
Feldman, J.B. 154
Finke, J. 3, 5, 18
Flavell, J.H. 186
Freud, S. 171
Freyd, J. 119

G

Gendlin, E.T. 3, 17, 18, 23, 25, 26, 27, 30, 39, 40, 52, 65, 67, 75, 80–81, 99, 104, 105, 116, 118, 119, 120, 156, 162, 163, 166, 179, 182
Gertrude 172, 173
Gibson, J.J. 97–98
Gilligan, C. 119
Glick, M.J. 64
Gödel, K. 118
Gold, J. 63
Goldberg, J. 16
Gopnik, A. 7–8, 12
Grant, B. 5

Grawe, K. 24
Greenberg, L.S. 21, 54, 74, 75, 77, 125, 138, 170, 181–182, 183, 186

H

Hamlet 170–174, 187–188
Haney, C. 39, 147
Hankin-Wessler, S.W.R. 172, 178, 179, 181, 185
Harré, R. 91
Hart, J.T. 68
Hawking, S. 148
Hedges, C. 31
Heidegger, M. 16, 37, 94
Held, B. 143
Hendricks, M. 100, 105
Henschel, D. 52
Hersh, R.H. 47
Hitler, A. 44
Hofstader, D. 118
Holland, S. 14
Holton, G. 26
Horvath, A.O. 155
Howard, G.S. 184, 185

J

Jaffe, Y. 179
Janoff-Bulman, R. 176
Jeffers, R. 142, 144, 149
Johnson, D.H. 99
Jones, E.E. 174
Joyce, J. 93, 130
Jung, C. 26

K

Kahneman, D. 98, 187
Klein, G. 98
Kleinman, A. 24, 102–103
Kohlberg, L. 47, 52, 182
Kruglanski, A.W. 179
Kuhn, T.S. 114, 115, 118, 119
Kurzban, R. 90

L

Lakoff, G. 176

Landrine, H. 95
LaSalle, M. 147
Lazarus, A.A. 23, 175
Lebow, J.L. 48
LeDoux, J.E. 113
Leggett, E.L. 185
Leicester, G. 33, 38
Leitner, L.M. 11
Le Texier, T. 39
Levitt, H.M. 136
Linehan, M.M. 25, 78, 138, 162
Livingstone Smith, D. 13
Loesch, M. 57–58, 131
Luyten, P. 48

M

Mackrill, T. 59, 82–83
Mahoney, M.J. 113, 118, 120, 175, 179
Mahrer, A.R. 115, 116
Markus, H. 181, 184
Martin, M. 84, 87
Masten, A.S. 186
McCrae, R.R. 113
McDermott, D. 166
Mearns, D. 34, 36, 107, 110–111
Meichenbaum, D. 175, 178–179, 187
Messer, S.B. 133
Michelangelo 131
Mickler, C. 82–83
Milgram, S. 147
Miller, W.R. 18, 24, 60, 75
Miller, D.T. 174
Moon, K.A. 5, 137
Morrison, J. 171

N

Neville, B. 12
Nisbett. R.E. 98
Norcross, J.C. 148
Norem, J.K. 143, 180
Nurius, P. 181, 184

O

O'Hara, M. 11, 12, 22–23, 26, 33, 38, 72, 84

Ophelia 170
Orlinsky, D.E. 24

P

Parks, B.K. 24
Perls, F. 73–74
Perry, W.G. Jr 47
Phillips, J.R. 105
Piaget, J. 47, 52
Pol Pot 44
Porter, C.A. 174

R

Reagan, R. 146
Rennie, D.L. 136
Rice, L.N. 183, 186
Richards, K. 131
Rogers, C.R. 10, 12, 13, 17, 18,
 21–22, 25–27, 29, 31–36, 41,
 46, 48, 51, 53, 54–55, 61, 62,
 63, 65–67, 68, 69, 71, 73, 79,
 81, 82, 83–86, 90–112, 115,
 135, 136, 145, 157, 166, 172,
 182, 183, 186
Rollnick, S. 18, 24, 75
Rosenbaum, R. 137
Ross, L. 98
Rowling, J.K. 94
Rusk, G.S. 25
Rychlak, J.F. 184

S

Sabat, S.R. 21, 42
Safran, J.D. 182, 183, 185
Sagal, K. 111
Sanford, R.C. 84
Saperia, E.P. 183
Sarbin, T.R. 185
Sartre, J.-P. 36, 94
Schmid, P.F. 5, 13, 20, 34–38, 140,
 145, 149, 166
Schön, D.A. 73
Segal, Z.V. 183 , 185
Seligman, M.E.P. 185
Shapiro, F. 23, 24

Shapiro, S. 111
Shaw, G.B. 131
Shostrom, E.L. 41, 66, 74, 82, 92, 135
Shotter, J. 119
Simons, D. 135
Smith, D.L. 13
Smith, T. 94, 105
Solovey, A.D. 25
Sommerbeck, L. 139
Spence, D.P. 99
Spenkle, D.H. 48
Sprong, S. 147
Stalin 44
Staudinger, U.M. 40, 46, 79, 81, 82–83
St Clair, M. 172
Sternberg, R.J. 29, 46, 47, 78, 81
Stiles, W.B. 64, 155
Stricker, G. 63

T

Tallman, K. 25, 28, 33, 36, 65, 89
Taylor, S.E. 174
Thomas, D. 97
Todd, J. 183
Tomlinson, T.M. 68
Traugott, C. 111–112
Trump, D. 44, 144, 145–148
Tulving, E. 184
Turner, R.H. 95
Turrell, J. 131, 157
Tversky, A. 187

V

Vonnegut, K. 4

W

Wachtel, P. 73
Wampold, B. 13
Watzlawick, P. 114, 173, 179, 186
Weitzman, S.M. 73
Wessler, R .L. 170, 172, 178, 179, 181, 182, 185
Wile, D.B. 48, 162, 179, 186
Wilson, T.D 98

Witty, M. 5, 7
Wood, J.K. 26, 30, 33, 38, 39, 43, 52, 78, 92
World Association of Person-Centered and Experiential Psychotherapy and Counseling (WAPCEPC) 3, 60, 90, 142, 159

Y

Youngblood, J. 165, 166

Z

Zilbergeld, B. 23
Zimring, F. 28, 30
Zirkel, S. 184

Subject index

A

acceptance 68, 82, 104, 152–53, 157, 172
actualisation 38, 145
agent/agency 14, 124–25, 153
Alzheimer's disease 21, 42
anorexia 31, 44
anxiety 14–15, 45, 76–77, 128–29, 159–63, 169
assimilative integration 133, 137–39
attention
    narrowed, 51, 150, 187
    open, 9, 50, 108–10, 157
authentic source, own experience 21, 54, 77, 130, 138
authenticity 35, 94, 123–24, 130
avoidance 159–62, 166

B

balancing 30–31, 47, 57, 80–81
becoming a person 36–39
behaviour
    dysfunctional, 25, 28
    unwise, 30–31, 44, 49,
behavioural
    self-blame 126, 176,
    therapy/approaches 25, 58, 175–78
Berlin Wisdom Paradigm 47, 49
borderline personality disorder 21, 134, 137, 162

C

change
    first-order, 115
    second-order, 114–15, 120–22, 173
characterological self-blame 176
children
    cruelty towards, 146
    development 106, 172
    impact of, 127–28
    resilience of, 165
cognitive
    behavioural therapy (CBT) 16, 76–78, 123–24, 131, 134
    development (Piaget's model of,) 47, 52
    therapy 58, 100, 126, 128, 151, 172–75, 181–83
consciousness 47
confrontation 180
congruence 35, 40–41, 54, 68–69
connected knowing 71, 73–74
constructivism 33, 145
contextualism 28, 56, 80–81, 116
control 87, 143, 154–56, 166
courage, of clients 152–53, 156, 159
creativity 12, 24, 29, 47, 58–59, 123
    emergence of, 42, 51, 78, 82–88
    fostering, 33–34, 80–81
    process of, 38
culture 82, 86, 91, 93, 95, 102, 104

D

danger orientation 187
decentering 183, 185–86
defensive pessimism 144, 148, 152, 154, 157, 180–81
defensiveness 50, 100
depression 104, 160, 176
dialogical 18, 140, 155–56
dialogue 30
  integrative, 52
  with life role 120
  role-play 58, 103
  whole person approach 66
  wisdom 42
  with self 183
  with therapist 5, 7–10, 34–40, 72–75
  with world 17, 155–56
disowning 174, 181
dominant paradigm 3, 9

E

emotion-focused therapy 18–19, 58–61, 73, 75–77, 129
emotions 49, 51
  in touch with, 9, 52, 57, 97
  processing, 125, 129
empathic
  responses and reflections 12–13, 17–19, 32
  listening 33–34,
  understanding 40–41, 54, 68, 89, 101–04
  responding 139
  witnessing 105
empathy 51, 60–69, 101, 122, 138, 148, 160
empathy-based psychotherapy 70, 74
empty chair role-play 58
encounter 35–37, 39–40, 67, 74, 94
engineering 16, 124–26, 129–30,
evidence-based therapy 123, 148
existential therapy 73, 83
experiential 80
expert stance, of therapist 61, 63, 70, 74, 76–77, 123
expert, client as 63–65, 74, 99
exposure 58
eye movement desensitization and reprocessing (EMDR) 23–24, 39

F

false self 67, 90–91, 121, 130
feeling unsafe 45
felt senses 52
first-person science 99
focusing 23, 30, 33, 39, 76, 105
focusing-oriented therapy 18–19, 75

G

genuineness 21, 55, 99, 104
Gestalt therapy 38, 183
'granfalloon' (Vonnegut) 4–5
growth tendency 16

H

hope 142, 149–50, 155–57
human cruelty 145
humanistic 94
  therapy 11, 126, 130, 182–83

I

implicit knowledge 63
inner voice 163
integration 177, 183, 186–88
integrative-process approach 184–86
intelligence, components of 29, 47
internal critic 171–88
internal generativity 84, 124
interventionism 17, 53, 61, 63–64, 66, 69–72, 153–55
  therapy as, 9–10
introjection 174–75, 177

K

knowing 52, 71–74, 93
  implicational, 26, 118
  of self 92, 97

Subject index   209

L
liberation philosophy 14, 18
listening, receptive 33, 140, 155–56

M
mechanistic views/practices 75
meeting of persons 20
  therapy as, 10, 17–18, 32, 40, 66–70, 75, 103
meta-cognition 186
meta-model of therapy 63
meta-perspective 134, 137
mindset 61, 63–64, 73, 133–41
motivational interviewing 18–19, 24, 60

N
nature of change in psychotherapy 113
non-directive stance 61–63, 183
normative judgements 14

O
object relations 121, 171–72, 174–75
openness 109, 152–54
  inner, 33
  lack of, 31
  to others 35
'Other', the 36–37, 41

P
paradigm
  revolution 115
  shift 120
parenting 7–10
perfectionism 177–80
person-centred 12–25, 34–36, 61–68, 74–76, 82–84, 100–01
person to person 35, 67, 74–75, 94, 105, 139
personhood 34, 37, 39
perspective taking 47–49, 51–52, 56–57, 59, 98
phenomenology 13, 96–98, 110
possibility, openness to 49, 144, 154
potential 122

post-traumatic stress disorder (PTSD) 126
power 36, 66
  client's, 75
presence, therapeutic 22
pressures towards uniformity 51
process perspective 184–85,
psychodynamic therapy 7, 100, 131–34, 177
psychopathology 78, 159–60, 166–69, 185
psychotherapy integration 14, 43, 60–63, 89, 133, 170

R
rational-cognitive therapies 176, 182
rational-emotive therapy 171
real self 90–92, 95–96, 98, 121, 130
reflecting
  by clients 11, 37, 47–49, 51–55, 57, 65, 106, 172
  by therapists 10, 89, 122
reframing 120, 173, 184
relativism 47, 53
respect
  for client 16–7, 54, 62, 68, 73–74, 138
  for self 161
responsiveness 155
rigidity 31, 181

S
safe space 12, 33, 54–55
safety 160, 172
schemas 14, 49, 56, 96, 114–24, 185
schizophrenia 17, 21, 42, 149
self, the 39, 90–94, 113–21
self-criticism 28–29, 163
self-healing 22, 24, 32, 60
separate knowing 71, 73–74
'shoulds and oughts' 16, 32, 174, 182
socratic questioning 58, 176, 180
splitting 47, 138, 187,
sub-person mechanism 13–14
subjectivity 100, 123–26, 130–31

T

techniques, use of 62, 64, 68–69, 75–77, 140
thinking
   contextually 56–58, 80–81
   multidimensionally 48, 50, 52
thou-I (and I–thou) 13, 42, 140
true self 93, 96, 121, 130, 174
two-chair technique 7, 58, 69–70, 171, 181, 183

U

unconditional positive regard 32, 40, 54, 68, 138, 145
unfolding, process of 24, 122

W

whole person 5, 7, 9, 13–14, 40, 66, 124
wisdom-facilitating 34–35
wisdom-making 21, 24–25, 53, 82–88
wisdom
   components of, 79
   ecological, 28–29, 32
   models of, 12, 26
   organismic, 22–23, 25–28, 38–41, 52, 175, 182
   self-organising, 31, 34, 38, 43, 46